D1474185

Political Theory for Mortals

SHADES OF JUSTICE, IMAGES OF DEATH

JOHN E. SEERY

Cornell University Press

Ithaca and London

First published 1996 by Cornell University Press.

Printed in the United States of America

⊗ The paper in this book meets the minimum requirements
of the American National Standard for Information Sciences—
Permanence of Paper for Printed Library Materials, ANSI Z39.48-1984.

Library of Congress Cataloging-in-Publication Data

Seery, John Evan.
  Political theory for mortals : shades of justice, images of death / John E. Seery.
    p. cm. — (Contestations)
  Includes bibliographical references (p.   ) and index.
  ISBN 0-8014-3259-6 (cl. : alk. paper). — ISBN 0-8014-8376-X (pbk. : alk. paper)
  1. Death—Political aspects. 2. Political science—History. 3. Justice.
I. Title. II. Series.
HQ1073.S43 1996
306.88—dc20   96-14524

The publicly manifest Spirit has the root of its power in the nether world.
—Hegel, *The Phenomenology of Spirit*

Contents

CHAPTER ONE

The Academy

In the future of these States must arise poets immenser far, and make great poems of death.

—Walt Whitman, "Democratic Vistas"

This is a book about death and politics. Here is the theme to start: Political theorists today, those scholars who think and write broadly about politics (I count myself among them), have been largely silent about death, and that vast omission ought to be largely reexamined.

Before I beat this topic of death to death, or bore some readers to nearly the same fate, I might take just a few paragraphs to step away from the usual academic conventions, disrupting the standard rhythms and flow of scholarly prose (engrossing as such prose may be) in order to reveal my initial prompting toward this possibly morbid, possibly taboo topic. I find myself, at this very moment, writing in the field of political theory, and it is indeed strange to imagine oneself so situated—as if a ready readership lurks off in one corner of the great marketplace of ideas, a group of fellow travelers more or less similarly schooled and versed in the same issues, names, and dates. Although far from like-minded, we speak the same language, or are at least able to communicate with hand signals. I well remember why I was originally attracted to this odd bunch of scholars, why I sought to join their ranks. Political theory seemed to attract scholars who quietly demanded from their academic activity more than simply a life of disinterested contemplation. To a person, they seemed like a friendly lot, a little more decent and humane and outgoing than many of their colleagues, occasionally charismatic, certainly more dilettantish (in a good sense) and global and urgent and creative and pretentious (in a good sense) in their outlooks, even though they would value immensely the kinds of academic accomplishment that occur only in fits and starts—slow, steady, stepwise gains in insight, bounded but detailed, respectable through and through, even if limited in scope. The very name of the discipline—political theory—is itself a potential contradiction in terms, inviting an occupational tension between real engagement and idle speculation. Such scholars might be ensconced in academe, or fruitfully resigned to the ivory tower, but they would at least have one foot out the door, or would at least spend blocks of time staring out the window, brooding. They seemed self-questioning, thoughtful, oppositional, Socratic. They exuded an uneasy integrity.

I find myself today, however, growing more and more impatient and peevish as I read the stacks of essays in political theory as they roll off the presses. To be sure, there is hustle and bustle in the field, it is alive and in that sense exciting, many players and disputes, rumblings and whisperings—now and then a truly new insight takes hold. But how rare, sadly, does an essay these days capture my imagination for an entire day. Maybe it's my fault, the result of constitutional captiousness; but increasingly I become indignant, even embittered, if a fellow political theorist wastes my time (I fret about my own work so). Too much of the writing is predictable and formulaic, stocked with stock argumentation, rehearsals and regurgitations, uninspiring echoes. Too much time is spent scoring points, establishing professional authority, promoting career concerns. Many pieces are impressive in the sheer amassing of material, duly and dutifully footnoted (as if cross-referencing means consensus or confirmation[1]); but too often such studies are all windup with no punch—or else the self-centering, semi-disguised because falsely modest subtext becomes all too transparent: "I'm smart. I've read a bunch of books. Respect me as a scholar."

Alas, life grows too short, literally. (I sometimes entertain the revenge fantasy of carrying on a Lucianic dialogue with these writers after our deaths, rebuking them for their wasteful words.) Sterility passes for rigor. Specialization on narrow topics passes for profundity. Minute distinctions abound, only to be later collapsed in another display of self-justified verbiage. The contemporary game is simple enough, and avid participants know the rules: Carve out an arcane niche, call it a contribution. My point is, the recent academicization of political theory is not necessarily a blessing. The appearance of more elevated, more sophisticated, high-tech discourse may be only that. I could accept more graciously, and would even participate more readily in these overworked debates—individualism versus community, the right versus the good, liberalism versus republicanism, mind versus body, nature versus convention, text versus context, male versus female, the one versus the many, the analytic versus the deconstructed—if they exhibited a sense of perspective about the irony of these lives—pale shades—that pore over pages while presuming that politics is the point. Should I read yet another study that resurrects a lost theoretical hero (while seldom acknowledging that this exegetical autopsy is hero worship or second burial)? Should I read one more period piece that slyly assumes privileged access to a time and place now removed? Should I peruse the arguments of another work that disingenuously tries to sacralize and monumentalize some forgotten text? Lifeless words, dead letters, printed in ink, not blood. One advocates this or that, one's methodology goes here or there, codes and conventions become the apparent end-all and be-all. Should I take them to heart, as if I were reading a good novel, which at least announces itself as fictional? So much earnestness and expenditure—for what? (Reading yet again Weber's *Wissenschaft als Beruf*, or even Wolin's heroic "Political Theory as a Vocation," hardly puts such questions to rest.) I know that I am not alone in holding these dissenting sentiments, for other, mostly wayward political theorists have voiced (in hushed tones, behind closed doors) similar broadside questions about the current fin de siècle: What is the meaning, what are the ultimate, or even pragmatic, purposes of such intensive academic labor in light of our impending bodily deaths, the foreshadowed certainty that such busy-ness shall someday come to an abrupt, seemingly inexplicable halt?[2]

Like other pilgrims, I have reached midway in life's journey, an age at which I find that my political theory mentors, members of an older generation, most of them émigrés from war—"survivors" in the sense used by Jews, obituary writers, and rape victims—happen to be dying at an alarming rate. Every other month, it seems, I read another eulogy listing their publications and accomplishments—call it a life—and I think to myself, something has been lost in the translation. I knew these people well, they weren't just pedants and pundits—they were real *Menschen* (men and women alike)—and it will never be the same without them. But then so many up-and-coming theorists today, perhaps because of recent market pressures for career advancement, seem all too eager to aspire to imitated lives of scholarly asceticism, yet apparently without the tragic sense of survivorship formerly underwriting all such work ("publish or perish" concerns notwithstanding). Zombies, the walking dead, pop up in almost every department, and many of these latter-day Wagners (many have never read *Faust*) consider scholarly contestation to be but war by other means. Departments and entire schools reveal their vampiric tendencies, crying out for fresh blood and new bodies every few years. The academy is, for those who like analogies, more than a minimum-security mental institution or a penal colony or a museum; it is a cemetery. Libraries are huge sepulchers. Books are tombstones. We who have aged a few years start to know where the bodies are buried, but others rush around trying to forget the carnage. Students, who have little sense of historical progression and the march of time, do not realize that ghosts sit next to them in every classroom, or that some of their professors are wearing X-ray specs, seeing right past their youthful Gretchen-like bodies to the skulls and bones beneath. Meanwhile, outside in the town below, gangland violence kills at a slightly faster pace and the bodies pile up, providing a fresh source of stimulation for a seminar discussion in political theory. The subject then runs its course. The bell rings, another hour has passed. So it goes.

Here is, nevertheless, yet another book, another book of political theory that implicitly presumes to compete for a reader's precious spare time. What might it accomplish? My own Sisyphean spirits, once so full of energy and possibility, have diminished since entering the field. My generation wasn't a war generation, but we grew up under the threat of nuclear annihilation. That memory has faded, as the cloud lifted. Those nuclear books—I know this too well!—have now been relegated to the ash-heap; they had a half-life of two or three years (better dead than read). So what, we quip in quick retrospect, if the world might have been blown up back then? Big deal! Let's move on to another topic; and indeed another death threat has emerged as a contender for our attention, inching out environmental degradation. Namely, many of my colleagues in the academy have succumbed to AIDS; but I do not believe that that plague has created a general climate, a substitute awareness of survivorship among my professional peers. With the chastening lessons of death mostly ignored, with no one around anymore to pronounce the entire field of political theory moribund, many young writers are choosing to blend in, to become boring and tedious; or a few dare to aggrandize themselves, killing off rival theorists, installing themselves as successors, going for the jugular, committing acts of textual violence, becoming serial murderers in successive chapters of Oedipal books. We've already become expendable human beings, we mid-life writers, we end-game academics, we second-order theorists. Under such gloomy, even dangerous circumstances, what is the purpose—I ask again—of producing yet another book? To be remembered through one's words? To contribute some meager benefit to an ongoing community? To immortalize oneself, to offer a living testament, to fantasize oneself already as a dead person, to revel prematurely in the remote possibility of posthumous recognition? To hang one's hopes on the distant, dim future? Let's read the handwriting on the wall: The word is doubly dead these days, and book writers and readers are dying breeds. No honest writer these days can present himself or herself as writing, even secretly, for the Thucydidean ages.

Myself, I no longer write mainly for the living, or for their children. Rather, I've come to realize that I write, and write cheerfully, for the dead. They renew my spirits, they restore my sense of purpose, they provide political direction. They take criticism well. It is a thesis of this book that I, as a political theorist, am not altogether unusual in this undertaking.[3] Instead, I hope to showcase the idea that this peculiar enterprise of writing and reading political theory is populated by persons endlessly fascinated with attempts to consult, even to carry on cryptic dialogues with dead authors, dead issues, dead books.

Dead Theory: Hobbes, Arendt, Foucault

Death figures importantly, to say the least, in the canon of Western political thought—the extended corpus—even if it hasn't been sufficiently and explicitly addressed in much contemporary material (one reads an occasional feminist aside referring to the "problem of death" as a male preoccupation, but that's about it). To start, Socrates famously referred to all of life as a preparation for death, and Plato insisted that the purpose of philosophy was to teach people how to die. Cicero repeated the point, and Montaigne said it again, citing Cicero. Christian theorists, as Nietzsche put it, had to struggle with the logistical difficulty involved in trying to emulate and follow a dead leader. And, to complete this barest of surveys, Hobbes, as Hannah Arendt claimed, is the only political philosopher in whose work death plays a crucial role.[4]

Hobbes

Maybe Hobbes, in seeming to have had the final word on death and politics, is to blame for the eerie silence on the topic today. His theory, which forms the basis for much modern contractarian theory, much thinking about sovereign authority, about power politics, about community and civil society, about equality and fairness, and war, and science, and language (the list could go on) all famously revolves around an allegedly primordial and potentially pan-human fear of violent death.[5] The Hobbesian premise is that modern politics can establish its rational mechanism, a superintending albeit earth-bound authority, by building upon this basic fearfulness. As Norman Jacobson has argued, Hobbes so overwhelms his typical reader with the specter of violent death as "the greatest evil,"[6] that the fear-inducing experience of reading about such fearfulness seems to confirm the point.[7] Perhaps we latter-day readers have acquiesced too readily in Hobbes's seemingly self-fulfilling depictions. Perhaps, too, the experiences of world war in this twentieth century, the unprecedented fear of global catastrophe, and the daily terrors of urban violence have inured us to the horrors of his account and seemed to reinforce his perverse vision. We don't, by and large, resist and contest his views on death (except, again, to read them lately as a function of gender[8]). Surely it seems commonsensical to be fearful about violent death—and if any bedrock or lowest common denominator, a ground for rational theory, is to be found and struck, fear of violent death seems a pretty safe bet. Most of us, especially those in the prime of life, don't welcome death in any Socratic sense; and even Socrates' skeptical appraisals about death must be viewed in context and with a grain of salt, since he spoke after all under the threat of a death sentence. Most of us Westerners view non-Western cases of political suicide as culturally pathological, and we generally lump together "terrorists," guerrilla fighters, *sati*, and *satyagraha* as crazed fanatics. Joyous Day of the Dead celebrations we dismiss as dark-skinned exotica. Yes, if we really must think about it, Hobbes was probably right about the Grim Reaper in some fundamental way—and we therefore intuitively accede that political theory can build on this basic fearfulness.[9]

That Hobbes bases sovereign political authority largely on fearfulness of violent death has become a commonplace. It is probably fair to say that Hobbes was thoroughly successful in establishing himself as the author of much modern political thought and practice: power depends upon the sword, upon the threat of bodily punishment; the maintenance of civil order requires nothing less than "the power of Life and Death."[10] This power, Hobbes insists, must be absolute: "It is impossible a Commonwealth should stand, where any other than the Sovereign, has a power of giving greater rewards than Life; and of inflicting greater punishments, than Death."[11] Yet if we probe further into Hobbes's writings about this bedrock notion of fearfulness toward death, we notice that cracks start forming in the edifice of what is supposed to be a sturdy structure. Hobbes starts making all sorts of concessions and qualifications to this sweeping idea of a natural fear of agonizing death at the hands of other humans. Maybe in the end he successfully plasters and paints over these cracks, so that today we hardly notice them; but alerted to these crevices in his thinking, we start to worry that the once-sure foundation of modern politics might eventually give way.

First, as many commentators on Hobbes have pointed out, Hobbes's attempt to remind his readers that death is to be feared was more exhortative than descriptive, since a great number of Englishmen around him, in his own day, were not in fact, he felt, sufficiently fearful about death. The problem for Hobbes was that people were too willing to tempt fate and to risk death, as evidenced in their willingness to die in civil war. It was easily demonstrable that various countervailing passions routinely provide sufficient motive for defying the fear of death; and Hobbes was well acquainted with Francis Bacon's essay "Of Death," which held that the fear of death is in fact the weakest of considerations.[12] So Hobbes's rudimentary task was to convince his fellows that death was ever to be eschewed.

Death itself, just any old death, isn't the *summum malum* in Hobbes's view; nor does he simply adopt Augustine's view that eternal death is the greatest evil.[13] Rather, he insists that the great fear humans hold (and should hold) is fear of agonizing death at the hands of other humans.[14] Violent death is repulsive to humans, one presumes, because it is painful and premature and thus avoidable; and yet Hobbes isn't concerned with questions of medicine and disease prevention.[15] Moreover, he allows that there are several conditions of life under which death would be preferable: "though death is the greatest of all evil (especially when accompanied by torture), the pains of life can be so great that, unless their quick end is foreseen, they may lead men to number death among the good."[16] Suicides are distracted by an "inward Torment or Apprehension of somewhat worse than Death."[17] In addition to physical pain or "inward" torments, Hobbes recognizes that various kinds of shame, dishonor, and scorn may make life not worth living.[18] He compiles so many exceptions to the rule, one begins to wonder whether the rule is true.[19]

For a covenant to bind parties together, Hobbes explains, a fear of the consequences of breaking it must be in force; mutual good will is insufficient.[20] Fear can be fear of powers visible or invisible; and Hobbes identifies religion as fear of the invisible, whereas fear of other men counts as a visible deterrent. Such remarks have led many of Hobbes's interpreters to conclude that religion, in particular Christianity with its doctrine of the immortal soul, presents the biggest obstacle for Hobbes in his mission to find a basis for civic convenanting.[21] Persons who view death not as finality but as a commencement into an afterlife, an afterlife that may indeed hold greater rewards and punishments than this one, will not obey a sovereign if push comes to shove. Diehard Christians are too willing to die, and thus they pose a threat to civil order. "For no man can serve two masters; nor is he less, but rather more a master, whom we believe we are to obey for fear of damnation, than he whom we obey for fear of temporary death."[22] According to this once-prominent view of Hobbes's deathly motives, Hobbes wishes to remove superstitious fear of religious consequences so that men will be more fitted for civil obedience. In short, Hobbes is more or less warring with Christianity.

But here again our reading of Hobbes becomes muddled and complicated. To be sure, much of his theory can be read profitably as a calculated response to prevailing Christian views of immortality and life-after-death. But instead of simply dispelling or discounting Christian accounts of death, his strategy may be to rewrite them to his political advantage, so that the Christian becomes coopted into Hobbes's civil order. Recent Hobbes scholarship has proffered the view that there may be much that is compatible between the "civil" and "ecclesiastical" chapters of *Leviathan*.[23] Hobbes's particular theological brand of mortalism may be reconcilable with his secular materialism: the body *and* the soul cease all operations at the time of biological terminus (the incorporeal soul does not abide in some limbolike state), and then the body and soul are simultaneously reconstituted at the time of Christian resurrection.[24] Hence the Christian believer has something at stake at the time of death, namely, the threat of body/soul oblivion.[25] Hobbes radically reconfigures one's postresurrection plans as well. He portrays heaven—a conception which he admits is novel—not as a place remote from earth, somewhere off in an Empyrean among the stars, but as a kingdom on *earth*—a "Civil Common-wealth, where God himself is Soveraign."[26] The Christian resurrection, then, is a resurrection not only of the soul, but, Hobbes contends, truly of the body as well (albeit no longer subject to death, if saved). These considerations about the nature of heavenly immortality, he notes, bear directly on the question of the authority of the sword and whether the commands of the civil laws should be obeyed by all.[27] Good Christians, in other words, should toe the line; or at least they cannot neglect the fate of their bodies for the sake of some otherworldly conception of imminent, immaterial bliss.

Hobbes seems to deploy a similar strategy with respect to the damnations of hell. Remember, if otherworldly punishments seem potentially more tormenting to a great number of citizens than do visible threats and punishments, civil authority will break down. Moreover, Hobbes states clearly that one need not obey the sovereign if obedience means risking eternal damnation.[28] Following a lengthy analysis of hell, Hobbes concludes, based on scriptural evidence and simple reasoning, that hell's torments will not be eternal after all. Bodies are finite and thus can be burned only once.[29] The wicked are subject to a "Second Death"—a postjudgment state of total oblivion, at which time one's entire entity is burned once and for all. If one wishes to call Second Death an everlasting death, Hobbes will allow it; but strictly speaking, the second dead are doubly dead, and there are no more bones about it. The torments of Christian hell, then, are more in keeping with the plain threats of bodily death—both produce oblivion—but then one wonders why oblivion, first or second time around, is to be the object of so much fearful projection.

Perhaps the most curious item among Hobbes's many musings about the politics of death involves his invocation and rewriting of the Leviathan image, borrowed from the Job story in the Hebrew Bible. In the biblical version the Leviathan is a monster, but now Hobbes calls it a God of sorts, namely a "mortal God." Commentators have interpreted this insertion of *mortal* to mean that this Leviathan is a human construct, an artificial God or God-like but humanly generated authority. *Mortal* thus means *human*.[30] But the critical passage doesn't read "artificial God" or "human God." Instead, Hobbes's oxymoron "mortal God" is cumbersome, for most gods are, by definition, not mortal.[31] Rather, I suggest that one of

Hobbes's intentions here is to emphasize that the Leviathan is subject to *death*. Therein might lie the most fearsome quality of all concerning Leviathan's authority: although awesome, it is destructible.[32] The fragility of Leviathan's authority means that humans cannot put their natural fears completely to rest anytime soon; the entire order could crumble. Falling back into a state of nature is always a possibility,[33] and thus humanity's terror (or its memory) must be perpetual and ever-vigilant.[34]

Finally, Hobbes doesn't present a sustained argument about why death, however construed, is necessarily to be feared. He discounts speculation about "ghostly" or "imaginary" matters; and he contends that no natural knowledge of man's estate after death is possible. Still, fear isn't the only logical conclusion one could draw under such conditions of imperfect information. Socrates and Pascal, for instance, both expressed a skepticism about ever knowing what death might mean, but they were led toward very different dispositions than fearfulness, namely, ambivalence and hopefulness, respectively. Hobbes seems to complicate his own position with other qualifications, concessions, and contradictions; for instance, George Kateb has seized upon the paradox that while Hobbes condemns civil war, he sanctions war between states.[35] At times the individual must give up his right to self-preservation and lay down his life for the sake of the nation.[36] All told, Hobbes seems to collapse many fears into one wholesale aversion surrounding death: fear of the unknown,[37] fear of oblivion, fear of pain, fear of humiliation, fear of opportunities lost, fear of Leviathan's death, fear of external conquest. Instead of exploring these many fears, Hobbes is largely silent on his own underlying views on why death is to be so dreaded, and we latter-day political theorists don't so much accept his views and assumptions about death as we share his aversion to confronting the issue directly, to looking death square in the face, as it were. We share his silence, or we slip and slide around the issue. Given all of these inconsistencies, opacities, and silences, Hobbes, in the final analysis, cannot have the last word on death and politics.

Nevertheless, while we may question his paranoia, his cleaving to life at virtually any cost, we also want to recognize that Hobbes may have something profoundly important to teach us about modern politics (a point that may be lost in the rush toward postmodern excess): civil order cannot accommodate too much self-inflicted killing. If politics means anything, it must marginalize or minimize, not coolly accommodate, our deathly impulses. Violence is unacceptable (even if politics is war by other means). In his own way, Hobbes wants to teach us a respect for life that doesn't simply invoke transcendental, categorical, or sacred imperatives. Nor will it do simply to concentrate on life's felicities, interests, or needs. Politics must confront death, the fact of human mortality, along with the power of humans to kill one another. Hobbes wants to found civil order out of a reverence for life that employs uniquely human tendencies, tendencies that perhaps only precariously scare off other vanities and desires leading toward self-destruction.[38] Peace is paramount. For our part, at this juncture in our inquiry into the politics of death, we might consider whether such an ambitious project as Hobbes's must be based upon a necessarily fearful and aversive stance toward death. Must we condemn the idea of death in order to teach a global respect for life?

Arendt

Hannah Arendt seems a likely candidate to fill in the blanks about death. Her work on the life of the mind is thoroughly preoccupied with the importance of death for the practice of philosophy, for Arendt follows Hegel and Heidegger in claiming that human thinking itself, the life of the mind, is due to the human animal's capacity to anticipate death.[39] Anticipating a past-to-be, the will can become an object of its own reflection. But philosophical thinking doesn't necessarily translate into political action, and death for philosophy (which typically represents the release of the sentient soul from the body) doesn't necessarily speak to death for politics (which requires an attachment to, not a release from, worldliness). Still, there is much in Arendt's political work that raises hope that she might redress the lack of theoretical commentary on politics and death. Her various works on Eichmann, death camps, extermination campaigns, war, revolution, and violence stir such hopes. She closes *On Revolution* with the lines "not to be born prevails over all meaning uttered in words; by far the second-best for life, once it has appeared, is to go as swiftly as possible whence it came."[40] Kateb opens his book on Arendt with those lines from Silenus,[41] and he suggests that Arendt had come to believe that without the polis and the life of action, no one, especially she, could bear life's burden. Knowledge of our mortality—death—is the worst burden of life. Only political action, with the chance for worldly memorialization, makes life worth living. Politics is nothing less than a way to combat death, or at least to withstand the wisdom of Silenus for the time being.

Arendt's repulsion toward death is clearly outlined in her work *The Human Condition*, wherein she insists that death and politics are categorically opposed. She explains that the existence of the polis, the world of political action, transforms the naturally cyclical character of human birth and death:

> The birth and death of human beings are not simply natural occurrences, but are related to a world into which single individuals, unique, unexchangeable, and unrepeatable entities, appear and from which they depart. Birth and death presuppose a world which is not in constant movement, but whose durability and relative permanence makes appearance and disappearance possible, which existed before any one individual appeared into it and will survive his eventual departure. Without a world into which men are born and from which they die, there would be nothing but changeless eternal recurrence, the deathless everlastingness of the human as of other animal species.[42]

Death as we understand it, that is, death of unique individuals—as opposed to the deathlessness of other animals (Arendt's theory is incorrigibly anthropocentric)—depends upon the existence of a common world. Death so understood is not simply a process of nature. But while the existence of a world may transform and dignify natural death, natural death apparently offers nothing in return to the political world. It only detracts. Such is not the fate, however, for the other "natural" feature of human existence in Arendt's thinking, namely birth. Arendt often couples birth and death, natality and mortality, in her thinking about the political realm. But death attests to the "futility of mortal life and the fleeting character of human time."[43] Death is an ending, not a beginning, and thus brings one back closer to the cyclical, repetitive, nameless ways of nature. Natality, however, Arendt closely associates with human labor, work, and action. Most important, natality productively serves the political realm of action; the naturalness of birth inspires new beginnings, novel initiatives, and second births in the political arena:[44] "action has the closest connection with the human condition of natality; the new beginning inherent in birth can make itself felt in the world only because the newcomer possesses the capacity of beginning something anew, that is, of acting. In this sense of initiative, an element of action, and therefore of natality, is inherent

in all human activities."⁴⁵ And here, in Arendt's thinking about the
polis, birth and death part ways dramatically.⁴⁶ Death has nothing to
do with politics as such, and can provide no similar inspiration:
"Moreover, since action is the political activity par excellence,
natality, and not mortality, may be the central category of political,
as distinguished from metaphysical, thought" (p. 9).

Arendt continues this tirade against death in her discussion of
political equality. Death she deems to be part of the "outside" forces
of "nature": "The equality attending the public realm is necessarily
an equality of unequals who stand in need of being 'equalized' in
certain respects and for specific purposes. As such, the equalizing
factor arises not from human 'nature' but from outside, just as
money—to continue the Aristotelian example—is needed as an outside favor to equate the unequal activities of physician and farmer.
Political equality, therefore, is the very opposite of our equality before death" (p. 215). Although earlier she seemed to discount metaphysical speculations about death, here she smuggles into her discourse her own ontological assumptions about conditions under
death: "In these instances [equality before death or God], no equalizer is needed because sameness prevails anyhow; by the same token, however, the actual experience of this sameness, the experience
of life and death, occurs not only in isolation but in utter loneliness,
where no true communication, let alone association and community, is possible. From the viewpoint of the world and the public
realm, life and death and everything attesting to sameness are non-
worldly, antipolitical, truly transcendent experiences" (p. 215).

For Arendt, in sum, the polis is a place that abides in space and
over time, although individuals will, of course, pass away.⁴⁷ The
polis creates the conditions for heroic storytelling and remembrance, spectacular and spectatorial activities that distinguish
the human animal from other animals. But a great deal of what
Arendt has to say in favor of the permanence and order and meaningfulness of the political realm turns, upon inspection, on an extremely thin and yet tendentious view of conditions under death.
Human finitude is frustrating and debilitating for her, and nothing
more.⁴⁸ Her notion of politics pushes death out of the picture alto-
gether.⁴⁹ At times she seems to recommend action in the public
realm not so much for its eudaimonistic, self-referential, noninstrumental qualities but, rather, simply because the polis endures and
becomes the repository for ongoing stories and remembrance.⁵⁰
Perhaps this is why she disparages public realms that emerged in

episodic moments of history but failed to institutionalize themselves for any length of time (e.g., the Paris commune, the early American councils, civil disobedience movements). Political freedom, evidently, must not be fleeting and finite (Arendt could hardly agree with Thoreau's transcendental comment that an act once well done is done forever[51]). Even though many Arendtian writers today applaud her championing of antiessentialist action and worldly pluralities, when evaluated from the vantage of death, Arendt's memorialist politics look remarkably like religion by other means.[52] We still need to say more about the possible meaning(s) of death for politics.

Kateb has continued to press Arendt precisely on this sore point of death. Despite Arendt's rhetorical demand that all deathliness be exorcised from properly political concerns, Kateb detects an unacknowledged ambivalence toward death on her part. He believes that Arendt doesn't divest all deathliness from her categories of political action as she contends but, rather, leaves such deathliness very much (if silently) intact. Indeed, her notions of political action and of contracting through the act of promising reveal a parasitic commitment to a politics of deathliness, a not-so-secret "death pact" among citizens: "I not only think this scorn [Arendt's toward the American Constitution] was determined by her commitment to the unique excellence of direct citizenly involvement, I also think that—and this, though mostly speculation, is my basic point—this very commitment, which issued in a magnificent theory of political action, has a dark underside. That underside is a barely indicated sense that whenever the threat of death is missing, political action is not truly present."[53]

Kateb modifies his strong charge. He explains that he isn't contending that Arendt's ideal of political action is "bloody and death-minded." Rather, he notes a recurring tendency apparently informing many of Arendt's writings: What seems to give political action its uniquely admirable quality over other kinds of worldly action is the chance that "death may be encountered along its way." Death ties together many otherwise disparate Arendtian motifs. Kateb sees death looming in the background of Arendt's theory in the following themes: Her insistence that the life of citizenship must overcome the urge for mere survival, mere self-preservation; her praise of courage, along with glory and suffering; her repeated fascination with political action that revolves around wars of city-states and modern revolutions, the extraordinary as opposed to the ordinary;

even her preference for direct democracy over representative government, insofar as self-sacrifice is experienced in the former as an element of citizenship, not stately obligation. Indeed, Kateb finds Arendt explicitly toying with death in one of her last writings: "For public interest always demands a sacrifice of individual interests which are determined by life's necessities and by the limited time which is given to mortals. The necessary sacrifice of individual interests to the common weal—in the most extreme case, the sacrifice of life—is compensated for by public happiness, that is, by the kind of 'happiness' which men can experience only in the public realm."[54] In the Arendtian scheme of things, political action may withstand Silenus's pessimism and provide a humanly generated response to nature's fatalism and the downward cycle of death, but that renewable political optimism is curiously underwritten by a readiness to die. Hence for Kateb, Arendt's ambivalence about death betrays a *death-dynamic* that actually animates the *vita activa* of politics: "What makes it good to have been born is thus what carries with it the chance that one will die young."[55]

Arendtian exegetes lately have been returning to her texts to reclaim a Nietzsche-inspired version of agonistic, contestatory, pluralized action that sustains the public realm of politics. Although these commentators astutely gesture toward Nietzschean cruelties implicit in such enterprises, they tend to soft-pedal the possibility that the Arendtian agon might require a background practice of annihilating some of its participants, or parts of the self, or stories thereof. Instead, the point of recognizing Arendt's debt to Nietzsche is to suggest that the Arendtian agon might ventilate and creatively transform the latent death-wishing and *ressentiment* bequeathed to the West by Socratism and Christianity. Competitiveness and commonality can go thus gloriously hand in hand, and Kateb's warning about dangerous saber-rattling as a darkly binding sentiment goes unheeded.

Yet for Nietzsche, Homer's contest circumscribes an agon that isn't simply the harmless interplay of (and thus nonresentful recognition of) various selves, identities, disturbances, and conflicting points of view. The contest emerges out of pre-Homeric deathliness, and it can always degenerate back into a terrifying savagery of hatred (hence the need for occasional ostracism should a clear winner emerge).[56] Death foregrounds and threatens the Homeric agon for Nietzsche, even if it isn't quite the same space as the Iliadic battlefield. Can one even imagine, however, Nietzsche imagining

Homer's contest in a historical vacuum, teleported away from its pre-Homeric (i.e., deathly) context? The idea that the fighting is sublimated or rechanneled is key. The stakes are still, in a way, life-or-death stakes; the healthy, life-affirming ethos still draws much of its sustenance from death. Invidious competitiveness does characterize Arendt's political ideal;[57] the Greek public realm, she explains, was permeated by a "fiercely agonal spirit" where one vied to demonstrate one was the "best of all."[58] Yet Arendt, and some of her followers, apparently wish to adopt the humane side of Nietzsche's how-to manual on the Greeks (how to diffuse envy, cruelty, violence, resentment) without the requisite background of violence and annihilation.[59] Such readings run the risk of making the modern agon into a bloodless, gutless version of politics: suspiciously, as scholarly debate by other means.[60] (As rancorous as such debates might sometimes become, that model of politics as scholarly disputation provides, as the saying goes, a politics where the fighting is fierce precisely because the stakes are so low.)

The problem for Arendt and Arendtian scholars may be that Arendt has a hard time of openly incorporating death, the idea of human mortality, into a viable notion of politics.[61] Instead, she must insist upon a categorical separation between the two, death and politics. Apparently she has taken Hobbes's lesson to heart (while resisting Heidegger's[62]): death is to be avoided, combated, transcended. Death always represents a point of closure, a final ending, a defeat of human efforts, a verdict of doom and ruin; the countervailing actions of Arendtian politics must therefore open up those closures, now deploying the use of creative births, memorable foundings, heroic undertakings, and novel initiatives as a way of disrupting the march toward mortal doom. Human communities can and must *defy* the natural fact of human mortality. In one form or another, whether as combatants or contestants, Arendtian actors must fight to the death, paradoxically, in order to defy death. But as with our reading of Hobbes, we wonder whether the original formulation, the necessary and too adamant separation of politics and death, doesn't already contain the seeds of its own theoretical demise.[63]

Foucault

A notable exception to the prevailing post-Hobbesian skittishness to talk about linkages between death and politics is Foucault. In much of his writing Foucault focuses upon death;[64] and in volume 1 of his *History of Sexuality*, he issues a stunning analysis which breaks the contemporary silence on the politics of death.[65] Foucault turns his attention toward a brutal paradox today: How is it that political theorists can be so animated about managing civil affairs according to sanitized "original positions" precisely during the century that has featured the bloodiest massacres and the worst-imaginable genocides heretofore?[66] Amidst all of these population slaughters, internecine conflicts, and advances in the technologies and economies of destruction, there is precious little death talk in political theory circles. Although Foucault has finally broached the topic, his treatment hasn't exactly unleashed torrents of discussion on death in contemporary political theory circles. His analysis of the relationship between politics and death, however, includes at the same time an explanation for the dearth of death theory today (but which actually may compound and contribute to, rather than relieve the situation).

In his chapter "Right of Death and Power over Life," Foucault contends that the nature of power shifted from the classical to the modern period and, moreover, that that power shift was accompanied by a fundamental change in the political uses of death. Once upon a time (to shorten Foucault's impressive tale) sovereign power was located and visibly concentrated in *sites*, and power meant that that sovereign body had the ultimate right to kill: to take a subject's life, to enlist a person in state warfare, to mete out a death penalty as punishment. Hobbes and Arendt, it might be said, both grapple with this old conception of sovereign power; and the difference between them is really negligble, since both understand post-monarchical sovereignty in a similar fashion, namely, as *situated*. Once the king is dead, and political sovereignty is seen as residing somehow in mutually consenting people, the question is merely how to draw the lines of that reimagined, reconstituted sovereign body. Hobbes hands the sword to an imaginary Leviathan; Arendt thinks of empowered people acting within spatial/temporal territories. Within these larger bodies are discrete, smaller bodies, on which power supposedly rests ultimately. Both Hobbes and Arendt are body counters. Both ask of power: Who (i.e., what sovereign body) has the ultimate right to play executioner or to wage war?

The features of Foucault's new conception of power are well known: modern power is dispersed, decentered, multiple, capillary, polymorphous, self-disciplinary, normalizing. Foucault emphasizes the change in content from old power to new: new power doesn't present itself as so possessed with killing as a demonstrable aspect of the exercise of power. Power now stakes a claim over all of *life*; it purports to manage life itself, and thus extends its reach beyond the legal subject over whom the ultimate dominion formerly was death. New power is "bio-power" because it attempts to master *living* beings; it attempts to gain access to living bodies themselves. To be sure, even though biopower presents itself as administering a positive influence on life, wars are still waged and much death ensues; but such wars "are no longer waged in the name of a sovereign who must be defended; they are waged on behalf of the existence of everyone; entire populations are mobilized for the purpose of wholesale slaughter in the name of life necessity: massacres have become vital" (p. 137). The managers of life now expose, for instance, entire populations to the threat of atomic death, all in the name of accelerated global survival.

Power is now organized, according to Foucault, around the management of life rather than the menace of death (p. 147); it has shifted from "a symbolics of blood" to "an analytics of sexuality" (p. 148). In the process, talk of death has apparently subsided. But this decreased interest in talking about death isn't because power has become in fact less bloody. "That death is so carefully evaded is linked less to a new anxiety which makes death unbearable for our societies than to the fact that the procedures of power have not ceased to turn away from death" (p. 138). Power simply cannot admit its continued fascination with wars and punishments and executions lest it might appear hypocritically deterred from its life-supporting mission. So talk of death is politically out-of-bounds. Death is now construed as power's limit; it is deemed a *private* matter, a secret aspect of an individual's existence; accordingly, suicide is construed no longer as a crime but rather as an emerging individual right against biopower. The difference is that power's morbidity today is concealed, masked, hard to pinpoint.[67] Holocausts still happen, but it is increasingly hard to identify and distinguish among the perpetrators, culprits, and victims.

While his own analysis of the political genealogy of death is breathtaking, and while he helps explain why few such discussions have been forthcoming lately, Foucault doesn't provide us with a political rationale for reopening our investigations into the politics of death. If anything, the inference to be drawn from his analysis is that such inquiries are purely retrospective and thus antiquated, for the nature of power has since moved on. Biopower has relegated death to the margins of society, and there it shall remain—as a private, quasi-secretive, subject-centered matter. Our current politics by their own normalizing terms preempt such brooding discussions:

> It is not that life has been totally integrated into techniques that govern and administer it; it constantly escapes them. Outside the Western world, famine exists, on a greater scale than ever; and the biological risks confronting the species are perhaps greater and certainly more serious, than before the birth of microbiology. But what might be called a society's "threshold of modernity" has been reached when the life of the species is wagered on its own political strategies. For millennia, man remained what he was for Aristotle: a living animal with the additional capacity for a political existence; modern man is an animal whose politics place his existence as a living being in question.[68]

Suicide might be viewed as a promising strategy of individual resistance against biopower, but for the most part, death is, politically, a dead topic for Foucault (notwithstanding his own interest in the topic, especially toward the end of his own life[69]): "What we need, however, is a political philosophy that isn't erected around the problem of sovereignty, nor therefore around the problems of law and prohibition. We need to cut off the king's head: in political theory that has still to be done."[70] In turning toward an analysis of the politics of sexuality and thus away from the politics of death, he takes us back virtually to where we started in our survey of Hobbes and Arendt. We have come to a dead end, Derrida's *aporia*.[71]

Other Fields

I dare say that other academic disciplines have taken death more to heart or to task. Religious studies and metaphysics have always been morosely fixated on deathly issues, and a quick study of Buddha, Moses, Mohammed, Aquinas, and Pascal easily confirms the point.[72] Yet the antimetaphysical, deconstructive, and poststructuralist turns in much recent philosophy have drawn new attention to death.[73] Hegel's and Nietzsche's respective pronouncements of the death of God, and Nietzsche's explicit concern with exposing the secret death wishes informing Socratism and Christianity, have led many post-Nietzscheans to try to theorize a fresh kind of attachment to life divested of any lingering resentment over the idea of human finitude.[74] Much in Heidegger's work teaches a way to view death as a constant presence in life. Cleverly following the death of God as well as Nietzsche's analysis of the historical construction of Western selfhood, several commentators have issued their own pronouncements about the death of the subject or the death of the author. Death is a growth industry. Distracted or overwhelmed, however, by the various technologies of destruction now at their disposal, such scholars have seldom talked about the implications of politics in the wake of so much theoretical death.

Certain writers in the fields of psychology, sociology, and anthropology have been a little more forthcoming, teasing us toward issues of politics and death. The Freud and Jung disputes over the symbolic significance of death are legendary, and subsequent psychological investigations have contributed a great body of literature surrounding the issues of death, dying, and bereavement. Much in the post-Freudian works of Norman O. Brown and Jacques Lacan turns on the otherness of death as well.[75] Sociology, especially the sociology of religion, boasts a strong and abiding interest in death; and sociologists have ingeniously looked at death as an indirect way to read into the workings of society, in a tradition starting from Malinowski and Durkheim.[76] Robert Hertz, following Durkheim in particular, viewed the death of a political leader as a disruption of the social fabric which presents a possible crisis of legitimation and succession; subsequent studies of "second burial" funereal rituals have been connected intimately to the political landscape of various societies.[77] Philippe Ariès famously chronicled the changes in Western attitudes toward death from the high middle ages to the mid nineteenth century, during which time the deathbed chamber ceased to serve as a site of public mourning.[78] Others—such as Charles Jackson, Elisabeth Kübler-Ross, Ruth Harmer, Evelyn Waugh, Herman Feifel, Geoffrey Gorer, and Jessica Mitford[79]— then examined this trend toward the increasing professionalization and privatization of Western funereal rituals. Death in the West especially, they tell us, is expensive.

Anthropology, as might be expected, presents the widest array of case studies into death from which we gain valuable cross-cultural ethnographic data—complicating to no small degree our preliminary assumptions about the possible political significance of death. Arnold van Gennep's notion of liminality and the rites of passage,[80] along with James Frazer's famous study of the Golden Bough in Egyptian death cults,[81] paved the way for numerous other studies that viewed death as a key required for reading the symbolic system of various cultures (and one wants to include here the names of Victor Turner, Jane Harrison, Maurice Bloch, Mircea Eliade, Mary Douglas, and many others[82]). To the outsider, it seems that mortuary rituals display most tellingly native cultural practices that try to negotiate and negate the contingency of individual death and thereby provide a royal road toward cultural interpretation.[83] At these liminal moments one typically might find the ways political authority is sacralized and reinforced, for instance, when the dead are transformed into a naturalized cosmos (as in a fertility cycle) upon the basis of which a governing mandate might be claimed by some social elite.[84] Death may be a given of the human condition (though numerous cases on record contest even that basic Western, allegedly biological assumption), but the meaning of death must be socially imagined and constructed—and these meanings can vary greatly, the anthropologists teach us.[85] In taking a peek into and beyond the grave, we therefore may be opening a can of worms.

Problems of Studying Death

To the initiate, a few stern warnings are in order about dangerous pitfalls that lie ahead in any investigation delving into death. First, the topic is unbearably vast. Two prominent studies on death start out with this disclaimer:

> What could be more universal than death? Yet what an incredible variety of responses it evokes. Corpses are burned or buried, with or without animal or human sacrifice; they are preserved by smoking, embalming, or pickling; they are eaten—raw, cooked, or rotten; they are ritually exposed as carrion or simply abandoned; or they are dismembered and treated in a variety of these ways. Funerals are the occasion for avoiding people or holding parties, for fighting or having sexual orgies, for weeping or laughing, in a thousand different combinations.[86]

There is too much to cover, it is a topic that cannot be exhausted in one tidy book. Were I to attempt a more thorough treatment of the subject (devoting my entire life to it), a number of categories would need to be fully examined on their own terms: ghosts, mummies,

vampires, devils, resurrection, reincarnation, reanimation, transmigration, channeling, cryogenics, cloning, cannibalism, human
sacrifice, cemeteries, tombstones, epitaphs, black humor, millennial-
ism, apocalypse, Thanatology, depth psychology, near-death, pla-
gues, murder, war, suicide, martyrdom, death in plays, art, film,
lyric poetry, music, death metal, the Grateful Dead, and so on. In
politics a general survey would surely need to include careful comparative studies of state monuments and tombs, from Washington
to King Mausolus to Napoleon to the Taj Mahal to the pyramids;
important figures and dead bodies, such as Grant, Lenin, Che
Guevara, and Marilyn Monroe; and a history of pastoral versus urban cemetery practice. Such a grand study would in addition need
to display sufficient concern about deeply emotional issues of grief
and personal loss.

Next, there is the whole problem of definition. Delineating what,
exactly, death is is not as easy as it may seem at first blush. We are
heading into a legal, medical, conceptual, philosophical, and anthropological thicket. The legal and medical professions view the
messy matter of definition as anything but settled.[87] Brain-dead but
fetus-bearing bodies, for instance, keep popping up and testing legal
precedent. New technologies prolong comatose lives, and new sur-
gical procedures transfer, recycle, and replace blood, bones, and or-
gans from one being to another (human and otherwise). New drugs
hint at reversing the aging process. Cloning and biogenetic insights
blur the boundaries of cessation. We hardly need a professional deconstructionist to intervene for us in order to challenge most claims
to a stable, unitary, commonsensical definition of death.

Asking biologists for a bedrock definition of death barely helps,
either.[88] What exactly constitutes a dead organism is necessarily
bound up with the definition of an organism, and that, it turns out,
is related to the definition of an orgasm (pun intended). Death and
sexuality are intimately linked,[89] in ways apparently seldom considered by modern feminist theorists who want to reject out of hand
any such linkage.[90] George Wald and Georges Bataille have both
pointed out that the idea of death, starting with the development of
authentic corpses, seems to have been a late invention in evolution.[91]
One-celled, asexually reproducing organisms at the beginning of
the evolutionary chain do not die as such. Not until the emergence
of sexually reproducing organisms does biology begin to speak of
unique, discontinuous entities that, as it were, die. For that matter,
individual bodies are hosts to a host of other organisms, parasites,
and dividing and sloughing cells; many of these lesser organisms

manage quite nicely, thank you, upon the death and decomposition of the host body. The pronouncement of physical death, moreover, can lag behind, rather than temporally precede, sociocultural definitions, as in the case of Hindu ascetics.[92]

Anthropologists point to peoples such as those in the Amur Basin who evidently observe no distinction between life and death, no great conceptual divide or existential boundary between the two.[93] Dead family members still live amidst the others who happen to comport themselves somewhat more energetically; the dead (as it were) are fed regularly for several years after "death"; and what outsiders might deem to be death is viewed only as a change of life. In many cultures, practices of divination and oracle consultation, not to mention prayer, ancestor worship, and simple remembrance, can be viewed as ways in which the dead are never really dead among and for the living.[94] Cults of the dead, such as the Orphics, routinely offer ways, often poetic and not at all mystical to Western ears, of communing between past and present.

Philosophers and psychologists often vex us with epistemological enigmas about death that could potentially impede our study.[95] Freud held that it was impossible to imagine your own death, and if you try, you can imagine yourself only as a spectator, not as the actual participant in death[96] (hence, no one really believes in one's own death—all reports and beliefs are secondhand and premature). Wittgenstein likewise declared: "Death is not an event in life; we do not live our death."[97] La Rochefoucauld wrote that humans "cannot look directly at either the sun or death," and Jacques Choron claimed that the idea of death is simply not tolerable. Ernest Becker contended that any secular attempt to address the primal mysteries of life and death will end only in lies and denials.[98] Mark Twain, on the other hand, reportedly quipped that suicide is the most sincere form of self-criticism.

We must also heed at this outset Foucault's implicit warning about any presumption that an inquiry into death (like sex) will reveal some deep, dark secret, a truth about human existence, or a core revelation about private individuals.[99] Maybe as well, along Foucaultian lines, a concern with the death of bodies is today passé given that such an inquiry focuses so intensely on individual subjects. Death has been normalized and routinized and more or less accepted in the late modern world—why dwell on it? Deathbed recitations and accompanying melodrama have receded from the scene since the eighteenth century; the king is dead, the subject is dead, the subject of death is probably dead. Like Elvis, perhaps it should be kept that way.[100] Complicating Foucault's linkage of western sex/death with the notion of a well-defined, unitary subjectivity are the occasional Chinese Taoist and North American Eskimo beliefs that each person comprises three or four souls which live on in multiple fashion.[101]

Such pointers about the problems of studying death are meant not only for the reader's benefit but are reminders for authors of death as well. I will add a few other considerations to the list. A move toward death as a way of thinking about politics should raise our initial suspicions. It could easily degenerate into a search for a ground or foundation of discourse that claims for itself a necessary privilege. The search for a politics on the basis of death might reveal a strategy of trying to move one's theoretical designs closer to supposedly unassailable dictates of "nature" or "biology" or "sexuality" (or "feminism" or "third-worldism"—or any of a number of other coded associations). Death might, for some theorists, hold out the promise of discovering new standards of universalism; or Dionysian community; or democracy (death as a profoundly democratic condition); or equality (the "great equalizer"); or it might attest to human shortcomings and frailties (life as a vale of tears); or it might be used to shore up a repressive politics (Marcuse's worry[102]); or it might exacerbate an anxiety about the need for worldly distinction and individuation (eat, drink, and be merry today, for tomorrow . . .).[103] It might be tempting for some to use the specter of death as a new regulative ideal, a way to claim a cognitive advantage, a way to effect closure or to reach an Archimedean point from which to do theory.[104] Death could serve as a tabula rasa on which an enterprising theorist could map or project about any position. Silence about death has been a big problem, to be sure, but we must be careful not to speak to that silence too glibly, especially since the topic tends to call forth many of our most touching or disturbing memories and emotions. A book about death and politics must not be manipulative, mawkish, or cheap. Leonardo da Vinci cut up dead bodies to discover the essence of human existence, and all he found inside were blood and guts; the eyes of his figures sketched thereafter—blank, distant, weary—tell the story of a death study gone foul.

Liberalism

Much as one who has experienced hell and lived to tell about it, we are now, after having completed our brief excursion into problems of studying death, in a better position to refine our thesis and reorient the direction of the project. Silence about death in political theory is a relatively recent phenomenon; surely the silence is silence under the particular conditions of liberal, secular democracy. Silence about death in political theory mirrors a contemporary silence about death in politics at large, or rather a silence in American political liberalism. We can easily develop a plausible account for such silence. The hallmark of liberalism, to use a commonplace if contested shorthand, is that it is a system that considers "the right" to have priority over "the good." The state·strives to maintain procedural neutrality on positions of substantive goodness, especially where rival versions may conflict. Even to the extent that the state intervenes in substantive issues of the good, it must confine its commentary to the "vital" concerns of survival, resource distribution, and worldly matters in general; commentaries on death ought to be reserved for the spheres of religion, theology, and metaphysics. As such, they are best confined to private, not politically public, realms. Narratives of and beliefs about death and life-after-death are thus best left privatized and pluralized. The boundary between matters of life and matters of death is conspicuous, hard to deconstruct, easy to respect.

Hence a Durkheimian analysis of death, one that reads into the structure of society by indirection, doesn't really apply to liberal politics. Durkheimians and post-Durkheimians typically presume that a common social structure underlies all political designs.[105] Death then alters social relations. Deathly disruptions in the political sphere thus require a funereal ritual to restore societal legitimation.[106] But political liberalism can remain silent on death, even on the death of a political leader, because the state neither presumes nor depends upon a coherent social order for its political standing. The state enjoys relative autonomy because of its professed neutrality.

Another way of accounting for this silence (and the attempt is admittedly speculative) is to extend Kantorowicz's famous study of the medieval king's "two bodies" into a theory of the modern state under liberalism. Like the double burial ceremony in Japan, the theory of the king's two bodies helped to solve, by camouflaging, the problem of succession and political continuity. Whereas the king's physical body would die, his corporate body would somehow live on (the king is dead, long live the king). Hence arose the idea of the political corporation, the people as a *universitas*, an entity that never dies, is never under age, is never senile, never sick, and carries on without sex.[107] The state is androgynous and self-reproducing and is exempt from all considerations about death. Many of those assumptions about the corporate status of the state, we might extrapolate, still characterize the constitutional status of the state under liberal democracy. The state need not develop a theory of death because it simply is not subject to death as such.

Individuals, even democratic individuals, still bleed and die, however, and death requires some response to the disruptions that it brings. But such functions of bereavement and coping (or celebration) are conducted by substate institutions and associations, and by private individuals who fend for themselves in the absence of a more public method. A wide variety of studies have described the institutionalism and privatization of funerary practice under conditions of American liberalism.[108] Such studies note, for instance, that the site of death has shifted from the private residence to institutional settings such as the hospital, the nursing home, the funeral home. Funerary rituals accordingly have become professionalized, often removing the place of burial from the local church cemetery to the commercial graveyard or mausoleum. The professional for-profit cemetery superintendent and funeral director, mediating between life and death, thus take over many of the responsibilities formerly directed by clergy and kin.[109]

Jessica Mitford and others have ghoulishly described the details of the professionalization and commercialization of the funeral industry in America in particular.[110] The rituals of death are now distributed according to market mechanisms—death is a commodity—and individuals pay and sustain the going rates, including insurance policies against death and pre-paid funeral plans. Mitford, Gorer, Christopher Lasch and other observers of the American funeral and aging business view the whole process as an attempt at denying the realities of death (embalming methods, cosmetic touch-ups, and copper caskets, for instance, mask such realities). Americans, these authors contend, generally refuse to talk about death; Americans banish the old and infirm to hospitals and nursing homes and to other such professional institutions because we can't stand the idea of death in the face of our buoyant, technologically successful, American style of individualism. Death is a downer; it is an embarrassment; it isn't polite. It means, when all is said and done, failure. Charles Jackson contends that Americans of the twentieth century no longer live their lives with the well-defined relationship to and

interest in the world of the dead that came to characterize the nineteenth century.[111] The forces of urbanization, bureaucratization,
mobility, and demographics have contributed to this separation of
the world of the dead from that of the living.[112]

While many of these authors speak sweepingly of denial, Philippe
Ariès sees a kind of heroism and genius in Americans' modern response to death and dying.[113] By turning to, in effect creating and
supporting, a modern commercial funerary establishment, American are trying, as individuals, to devise new rituals and institutions.
Ariès doesn't explicitly connect this development to his other major
claim, namely that death, once it left the bed chamber, ceased to be
a public matter and became privatized—and yet such a connection
could easily be drawn. Instead of denial and Lasch's contention of
symptomatic narcissism, American funerary practice could be, and
probably must be viewed in relation to, as a function of, the liberal
state's neutrality and lack of policy or public commentary concerning death. Clearly it would be contrary to all contemporary assumptions to suppose that individuals should look to or expect any help
from the state in their confrontations with the Reaper. The matter
is out of bounds. Civil society, separate from the state, in fact supports a profusion of alternatives for imagining and negotiating with
the prospect of death. Far from denial, Americans, we might submit, are fascinated and even preoccupied with death. Witness the
best-selling status of *Final Exit*, a recent how-to manual on suicide;
and yet another how-to best-seller on death, *How We Die*.[114] Or
observe the outpouring in popular materials, in films, books, music,
on the themes of violence and killing. The thirst for blood has
never been higher—death (like sex) sells!—even if erudite discussions of death don't appear in political theory journals or in the
chambers of Congress.

Some might raise the question at this point: If the silence of liberal theory on death reflects the silence of liberal practice on the
matter, and if liberal civil society copes well enough with death, why
do we even need a political theory of death (except, perhaps, to
recognize its proper apolitical standing)? I would answer along the
lines of Marx's analysis of the status of religion found in his essay,
"On the Jewish Question." The alleged autonomy of the liberal
state is incomplete and even disingenuous. Death policies do exist,
even if thinly veiled by official terms of neutrality. Furthermore, in
many policy matters, the state actually adopts substantive positions
on death. The state certainly intervenes when it provides a legal

decree of death; when it comes time to tax departing citizens; when it proclaims memorial days for those fallen in battle. But there are other times when political neutrality on death is impossible to maintain, when the state slips into taking very telling stances on the public significance of death.

Some of the political assumptions about death emerge only when liberal practice is put into comparative perspective. A few examples:

Property rights: The French Revolution transformed and democratized the notion of property by eliminating the intergenerational transfer of titles and offices. The contemporary liberal state clearly adopts a death policy when it regulates and taxes inheritance transfers. The mere notion of an estate that remains intact and abides even after the death of the owner requires political articulation. The definition of property is not simply a function of the processes of the market—what counts as property, who counts as legitimate economic actors, and what and how much property one can cling to beyond the grave are questions that can all be subjected to political negotiation and contestation. (Weber also makes a point of noting that the oldest paper money was used to pay, not the living, but the dead.[115])

Legal rights and contract: In many matters of libel law, tort and probate, dead persons have rights. Contracts don't expire after the death of a party to the contract, as if there were a built-in statute of limitations or expiration clause. But should it be lawful for one to extend deliberately one's contractual influence well beyond one's death? For instance, should a home buyer be permitted to finance expensive real estate by taking out a 100-year mortgage (as in Japan), thereby committing future generations of progeny to debt without their prior consent? By a similar token, should it be legally permissible for investors to buy out the life insurance policies of soon-to-be-dead AIDS and cancer patients?

Citizenship: For a period in ancient Greek democracy, the son could not vote until the father had passed away. Today we ignore the idea of family representation in favor of "one person, one vote"—even as the family becomes a renewed subject of political theorizing. Are there times, however, when democratic voting should be generation-specific (e.g., a referendum on the increasing burden of Social Security on a younger working generation, or a national tax policy that defers a huge burden of debt)?

Freedom versus enslavement: Orlando Patterson has argued

that slavery represents a societal substitute for death (captivity rather than killing in war, for example).[116] The slave experiences life in the liminal state of "social death" insofar as he or she is alienated from his birthright, family, ancestors, and descendants. Patterson's analysis of the slave's "institutionalized marginality" resonates with Derrida's analysis of the marginal or foreign figure as a "figure of death."[117] Our notions and practices of political, legal, and social standing are intertwined, these authors suggest, with our cultural conceptions of death.

Community versus individual rights: Laws on suicide, suicide-assistance, and euthanasia force the state to adjudicate between claims to an "individual's right to die" and the state's claim to preserving that person's live body. Demographic shifts toward an older U.S. population, along with the skyrocketing costs of health care, have worked to make these issues of dying more salient in recent years.

Medical ethics: In addition to life-prolonging procedures, new reproductive technologies have forced the state to make literally life-or-death decisions. Human sperm can be frozen and thawed—hence biological generations no longer need to be successive—and the issues have become practical, not just speculative. Who owns the sperm of a dead man? What are the legal rights and responsibilities of dead but actively procreative parents?

The rights of the unborn: Disputes over abortion, the environment, and the growing national debt all raise the issue of a nation's obligation to the future. In the case of abortion, the federal state sometimes claims procedural neutrality by shifting the right to states or women, but this move hasn't satisfied those citizens who see substantive rights for the nearly-born and yet-to-be-born. Especially in the case of abortion, substantive and procedural rights are extremely hard to disentangle.

National reparations: Reparations paid to interred Japanese-Americans have sparked a recent debate about whether reparations should be paid to the American descendants of African slaves; but this is not the first time in U.S. history that such a debate has occurred. National debts are in fact sometimes discharged beyond any statute of limitations. Names are cleared, the guilty exonerated, wrongs redressed. The Japanese recently issued an apology for wartime prostitution camps in South Korea. Canada returned large parcels of land to its native population. In the United States, the courts have been asked to retrieve bones of Native Americans on display in museums and return them to original burial grounds. The past is never simply past in the politics of a nation.

War and conscription: Any pretense that the state doesn't have a right to one's very life is swept away in times of war. The state can call upon its citizens to die (not just to risk death). Although many U.S. citizens insist on the constitutional right to bear arms, very few members of civil society are demanding that the (voluntary) military be completely privatized. Also, the state reveals a strong attitude about death in its obsession for identifying, securing, and repatriating the dead bodies of MIA's, sometimes decades after the end of a war.

Capital punishment: The state, quite simply, can punish you by taking your life. Although no longer viewed as cruel and unusual and unconstitutional, capital punishment can hardly be construed as a "neutral" commentary on the relative significance of life versus death.

Even beyond the above policy matters, liberalism draws much theoretical sustenance from stands, albeit inexplicit or poorly articulated stands, on death. The American democracy is, of course, not a plebiscitarian democracy but rather a constitutional republic. Constitutionalism is arguably a strong form of ancestor worship. Why we in the present ought to respect those words and practices from the past requires an elaborate theoretical storytelling that, in the end, somehow inspires living reverence for the work of dead men. More than one commentator has noted that Washington, D.C., the nation's capital and site of federal authority, is one huge boulevard of monuments, memorials, and museums—the Washington, Jefferson, Lincoln monuments; the Vietnam, the Holocaust, and other memorials; the Smithsonian and other museums; Arlington Cemetery, and so forth.[118] To someone from another planet, the nation's capital probably looks like a cult of the dead.[119] State and local capitals throughout the nation also draw upon a deathly monumentalist architecture, much of which glorifies war and killing. Dead people's pictures and lifeless statues hang in capitol verandas all across the country. It is not hyperbole to say that political institutions in the United States, on the local, state, and federal levels, reek of death.

Political notions of contract, community, individualism, ethics, and justice all betray an underlying stance about death. Edmund

Burke, for instance, was the only contractarian to extend expressly one's political obligation to past and future generations (although his influence on modern liberalism is virtually dead, replaced by Thomas Paine's claim that "it is the living, and not the dead, that are to be accommodated"[120]). Hegel felt that the notion of community emerges in the modern state only in times of war; people feel a sense of civic connection only in times of official extremis, as they engage in a collective meditation on death (Hegel forgot All Hallow's Eve). Some say that liberalism bespeaks a theory of robust individualism; but anthropologists and morticians will tell you that at the time of death, liberal societies radically devalue the individuality of the deceased—communities do their best to expel the dead body from their midst.[121] In political ethics, some theorists advocate a version of consequentialism—but such notions usually don't extend as far, for instance, as the Native American consideration for the consequences to the seventh generation beyond the present. Those who espouse an economics and psychology of self-interest usually employ an extremely foreshortened concept of interest, one that doesn't take aging and death much into consideration (try modeling Andrew Carnegie's motto: "The man who dies thus rich dies disgraced."[122]). Some post-Keynesian economists seek to extend the reach of self-interest into an intergenerational incentive, contending that a bequest motive spurs long-run productivity; but that particular holy grail has never been statistically demonstrated. "Count no mortal man happy until he is dead"—the eudaimoniac wisdom of the ancients—is lost on the limited egoists of the present (not to mention Aristotle's contention that the happiness of the dead can be altered after the fact[123]). Finally, considerations of justice have always drawn upon images and tales of an afterlife, however these might be construed. Dikē, for Sophocles' Antigone, was a god of the underworld. If liberalism is reluctant to speak about death, perhaps the topic of justice is not getting its full due.

Literary Alternatives

As a response to the virtual silence of liberalism and liberal theory on the politics of death, this book is not meant as anything more than a first step in the direction of speaking a bit more forthrightly on the subject. Yet there is still another turn in my argument and procedure. I propose that it is highly advisable in theorizing about death to rely especially on literary and admittedly imaginative strategies of analysis. I intend simply to circumvent many of the methodological and epistemological problems mentioned above by making generous recourse to fiction. I thus won't be attempting to look death squarely in the face. Here I borrow shamelessly from Rousseau's *Second Discourse*.

"Let us begin therefore by setting aside all the facts, for they do not affect the question."[124] More than any other sentence in Rousseau's writings, this opening sally rankles readers. How dare he disregard reality so brazenly! Such critics typically charge Rousseau, by the end of the essay, with proposing that humanity is naturally good or else perfectible, that his account of the state of nature is built on a new anthropology and benign but naive primitivism. They squirm to explain the seemingly obvious contradiction in his outlook between fantasy and facticity; they deconstruct his cleverness if they detect it. They apparently cannot accept his admittedly imaginative critique of former naturalisms, Hobbesian and Lockean. But Rousseau's method is quite sensible: If humans are creatures conditioned in good part by their surroundings, then it is impossible to theorize an aboriginal human "nature." Even one's perception of the "facts" of nature will be refracted through the lens of societal conditioning (which is to say, humans are situated and born into civil and social settings; there is no way not to be). In a sense, Rousseau virtually confesses, one *never* can reach a pristine state of nature outside of civil society; all arguments on the basis of nature are dubious. Should one wish to engage nevertheless in this kind of theorizing (if only to throw the burden of proof back upon Hobbes and Locke), one can do so only by indirection—by admitting the fictive, provisional, ironic, imaginative status of the enterprise. To get an outside perspective on ourselves (as it were), we theorists must project through fiction, we must construct our own Feuerbachian *Umweg*, we must visit other possibilities through a leap of the imagination. The point of such a tact is *not* to advocate utopian or idealistic schemes; rather, a literary approach, wherein one announces candidly the fictionality of the enterprise, is the only hardheaded way to proceed if one is deadly serious about being true to the full nature of politics (i.e., as an intractable yet irretrievable "second nature").

In the following pages I am therefore not attempting to embark on a new metaphysics of death for the sake of politics. Rather I am exploring and advocating admittedly imaginative excursions into death, as a way of theorizing about politics. My strategy is Rousseauian, except that I shift the focus from a state of nature to a state of death.

The approach is not new. There is a long tradition in the West of imaginative infernal traveling closely associated with political foundation narratives, from the *Epic of Gilgamesh* to Homer's *Nekyia* to Virgil's *Aeneid* to Dante's *Inferno* to Goethe's *Faust* to Nietzsche's *Zarathustra*.[125] Called variously the *katabatic* or orphic-epic tradition,[126] these speculative descents into nether regions allow theoretical travelers to examine political attachments as if from afar. The key to these deathly excursions is that the entrance into the underworld is gained by way of artistic expression and Orphic lyricism—called the Dionysian by Nietzsche, the archetypal by Jung, the carnivalesque by Bakhtin. Again, the appeal to literature and fiction need not represent a flight from realism and an escape into fantasy but, instead, can contain a very calculated approach for circumventing the epistemological and representational limitations imposed on theory by conditions of human finitude.[127] Science, by contrast, simply offers no reliable understanding about death; it can offer no interpretive account—it must remain mute; whereas literature can at least venture into such dark, uncharted territories. In politics, literary approaches characteristically attest, if through understatement, to the greater elusiveness of the subject and to the inherent limitations of theory. Literature can thereby offer a far greater commitment to realism, a sustained acknowledgment of on-the-ground complexity, than self-proclaimed realistic accounts, which, by contrast, often seem brutish, nasty, and short.

Underworldly accounts have been particularly good at providing a sense of linkage between past and present, for recollecting in the land of the dead the memories of lost lovers, neglected parents, and vanquished enemies. Dionysian forays, Aeschylean furors, Orphic excursions, and Rabelaisian carnivals commonly try to effect communion with the dead through a poetic spirit of festivity. Political theory could productively align itself more closely with this tradition since the importance of the past bears so heavily on the work of contemporary theory. But underworldly meditations with the dead need not be confined to knowledge of the past; through a similar exercise of imaginative consultation we can better forge speculative ties with and toward the future.

The preliminary fear, I suspect, for those not predisposed toward such an adventure is that it seems to provide shaky, flaky grounds for analysis. But I suggest that such reveries ultimately erase initial distinctions between the imaginative and the unembellished. For instance, Arendt's insistence that the category of death belongs outside of politics because it is hopelessly tethered to cyclical nature might be reexamined under an Orphic spell. Thus I can imagine a land of the dead wherein earlier notions about political equality are shown finally, after all is said and done, as having been based all along on supremely *political* constructions of the allegedly natural distinction between nature and politics—but dead souls appreciate this erasure only after the fact, after they have been removed from a political situation that masks its own conceptual triumphs. Similar deathly investigations might throw into analytic relief some of our deepest and yet occluded assumptions about personhood, agency, politics itself. A little act of the imagination can shed altogether new light on our political attachments and might even suggest new paths to take. To be sure, no final account, no single image (or cluster of images) can possibly account for human mortality; indeed, if it were possible to deliver a fully satisfying account of death, then political theorists would not have to resort to images, which are, by nature, incomplete and imperfect.[128] But it will not do simply to erase death entirely from the political narrative, to pretend that the business of politics isn't conducted in the shadow of human mortality. Richard Rorty, for one, wants us to stop telling big life-or-death stories because, he contends, such stories smack of metaphysics[129]; but Rorty doesn't seem to consider that one might descend poetically into death without yielding to a new metaphysical literalism. In turn, can his smaller, so-called pragmatic stories really lead us onward in light of death?

Yet I trust Rorty to be a potential ally of the present attempt to pursue and maybe to craft new political images. In *Contingency, Irony, and Solidarity*, Rorty in effect calls upon today's political theorists to become creative image-makers, for human solidarity is to be expanded through imaginative identification with others, not through supposedly unassailable appeals to unchanging and firmly grounded reasons. Older abstractions such as the appeal to "rational beings" have done an "enormous amount of good,"[130] but Rorty submits that a new, admittedly constructed *focus imaginarius* animating a sense of obligation would be "none the worse for being an invention rather than (as Kant thought it) a built-in feature of the human mind" (p. 196). Rorty names his utopian preference for a liberal polity whose cultural hero would be a "strong poet" (in Harold Bloom's sense of the term) (p. 53). Such a poet can inspire committed civic sensibilities even in this epoch characterized by contingency, irony, and disbelief. "A sense of human history as the history of successive metaphors would let us see the poet, in the generic sense of the maker of new words, the shaper of new languages, as the vanguard of the species" (p. 20).

So far so good. Where I take exception to Rorty's call for a new-found appreciation of the benefit of political *poesis* is in his insistence that the strong poet's main virtue is his or her strong fear of death. Rorty relies upon Bloom for this understanding of poetry: "every poet begins (however 'unconsciously') by rebelling more strongly against the fear of death than all other men and women do."[131] Rorty wishes to extend Bloom's definition of strong poets beyond inspiring versifiers, so that he might include Proust, Nabokov, Newton, Darwin, Hegel, and Heidegger as people also "to be thought of as rebelling against 'death'—that is, against the failure to have created—more strongly than most of us."[132] The strong poet's fear of death, Rorty explains, is "the fear of incompletion" which prompts the realization that one's works will always be marginal, parasitic, and therefore dependent for meaningfulness upon readers' good will and upon past writers' efforts (p. 41). Nietzsche, too, writes of a culture that supports the self-creating strong poet—but Rorty prefers the Bloomian poet as a "de-divinized" version of the Nietzschean hero. Accepting a "pathos of finitude" (p. 42), Bloom's poet builds upon a tradition of poems and poetry, past and future, ever mindful that no poem gets completed in a single lifetime, since "no such working out gets completed before death interrupts" (p. 42).

What, I want to interject, is the necessary connection between poetic image-making and fearfulness about death? Rorty's fearful formulation seems to exclude Whitman's democratic call for great poets of death—poets, it would seem, whose inspiration draws upon, confronts, maybe even celebrates human finitude (with all the contingency, incompletion, and uncertainty that death might confer). I largely accept Rorty's critique of modern theorizing for its failure to provide adequate and credible justifications for modern practice; and I welcome his call for a kind of poetic consultation that might better serve modern political practice. But I suggest that he has overlooked the political tradition of descent poetry, wherein death is not simply dreaded but also celebrated as the font of creative rebellion. Whitman called not only for new poems for a democratic America but for great poems of *death*. Who better to consult for appropriate images of death than the dead themselves? Hence as poets we travel into the underworld.

Case in point: Aristophanes' play *The Frogs* features a disguised Dionysus (pretending to be Heracles) who descends into Hades in search of a poet who can teach the people how to be better citizens. Orators, politicians, educators, sophists, and even contemporary poets have failed in this task; it is a decadent age. Thus Dionysus seeks inspiration from one of the classic dead poets of the city. The play is of course a spoof upon the descent tradition, and the main drama features an amusing contest of wits between Euripedes and Aeschylus as they stand before the Palace of Pluto. At the outset of the contest Pluto tells Dionysus that he can take one of the two poets back with him, but he must choose. Before the contest begins, Euripedes asks Dionysus, "What do you want a poet for?" To which Dionysus responds: "To save the City of course."[133] Aeschylus eventually wins, a triumph which the play portrays as a victory for wisdom over mere poetic cleverness (and that preference accords with the play's evident desire to end the bloodshed of war mongering in the land-of-the-living above). The comic Aristophanes makes a serious point, which apparently can be expressed only through comedic allusion, because the living are literally in no position to appreciate it: Dead poets are the best equipped to teach the living about politics. The living, by contrast, do not fully appreciate the long-term stakes of their own efforts; without the help of dead poets they are incapable of entertaining the big picture on things.

Although *The Frogs* demonstrates a poetic excursion into death for the sake of political counsel, it doesn't provide an adequate counterexample to Rorty's call for a strong poet who rebels against death—since *The Frogs* seems to be invoking dead Aeschylus to teach a commonplace about tragic limitations. Death, while portrayed poetically and comically, is still to be avoided. Thus I might call attention to another, trickier example from the descent tradition of political consultation, the point of which in this particular case isn't simply a blanket reverence for life (by deathly indirection): to wit, Machiavelli's *The Prince*.

Thanks to Sebastian de Grazia's excavating work, *Machiavelli in Hell*, we now realize that Machiavelli was entirely preoccupied with the descent tradition in Western poetry. De Grazia contends that Machiavelli was a frequent visitor to the underworld. "He often set up reports, communications, and journeys between this world and that one beyond the tomb."[134] Machiavelli described his own exile as a living hell, and he included references to hell in numerous works, especially *The Golden Ass*, *Belfagor*, and *Mandragola*. Like Dante, Machiavelli imagines hell as a political allegory; and like Dante, Machiavelli creatively rewrites the Plutonic narrative: "The most famous travels to the dead available to Niccolò in literature in one form or another would include Odysseus's in Homer, Er's in Plato, Orpheus and Aeneas's in Virgil, and Dante's guided by Virgil in Dante. All of these journeys are drawn out in lengthy sections of long works, cast with unhappy scenes. Niccolò's journeys are short, described in a paragraph, and anticipated with delight" (p. 324). Machiavelli's reconstructed hell "has a political philosophy, a statecraft, and a moral philosophy to go along with it. Further, he has revamped hell to make it less hot, well-governed, and pleasantly populated" (p. 340).

But perhaps de Grazia's most interesting claim concerns the famous letter Machiavelli wrote to Francesco Vettori in which Machiavelli reveals whence he got his material for *The Prince*, namely, through evening seances with ancient authors.[135] Commentators have read the letter as Machiavelli's imaginative and self-aggrandized if ambivalent identification with ancient princes—since the paragraph in question talks about "ancient courts of ancient men"— but de Grazia reads this "fantasy" (Machiavelli's word) as yet another of Machiavelli's otherworldly excursions. In the letter, Machiavelli refers to Dante in the same breath as *On Princedoms*; and the ancient authors referred to by name in the letter are all poets. No matter whether the ancient (i.e., dead) leaders in question are poets or princes, a most curious line in the letter states that while he is engaged in conversation with these ancients in his study, Machiavelli forgets all of his troubles, he is not bored, he does not fear poverty; and, "I am not frightened by death; entirely I give myself over to them."[136] In this transfixed mode, no longer frightened by death, Machiavelli writes down his notes for what eventually becomes *The Prince*.

Machiavelli, for de Grazia, is an infernal traveler *and* a new infernal image-maker for politics. But he doesn't name his new work *The Prince in Hell*. Machiavelli doesn't admit that the new death image is indeed a new death image (we have to surmise that from his letters). Machiavelli provides a post-Christian model of hell, a hell that is less tormenting, according to de Grazia, because he doesn't want new princes to love their souls more than their countries; he doesn't want them to avoid doing evil out of a daunting fear of hell. Yet

Machiavelli doesn't want to deprive new princes the useful tool of invoking fear of hell as a way of keeping common, god-fearing people in line. His new political image of hell is reserved, therefore, for a select company; otherwise he will keep quiet about his ulterior motives. De Grazia worries about Machiavelli's "sleight of hand" and whether "the revamped hell [is] but whistling in the dark."[137] Machiavelli wants to teach a new attachment to politics, one that doesn't necessarily depend upon fearfulness of death; and accordingly he looks to craft new images of death for modern politics. Yet there is a problem in announcing oneself as a self-conscious political myth-maker, especially in an epoch that clings tenaciously to the old images.

Machiavelli's inability to come clean may hold lessons for our era. Netherworldly theorists characteristically rely for their images of death upon the experts—the dead, mostly dead poets.[138] They present themselves as "channelers" for the dead, compensating for their own volitional or creative crises by reporting, as it were, secondhand accounts from sources that cannot be confirmed by the living. In the infernal tradition, theorists are freed of the burden of relying on their own diminished authority: they present themselves as simply reporting what the dead have told them, a secondhandedness that typically lends itself to comic, masked, or ironic modes of presentation. Although such secondhand theorists cannot resolutely fashion new political images, they are sufficiently creative to fashion an imaginative underworld in which they receive the teachings of shadowy experts. The infernal tradition thus shelters a moment of creative *poesis*, allowing theorists to acknowledge their own justificatory shortcomings while simultaneously continuing the project of political theory. Political theory is not dead, but it is well-nigh impossible without the help of the dead.

In light of the failures of contemporary liberal and postmodern theory to offer constructive images for our political practice, Richard Rorty nobly tries to recuperate these two theoretical projects by bringing them together into an unexpected alliance: Private ironism and public liberalism can coexist peacefully, even productively, he reassures us. But as sketched above, Rorty's uneasy reconciliation of irony and politics depends upon a poetic bridge that is built over a deep chasm: Rorty's private ironist and Rorty's public liberal share a common disposition toward *death*, namely, *fear*. Rorty rewrites Hobbes's rewriting of the Christian tradition of fearfulness unto death; but in the end, he, like Hobbes, is *too* parasitic upon that tradition he attempts to refashion. Maybe, however, postmodern irony and political liberalism can be brought together in a way— namely, following the descent tradition—that doesn't write death out of the poetic equation, as Rorty's poet-theorist rebelliously demands.[139] Still, Rorty's efforts are a far cry from those of modern, liberal, and postmodern theorists who blithely insist that human mortality presents no great obstacle to political theorizing and statecraft. For example, John Rawls (whom I consider to be one of the great image-purveyors of our time[140]) concocts an "original position" that effectively insulates theorizing from death by transforming mortal citizens into lifeless abstractions;[141] such liberal projects need to be linked to the Christian tradition of attempting to defeat, ignore, or redeem the idea of death. Rorty wants us to confront the vestigial Platonism that creeps into contemporary theory; I would add, we still need to confront our vestigial Christianity and, following Machiavelli's hell (which is reserved exclusively for macho men), our vestigial sexism. The rest of this book will thus review those respective matters in that order: Platonism, Christianity, feminism.

   To sum, political theorists customarily have paid insufficient attention to death in their studies of politics—and perhaps there is good reason for that tremendous oversight.[142] Politics (and perforce the study of politics) generally focuses upon issues of the day, involving the flesh-and-bones concerns of pragmatic survival, resource distribution, cruelty avoidance, and other such matter-of-fact concerns; whereas the study of death is usually related to the realms of religion, theology, or metaphysics—to the otherworldly.[143] The silence of the neutral liberal state also discourages or deflects much death theory, and the ghost of Hobbes has kept us quiet. But death is hard, ultimately impossible to ignore as an integral part of the human condition, as the final parameter for what counts as politically feasible or admirable; and thus no account is still an account, by default or omission, if an extremely thin account. If politics requires dedication and attachment to worldliness however defined, whether as power, as justice, as the common good, or as individual interest, then how can that dedication be sustained in the face of death? Just as Camus claimed that suicide is the only important question for philosophy, so must political theorists at some point confront the question of death (which looms ever silently in the background). What is our response to Silenus? If death defeats all hopes and purposes and aspirations for life in this world, doesn't it also mock politics as a matter of course, in due time? *Fiat justicia, et pereat mundus* [without justice, let the world perish] said Cicero, said Kant, said Arendt.[144] But their respective notions of justice, despite their admirable attempts to introduce justice into worldly affairs, all seem now a tad too transcendental. Maybe Cicero, Kant, and Arendt were looking in the wrong direction for Dikē. We need to start digging downward instead. As Aristotle remarked, the truly free life of *theorein* is life considered from the perspective of death.[145]

No Exit?

The order and rationale of the remaining chapters in this book follow the following scheme. For those readers (and reviewers) who wish to find my particular solution to the dilemmas posed above but who, for one reason or another, find themselves short on time, you may skip directly to the final chapter. There you will find my culminating and yet self-contained theory of Plutonic justice, the purpose of which is to provide a social contract for liberal-democratic theory that takes death more robustly into account than it currently does. The intervening chapters can be read on their own or as part of a more intricate tapestry. I present close readings (excavations/ exhumations/ resurrections/ reanimations) of three prominent death narratives in Western theorizing: Platonic death, Christian death, feminist death. In my own background research and thinking, I have not turned a blind eye toward non-Western death accounts; but most of these accounts, although immensely interesting, do not speak directly to the genealogy of the liberal-democratic political problems outlined above. There is much cross-cultural work to be done, but for now, I leave others to accomplish that vastly important work.

These three excursions into death—the Platonic, the Christian, and the feminist—all present idealisms that stem from an attentiveness to dead bodies. To speak very broadly, such idealisms still inform, if only as a dead weight from the past, the politics of contemporary liberal-democracy. On this score I am following Nietzsche's understanding of the murky origins of Western moralism, which, according to Nietzsche, can be traced in good part to particular interpretations of the deaths of Socrates and Christ. In numerous places I borrow from Nietzsche's reading, but in many other places I depart significantly; and in those latter places I try to draw forth the political implications of my alternative view. These texts— Plato's writings and the Christian Bible—still require careful rereadings. It might be noted that toward the end of his life, with deathly matters closing in around him, Michel Foucault similarly took up rereadings of Platonism and Christianity—this familiar Nietzschean territory—in order to articulate a "politics of the self."[146] In key places I push off from Foucault's insights as well. Into this sweeping discussion I also want to introduce an equally broad contribution by modern feminism, in particular the work of Donna Haraway. Like Nietzsche and Foucault, Haraway and other modern feminists want to identify expansively influential historical assumptions that still inform modern practice, sometimes silently and insidiously. Socrates' and Christ's understandings of death, as well as Nietzsche's and Foucault's accounts of them, can now be exposed as "male" readings of death. I am interested, then, in examining Haraway's reworking of Platonic and Christian death themes in order to gesture toward an alternative feminist account of the politics of death.

My own take on these texts is interpretive, often speculative, probably in some places provocative. I am not proposing a chronology or developmental scheme, though there are recurring themes that tie the various chapters together: the body, the underworld, sacrifice, resurrection, anticonsequentialism, democracy. Also, the idea of irony surfaces prominently in the Platonic and feminist chapters. Plato and Haraway, I propose, fashion their idealisms out of a death perspective via irony; whereas the Christian tradition, infamous for its lack of self-irony,[147] performs a similar act of indirection but now calls it the miraculous. In any event, I understand my own rereadings of these texts as carrying on a dialogue with each tradition, borrowing this, discarding that. That process of culling and weeding prepares the groundwork for the final chapter, where I selectively adopt many Platonic, Christian, and feminist themes and rework them into a new underworldly narrative. Much of this final chapter pays tribute to the work of John Rawls, though I understand my own efforts as complementing his constructivist-analytic approach with a self-consciously imaginative and literary approach to the writing of political theory. At that point I descend into my own land of the shades, envisioning a social contract written in a nether world of the departed dead.

CHAPTER TWO

The Cave

In Plato's cave, there is no word to designate death, and no dream or image to intimate its unspeakableness. Death is there, in the cave, as excess, and forgetfully; it arrives from outside into the words of the philosopher as that which reduces him in advance to silence; or, it enters him the better to set him adrift in the futility of a semblance of immortality, making of him a mere shade, the perpetuation of shadow.

Ironical death: Socrates's, perhaps—the death which death takes away with it and renders thus as discrete as unreal. And if the "possibility" of writing is linked to the "possibility" of irony, then we understand why the one and the other are always disappointing: it is impossible to lay claim to either; both exclude all mastery.

—Maurice Blanchot, *The Writing of the Disaster*

In this chapter I attempt to bring together, into an open confrontation and joint consideration, two features of Plato's philosophy that are usually left quite separate in secondary commentary: his passages on death and his apparent use of irony. We savvy readers, schooled in the ways of Socrates, certainly suspect that we detect an authorial irony when, for instance, Plato knowingly reports the now-dead Socrates as saying that "true philosophers make dying their profession" (*Phaedo* 67e); or when he cutely features Socrates as bemusedly admonishing his interlocutors not to "let our argument die and fail to bring it to life again" although that act might seem almost Herculean (89c). But my purpose is not simply to rehearse again the thesis that Plato, like Socrates, is an ironist—although he is an ironist who writes about an ironist and therefore is an ironist's ironist.[1] Rather, I want to ground Plato's irony especially for those for whom irony is nothing more than a hopeless enigma wrapped in a riddle. Spilling the beans, I shall violate everything I believe about the subtle charms of irony and simply blurt forth what I think it is about. Platonic irony, I now declare with the full force of my being, is about death. (Shout it from the rooftops. Tell your friends. Pass the word.) Moreover, I hold that an uneasy grasp of the ironies of death are crucial to an understanding of the politics of *The Republic*—although I must caution at this outset that my reading hardly reinforces the traditional political readings of that work.

Thanks mainly to the late Gregory Vlastos's last work, *Socrates: Ironist and Moral Philosopher*, analytic philosophers and classicists are expressing a renewed interest in the dynamics of Socratic irony.[2] But on the whole they seem vexed by their inability to arrest this elusive trope through their scrutinizing methods. When exactly is Socrates being serious? How can one tell in a particular passage? Is Socrates merely feigning ignorance, or is he truly ignorant? Is he being sincere when he says that he knows that he knows nothing? But isn't that a self-contradictory position? Is he holding a kind of superior wisdom in reserve? What is the basis for his apparent self-confidence? Might he be holding strong beliefs without holding knowledge as such? Why does such an ignorant, ugly puss still carry on conversations with his know-nothing fellows? Isn't this self-proclaimed gadfly really an arrogant, snobbish, antidemocratic malcontent who delights in tricking and teasing his interlocutors? What *are* his secrets? What does Socrates know of himself? Might Socrates be—at bottom—a complete mystery to himself? If so, how could any human being carry on under conditions of complete skepticism, ignorance, and mystery? Why should a blowhard buffoon, who got himself taken seriously, still be viewed today as a moral exemplar?

Whatever the debate brewing over the particular nature of Socratic irony, the prevailing opinion that seems to be emerging among learned Plato-watchers is that we all should concede an open-ended ironism to Socrates, at least to the Socrates of the early dialogues; but we probably shouldn't extend that same benefit of the doubt to Plato (even though Plato was the very author who took it upon himself to showcase in writing this ironical character of his). Perhaps Plato picked up a few tricks from Socrates, and hence we can recognize a few of his own ironic moves and moments in his texts; but all in all, Plato betrays the spirit of Socrates' slippery, ironical ways. Plato gives answers where Socrates gave us but questions and more questions. Plato wants to go beyond Socrates, he wants to solve the dilemmas bequeathed to him by Socrates, he wants to make Socratic philosophizing into a *system* of philosophy. In short, Plato is a Platonist (a dogmatist, a rationalist, a literalist), not a Socratic, not a true ironist, not an early practitioner of Kierkegaardian "absolute infinite negativity." The problem is that Socrates died having failed at politics, and Socrates' death exposed the limits of his irony; and hence Plato's profound appreciation of death cannot square with his countervailing appreciation of Socratic irony. One or the other must go; and irony gets the short stick. Plato, as writer, kills off the ironist for a second time. If Plato himself is at all ironic, his occasional irony, deployed in the service of nonironic Platonism, is performed largely at the expense of Socratic irony.

How did the international community of professional Plato readers arrive upon this provisional consensus—namely, on the insistence of a rigorous distinction between Socrates and Plato, and thus on a corresponding opposition between ironism and Platonism? Other ancient portraits of Socrates—Zenophon's, Aristophanes', Aristotle's, Plutarch's—have competed with Plato's through the ages, so that Plato's version of Socrates was never taken as the unexpurgated account. The modern author who is probably most responsible for influencing our joint readings of Plato and Socrates, along with the contrapuntal motif that distinguishes starkly between Socratism and Platonism, is G. W. F. Hegel. For Hegel, Socrates is the ironist par excellence, and Plato is the Platonist who leaves irony behind. We must review and maybe resist Hegel's reading, because it carries with it all sorts of nasty complications. Mainly, Hegel's interpretation of the relationship between Socrates and Plato impairs our ability to see any way to reconcile the often-conflicting claims of irony, death, and politics.[3]

For Hegel, Socrates mobilized a rudimentary spirit of negation in and through irony. Socrates' humorously dissembling ways effectively attracted and held the attention of others. He elicited the views of fellow Athenians by making a show of taking those views seriously. But out of the other side of his mouth Socrates contradicted and negated those views. Hegel thinks this process of criticism was helpful (viewed in long-term retrospect), for it shook the Athenians from their uncritical reliance on Homer, it broke their arrogance, and it made them think for themselves. Socratic irony was thus a form of dialectics, but it suffered from severe limitations. It never went beyond its corrosive negativity in order to produce something positive. Socrates took seriously the opinions of others only to trivialize them, and he left nothing in the wake of his destruction. His irony never went beyond a trivializing form of interpersonal banter, and it certainly never produced a viable politics. Socrates talked against people, but he didn't parlay that negativity into something more than mere sniping. Hence the Athenian judges were right, thinks Hegel, in their assessment of Socrates' general contribution to Athenian culture: He did little more than to corrupt the youth and to speak against the gods of the city.

Worse yet, Socrates' own example seemed to demonstrate that the reflective, self-questioning individual will always be at odds with the state. If we attempt, after the fact, to fashion his life into a doctrine, the abstracted lessons of his life—his irony—could be summarized, thinks Hegel, as follows: All in life is trivial. Focusing on the inherent triviality of all worldly attachments, Socrates then forced the issue with the state: Irony or Politics. One or the other must go. If all is trivial, if the philosophic individual is set permanently against the state, then irony can't productively serve politics. Hegel raises the stakes against Socrates by claiming that Athens was justified (from its own vantage) in executing Socrates. He was indeed detrimental to the state; in fact, his ironic teaching *required* his death. Socrates' death, Hegel concludes in a tidy formulation, proved the "antagonism between philosophy and politics"—an antagonism that Socrates was never able to solve, in theory or practice.

Plato, however, for Hegel, learned the lessons of Socrates' death. Plato wanted to solve the problem of Socrates' death by depicting a system wherein philosophic individuals would be happily reconciled with the state. Plato thus attempted to extend the legacy of Socrates, and in a way he was successful in advancing the spirit of Socratism. According to Hegel, Socrates attempted to give "objective significance" to "subjective morality"—a person's conscience, conviction, and self-examination were to be seen as valid in their own right, which meant that an "objective principle" now inhered within the subject.[4] Hence Socrates extended and yet combated the influence of the sophists, who also had promoted a concern for humanly negotiated standards of proper conduct; but the sophists had taught only that "man is the measure of all things."[5] Socrates tried to put human ethics on a surer footing (the point for Hegel is *not* that Socrates taught a nascent adherence to transcendental standards or that knowledge of such standards is "virtue"). Plato, then, took Socrates' anthropomorphic ethics and tried to make a general political system out of it. He was successful, thinks Hegel, in taking Socrates' implicit idea of subjective ethics and devising a system out of that buried teaching, but two problems persisted. One, the system, now incorporating the spirit of irony, undermined irony's critical impact (even if it withstood the problem of triviality); and two, the system generated a political ideal but made no provision for introducing that ideal into political reality. In the end, Plato's death revealed the same or similar limitations as Socrates' death. Plato gave us a blueprint for extending the idea of a new political system beyond Athens, but Plato in his own lifetime was never able to show how the ideal could be put into practice. *The Republic* addressed and tried to solve essentially a practical problem (how philosophy might be reconciled with politics, how theory might be introduced into practice), but it remained at the level of theory—a chimera, as Hegel calls it. Plato died—and died a failure—though as an author he indeed bequeathed to his survivors more than Socrates ever did.

Hegel's own magisterial system is impressive and often overwhelming, and thus it is sometimes difficult to achieve critical distance from it. But I want to suggest that Hegel may simply have missed the boat concerning Plato. He completely misses the inherent irony of Plato's own teaching, and he only scratches the surface of Plato's own awareness of the (political) problem of death. Hegel, writing for the ages, prematurely monumentalizing his own writings, in eager anticipation of his own death, misses the self-referentiality of Plato's writings. He doesn't seem sufficiently appreciative (and I well realize that mine is an ironic charge to level against the great philosopher of reflective hindsight) that he himself, Hegel, is a historian of death who is writing about a dead man (Plato) who was writing about a dead man (Socrates) who had proclaimed himself already dead while alive (well before Hegel's similar pronouncement) and who tried to break the reliance on another dead man (Homer) who had depicted an entire way of life built on men killing other men. Hegel was a lover of the spirit of negation but was an enemy of irony, especially as applied to politics. More than any other writer, Hegel was and is responsible for enshrining a lasting opposition between irony and politics; but now we, who are better positioned to know that Hegel's death hasn't brought about the end of history, can perhaps recapture the deferred meaning of Plato's politically ironic, and therewith deathly, writings.

Toward Death: *The Apology*

Following Hegel, commentators often reconstruct a rendition of the "early" Socrates (the ironic Socrates, the quizzical Socrates, the un-Platonic Socrates) based to a great extent on a reading of the *Apology*. Here Socrates presents us with his perplexing, and therefore fascinating claim that he is perhaps a bit wiser than the rest of his fellows because he is conscious that he is not at all wise (21b); he at least knows that he doesn't know (what is "noble and good") (21e).[6] Philosophers have made great philosophical hay out of this one epigram, and, as mentioned above, some analysts have been trying recently to shed epistemological light upon it by refracting it through the prism of irony. But in the text the entire discussion is set against a great discussion about death, which seems to be underplayed in the secondary literature (which is not to say that commentators haven't noticed that Socrates will be sentenced to death by the end of the dialogue). The question that Socrates returns to throughout the dialogue might be summarized as follows: Why does he persist in doing what he does, pursuing the philosophic life, in view of the eventuality of death? Or to put the question more generally: Why should anyone pursue goodness and justice when we all are subject to death? Throughout, Socrates stays committed to his life of philosophic inquiry and conversation despite his lack of any sure knowledge about anything and, in particular, despite his lack of sure knowledge about conditions after death. Instead of a thoroughgoing distancing from worldly engagement, however, we discover in Socrates an expression of unwavering resolve and devotion, a defense of his lifelong activities.

In the *Apology* Socrates responds to his silent detractors by claiming that he would have pursued questions of good versus bad, justice versus injustice, no matter what the risk to his person, even if he might have endangered his very life along the way (28b–c). Achilles likewise belittled the dangers of death, "fearing much more to live as a bad man" (28d). Here Socrates begins to expound a thesis concerning his fearlessness about death, a thesis that he will repeat in several other dialogues (*Rep.* 3.386, 6.486b; *Phaedo* 62–69). Too often overlooked is that his position of resolute fearlessness *grows out of* his much-ballyhooed skepticism, and thus we ought to follow carefully this counterintuitive stance. Socrates associates the common position of fearing death with a claim to a kind of wisdom—those who fear death must presume some kind of knowledge about what death brings. He then turns around this commonplace fearfulness by suggesting that greater modesty or skepticism about such matters would require all judgments about the state of affairs after death to be suspended. "For to fear death, men, is in fact nothing other than to seem to be wise, but not to be so. For it is to seem to know that one does not know: no one knows whether death does not even happen to be the greatest of all goods for the human being; but people fear it as though they knew well that it is the greatest of evils" (29a–b). That shifting the burden of proof, then, cleverly disarms the sophist, whose pursuit of worldly knowledge, honor, and riches (which together fall short of the pursuit of justice) presupposes an abiding anxiety about death.

Socrates says that he does not know sufficiently about the things in Hades, but he does know that it is bad and shameful to do injustice (29b). He has been trying to teach the city that virtue does not come from money, and he would go on teaching such things even if he were to die many times (30c). (The jury apparently grunts in disapproval at this remark.)

After Socrates is found guilty, one man proposes death as his punishment.[7] Socrates would prefer of course to live out his life with free meals at the Prytaneum. Exile or self-silencing, however, is out of the question, but he won't be able to persuade his accusers of this because they will think he's being ironic (38a). Nor will they ever be persuaded that an ironist might sincerely think that it is a very great good for a human being "to make speeches every day about virtue" and to believe that the unexamined life is not worth living. The Athenians are not in fact persuaded, and they vote to condemn him to death. But Socrates responds: *thatton thanatou thei*—villainy runs faster than death (39b). Now condemned to death, Socrates will, like Patroclus, Hector, and Achilles before him, issue a few death oracles. He predicts that sentencing him to death will not release the jurists from having to account for their actions. The spirit of Socratism will nag at them well beyond his death. Irony will live on.

At this point in the text (40c), Socrates turns the tables on those accusers who presume that death is necessarily a penalty. Death, rather, may be a good thing, he points out. Maybe death is like one great night of sleep, so that one might even be happier than the Great King of Persia (who was popularly believed to be the happiest of men because of his enormous wealth and empire[8]). Or maybe death is like a journey to another place where all the dead now reside. *That would be the greatest happiness*, says Socrates. In Hades one would thus find true justice among the dead (with better judges such as Minos, Rhadamanthys, Aeacus, and Triptolemus). Or what better happiness could one imagine than to associate with Orpheus, Musaeus, Hesiod, and Homer! (Note that these four, all poets of infernal traveling, are also poets well known for bringing benefit to humankind, despite their profound awareness of death.)[9] Socrates says that he is willing to die many times if death is like a great sleep or great journey. He would live his life in Hades in the very same way that he lived his life in Athens: "And above all I should like to spend my time there, as here, in examining and searching people's minds, to find out who is really wise among them, and who only thinks that he is" (41b–c). The text then ends with Socrates beseeching the jurists to punish his sons if they care for money more than virtue. "But now it is time to go away, I to die and you to live. Which of us goes to a better thing is unclear to everyone except to the god." (42a)

Nietzsche, evidently following Hegel's lead regarding the negativity of Socratic moralism, offers a trenchant critique of the *Apology*—but that reading, I want to propose, likewise assumes that Socrates' death proves that irony and politics are mutually inimical. Plato's text, I submit, is working instead to persuade readers that an ironic appreciation of death can serve politics productively.

Briefly: Nietzsche's critique of Socrates and "Socratism" is that Socrates gives himself over too eagerly to death. His embrace of death, in turn, entails a decadent, denigrating, pessimistic attitude toward all of life and living. That Socrates views life as a sickness to be cured is revealed in his last words in the *Phaedo*: "Crito, we ought to offer a cock to Asclepius."[10] But Nietzsche goes even farther, contending that Socrates in the *Apology* is suicidal: He isn't remorseful, he provokes his accusers, he actually wants to die! Such a punishment would be appropriate, thinks Nietzsche, because death is the logical culmination of Socrates' entire philosophy. His relentless questioning of all human instincts, his aversion to the body, his implicit demand that life be justified, his obvious contempt for his fellows—such moral exhibitionism barely conceals a secret death wish, a resentment toward life itself. Supposedly in order to justify and reform worldly conditions, Socrates concocts an impossible standard of "the good per se," a vague notion that isn't to be found anywhere in the world as we know it; and then he holds others to it strictly without admitting his own shortcomings. Let him die, then, if he really prefers the hypothetical justice of death to life.

Yet according to Nietzsche, Socrates demonstrates even more cruelty toward his interlocutors, for he isn't satisfied in securing his own death but wants his particular way of morbid moralizing to be passed on to others after his death.[11] He wants his pain to linger. So he engineers for himself a noteworthy, memorable death (and Plato falls for it[12]). In presenting himself as victim and martyr, he forces his survivors to feel guilty and baffled over his unjust execution. That guilt will then produce in his followers a similar voice of persistent self-reproach and self-examination. In the aftermath, we heirs to the Socratic teachings will take this ugly buffoon's death seriously as some kind of important watershed in the history of Western consciousness, and we will vex ourselves with similar pangs of unhealthy conscience in pursuit of remote standards that we dimly understand. Plato, in all of this, was the unwitting dupe of this dead white guy. Plato—pathetically—took seriously the quest for pursuing objective, universal, rational standards of morality, never realizing that that supposedly exalted pursuit for Wisdom, Nobility, Truth, Goodness, and Justice foundered on Socrates' murderous misanthropy and self-hatred.

Although Nietzsche speaks frequently of, usually railing against, Socrates' irony, he, like Hegel, seems to have missed it for the most part.[13] He interprets the Socratic project as attempting to reside literally in a land where the "good per se" rules.[14] Nietzsche doesn't seem to consider seriously the possibility that Socrates (along with Plato) might not believe in such quaint notions (notions drawn from the cultural soup of the day), or that Socrates might not really prefer death to life. Rather, Socrates' project may well be that he wishes to teach others to pursue an admittedly vague and admittedly unachievable notion of "the good" even while operating under conditions of skepticism, ignorance, and finitude—though realizing all the while that one need not believe literally in such farfetched ideals. The ulterior point of such strange activity may not be that he's trying to make his accusers feel guilty for not already being dead (that will come soon enough, as Plato knows) but, rather, to put their own worldly and political attachments—attachments that do conflict with Socrates' outlook—into a new perspective, using death as a foil. Viewed from the perspective of death (as it were), do their own concerns really amount to more than a hill of beans? By contrast, is there a way of being in the world that doesn't reveal itself to have been in vain all along once death descends upon us all? Or to put the issue in Nietzschean terms (for Socrates and Nietzsche may ultimately have more in common than not): Is there a way to live and to affirm life without being mocked and defeated by the prospect of death?

More Death: *The Phaedo*

Nietzsche's interpretation of Socrates' deathly pessimism is based largely on a reading of the *Phaedo*. Offering an alternative reading of the same material is Michel Foucault, who extracts from that dialogue not pessimism and life-denigration but, rather, cheerfulness and a theory of care.[15] Foucault's rereading is helpful, especially since he is no stranger to Nietzsche's dismal portrait, nor is he unsympathetic to Nietzsche's general critique of Socratism. Nonetheless, although his life-affirming reading of the *Phaedo* is long overdue as a corrective to Hegel's and Nietzsche's shared view of Socratic negativism, the particular lesson that Foucault reads into that text—care for the self—is perhaps misplaced. Let us take another look at a few key passages from that text, especially those passages concerning the death teachings.

Socrates remarks that he will try to offer a better explanation of his rather cavalier attitude toward death, his own death in particular, than he provided at his trial (63b). Crito warns him that the hemlock won't work too well if he talks too much and overheats, but Socrates insists and persists in talking to the very end. A philosopher who has devoted his life to philosophy in the proper way should be cheerful in the face of death, because he has been preparing himself, even looking forward to death, his entire life. Simmias laughs in a burst of black humor, remembering the common view that philosophers are half-dead already and thus would quite agree with Socrates that philosophers deserve what they get. But Socrates replies that ordinary people aren't "quite aware" of the sense in which philosophers already have one foot in the grave.

Socrates invokes the Orphic-Pythagorean view that death is nothing more than a release of the sentient soul from the body. Philosophers, he states, aren't concerned with the pleasures of the body—he mentions food, drink, sex, smart clothes, shoes, and other bodily adornments. Most people, he adds, think that a person who finds no pleasure in these things does not deserve to live (65a). But concern for the body also fills us with a lot of nonsense, distracting us from the activity of thinking. He mentions that wars and revolutions and battles are due simply and solely to the body and its desires. Wars are undertaken for the acquisition of wealth, and the passion for wealth is but an enslavement to the body (66d). Logic seems, then, to yield the necessary conclusion that true wisdom will be attainable only when we are dead and completely rid of the company of the body (Socrates seems to be pushing the envelope at this point, ironizing those who adhere to such tidy sophistic syllogisms).

Socrates winds his way through various arguments to prove the point that philosophers make dying their profession. The form of the argument is classically negative, disputing and dispelling popular bases for fear about death (but not necessarily proving that a positive good accrues to those who die). After a few rounds of such talk, Socrates concedes that "this is the best defense that I offer you, Simmias and Cebes" (69e). He tries to console his friends by saying that he shall find good friends and good rulers in a hereafter. Socrates agrees to continue after an additional query about the state of souls after death, but he admits that his discourse will sound ridiculous and worse than comic (70c). He claims to believe unshakably in the idea that the living come from the dead and that the souls of the dead exist (72e). But the group tries to reason itself into a firmer conclusion about the exact conditions of the body and soul after death. The "visible" part of a person stays, upon death, in the "visible" world, but the soul, which is "invisible" goes to Hades (*aides*), the true, unseen world (80e).[16] A soul that is "heavy" and "visible" is, upon death, weighed down and dragged back down to the visible world. What makes such a soul "heavy" is fear of Hades, the unseen; and such a soul hovers about tombs and graveyards. Ghosts are souls that still cling to the realm of the visible (81d).

These ghosts represent wicked souls, who in their lives had been attached too closely to the concerns of the body. In their craving for corporeality, they sometimes return to the land of the living and visible, imprisoned once more in a body. Those who were gluttonous, selfish, or drunken assume the form of donkeys. Those who were lawless and violent assume the bodies of wolves and hawks— or other appropriate animal forms. Those "happiest" people who had been good citizens, virtuous by habit only, however, not by philosophy, become some other kind of social and disciplined creature, such as bees, wasps, ants—or they might even become decent human citizens again. Knowing that the bodily thus entraps, philosophers abstain from all desires. They are not like the average person who "thinks of money first" and is afraid of financial loss or poverty. Nor are philosophers aiming for distinction, authority, and reputation (82c–d). All of these things—honor, ambition, wealth— belong to the realm of the "visible" and "bodily."

The problem in convincing other persons of the greater, largely unseen virtues of philosophy is that persuasion must operate in and through the realm of visibility, and at the same time an initiate must be slowly disabused of reliance upon visibility (82e–83e). Hence most people won't be persuaded. In fact, at this point in the text, Simmias and Cebes are presented as remaining unconvinced (84c).

Socrates laughs. If he can't persuade his best friends, how can he convince the outside world? Swans sing sweetly at the time of their death, but people are wrong to think that the swan song is an expression of grief. Swans rather are prophetic, believes Socrates, and they sing because they are joyous about the world to come.

This musical analogy also fails to convince. Simmias and Cebes tell Socrates that they think his theory has serious flaws in it (85e). They examine together the Pythagorean theory of the soul, and they refer to an "illustration" of a tailor (87b). Plato's text within a text, a dialogue in the dialogue, resurfaces at this point when Echecrates and Phaedo resume their discussion and pose their own questions about Socrates' argument (88d–89b). Socrates reinvigorates his discouraged interlocutors by warning against "misology." The argument eventually turns to Socrates' account of his own earlier genesis away from natural science and physical investigations. Such naturalist study is like watching an eclipse of the sun (99d); people really do sometimes injure their eyes. Socrates at the time started to make recourse to "theories" and used them in while trying to discover the truth about things. "Perhaps my illustration is not quite apt, because I do not at all admit that an inquiry by means of theory employs 'images' any more than one which confines itself to facts" (100a). I might suggest that the text is (deliberately?) confusing and self-undermining at this point; and the characters' skepticism seems to reinforce our off-balance reading experience, for they seem similarly suspicious of Socrates' point of view.

In one last gasp, Socrates attempts to convince his survivors of the need to attend to their souls by weaving a magnificent otherworldly account of reward and punishment. Departing dead souls take to the land of Hades nothing but their previous education and training. Socrates elaborates at length about the many paths to Hades, though he undercuts his own tale somewhat by admitting that "no reasonable man ought to insist that the facts are exactly as I have described them" (114d). But this account or a similar one presents a belief worth risking, a noble one. Such accounts we should use "to inspire ourselves with confidence." Instead of caring for bodily pleasure, or decking one's soul with "borrowed beauty," one should pursue "self-control," "goodness," "courage," "liberality," and "truth" (115a).

Is Socrates being completely serious in claiming that philosophers are practicing death? Is he recommending literally a stoical detachment from all worldly, bodily pleasures—the ascetic ideal—

so that one can participate more freely in his morbid eschatology? I think not. Readers may be reading him (and Plato) too straight. The irony I detect inheres in the fact, the shared readerly awareness, that such overtures toward death must be practiced by the living.[17] Socrates isn't recommending a fatalism or suicide. The virtues that he endorses—the pursuit of self-control, goodness, courage, liberality, truth, and care for the self—must be enacted by those who are still embodied. He leaves his instructions to survivors, not fellow death travelers. He doesn't ask Crito to drink the hemlock with him (although they are sacrificing the cock to Asclepius together). Likewise, Plato is writing for living readers, not dead ghosts.

What then is the content of his infamous, not to mention extremely difficult advice to avoid and even despise the pleasures of the body? Is that stance even possible for survivors? Or does Socrates try to put survivors into this impossible position out of contempt? Latter-day readers seem to follow Nietzsche blindly in viewing the sacrifice to Asclepius as finally revealing his aversion toward all of life, a statement against human mortality itself, a preference in turn for death. Foucault's countervailing, life-affirming reading extracts a positive theory of care for the self only by maintaining a strong soul-body dualism.[18] But if we look again at those passages in which Socrates rails against the body, we notice that he is quite specific in the kinds of pleasures that he proscribes: sex, ambition, reputation, power, and especially wealth. All of these pleasures he associates with "visibility"—whereas his admittedly inadequate "illustrations" of the greater pleasures of justice after death are "unseen." Consistently he inveighs and warns against the body in order, it seems, to instill the *particular* lesson that his survivors should eschew the visible badges of what now counts as worldly success; and in their stead he offers other, supposedly more exalted virtues, although the benefits of those virtues are hard to envisage and thus it will be difficult to persuade living people to pursue them. But clearly he is not simply teaching his friends to hate life and look forward to death. Nor is he simply recommending that they pursue an ascetic, hyper-rational, knowledge-seeking form of death-in-life. Philosophers evidently have read Plato's soul-body distinction here too sweepingly.

Other Platonic dialogues, referring to the lessons of Hades in particular, offer additional clues and insights into Socrates' and Plato's views on the lessons of the death teachings. In the *Cratylus*,

Socrates mentions that the name Pluto means "giver of wealth," and wealth supposedly comes out of the earth beneath (403a).[19] But people in general imagine that the term *Hades* (*aides*), the land of the invisible, is also a land below; and they tend to confuse these terms, Pluto and Hades. The suggestion in the ensuing dialogue is that persons tend to confuse these different forms of wealth, the seen and the unseen. People are afraid and confused about Hades, Socrates explains. He reasons that people are better chained to a spot by desire than necessity, so he asks, what chains of desire hold people to Hades once they are dead? The apparent answer: There is no desire stronger than the thought that you will be made better by associating with another (403d). That is the reason that no one who has ventured to Hades is willing to come back to us. That is why Hades is sometimes referred to as Pluto, the rich—because, although dead, Hades/Pluto has much more than he needs down there. Again at this point in the text, Socrates repeats the distinction between the virtues of the soul and the virtues of the body (404a)—but now the virtues of the soul are identified quite explicitly with the desire to associate with others and to be bettered because of that association. (It is not, as Alexander Nehamas claims, a care for the self that is strictly individualist.)[20] The lesser pleasures of earthly wealth-getting provide, by contrast, a pale alternative.

In the *Gorgias*, Socrates asks his fellows to listen to an otherworldly fiction that he takes to be fact, or so he says (523a). In this version of life after death, good souls go to the Isles of the Blessed, bad souls go to be punished in Tartarus. In the earliest days of this scheme of things, living men rendered judgment on the living, pronouncing sentence on the very day on which the marked men were to die. But such a system was flawed, for judges made bad judgments. The problem was that many who possessed evil souls were "invested with fine bodies and lineage and wealth, and when the trial takes place, many witnesses come forward to testify that they have lived righteous lives. So the judges are dazzled by these, and at the same time they are clothed themselves when they give sentence, their eyes, their ears, and their whole bodies acting as a screen before their souls" (523d). So Zeus decided that men must be stopped from foreknowing their deaths (a suggestion which Prometheus had already submitted). In addition, men must be stripped naked of all of these dazzling adornments before they are judged, and they must be judged after death. So, too, must the judges be already dead and naked. That will make the verdicts more fair. There will still be problems, of course. Fat bodies will be fat corpses after death, long-hair will still be long on corpses, former convicts will still bear scars on their naked corpses. "And, in a word, of the physical characteristics acquired in life all or the greater part are visible for some time after death" (524d).

But if judges can look past the dead body and judge on the basis of the virtues of the soul accumulated during and carried over from the life that had been lived, then the judgment will be more just. Not all bad souls will be eternally punished; some will be marked for improvement. But others will be subjected to terrifying tortures throughout eternity because of their misdeeds, "literally suspended as examples there in the prison house in Hades, a spectacle and a warning to any evildoers who from time to time arrive." The worst warning examples, and the worst eternal punishments, are reserved for those who performed political misdeeds—tyrants, kings, potentates, and politicians (525d–e). Because of the license they enjoyed, they are guilty of the greatest and most impious crimes. Socrates says that it is among the most powerful that you find the superlatively wicked—leaving open the possibility that some good persons can be counted among the powerful. But those cases are rare, because power so often corrupts. Yet by the same token, those who pass through life in righteousness when they have every license to do wrong deserve special admiration and maybe even the highest praise (nonpolitical philosophers and do-gooding private citizens will indeed go straight to the Isles of the Blessed, but Socrates, while clearly approving, doesn't mention any special commendation for them).

Socrates ends the story by saying that he wants to present to his judges a healthy soul, and thus he renounces "the honors sought by most men" (526d). Again he mentions that there is a real difficulty in demonstrating why "we should live any other life than this, which is plainly of benefit also in the other world." But despite all of the arguments and refutations, one thing remains steadfast: "Before all things a man should study not to seem but to be good, whether in private or in public life" (527b). Pursuing justice and virtue will win you "happiness both in life and after death." The dialogue ends on that triumphant note, and Socrates suggests that he and Callicles should invite others to join them in their pursuit, now that they've reached a conclusion about "the best way of life—to live and die in the pursuit of righteousness and all other virtues" (527e).

Hegel, Nietzsche, and Foucault all read the death teachings of the *Apology*, *Crito*, and *Phaedo* as a cycle, a more or less unified story. All three writers read strong individualizing Socratic tendencies into that cycle that separate the solitary philosopher from any kind of later (Platonic) political program. But as I've intimated, already in these teaching are numerous gestures toward politics (though not a politics based merely on habit, convention, and discipline). All of the themes, images, and motifs that we focused on in the *Apology*, *Crito*, and *Phaedo*—the idea of Hades as a meditation upon justice; the invidious comparisons between lives of wealth-getting as opposed to virtue; the extended plays upon visibility that humorously undercut the flow of argument; the dramatic highlighting of the importance of politics rightly pursued—come together and are fully exploited only in the *Republic*. Rather than seeing the *Republic*, from book 2 on, as Plato's declaration of independence from Socrates, I see the entire book largely as an extension of many Socratic death lessons, now attempted through writing (and thus intended for Plato's survivors); hence I see a continuity between the death cycle and the *Republic*. In the *Republic* as well we see the best evidence of Plato's own form of irony, which Plato apparently regards, I might suggest, as the appropriate writerly vehicle for attempting to connect the death teachings to the political virtues that he wants to promote.

A Politics of Death: *The Republic*

To start, let's agree about one very conspicuous, undeniable feature of the *Republic*: it reeks of death. From the first word to the last, the *Republic* consistently and relentlessly pursues death metaphors, death scenes, and dialogues among the dead.[21] There can be little question that from the beginning to the end the *Republic* is thematically unified by a series of underworldly descent (*katabaino*) scenes: the opening Pireaus scene, the allegory of the cave, and the final myth of Er (other *katabaino* stories include the ring of Gyges [359d], the divided line analogy [511b], and the helmet of Hades [612b]). Much of the work is preoccupied with the lingering influence of not only now-dead Socrates, but also now-dead Homer. As Eric Voegelin argues, the opening word *kateben* opens up a "symbolism of depth and descent" that recurs throughout the *Republic*, which apparently alludes to Odysseus's descent into Hades to inquire after his political return.[22] Voegelin and others find further evidence for this reference in the mention of the goddess Artemis-Bendis, who attends to souls on their way to the underworld.[23] But Voegelin reads into these netherworldly references a more or less straightforward expression of Socrates' overriding concern with the afterlife.

Yet clearly Socrates is already dead at press time, and Plato surely knows it. He has deliberately staged the scene as a dialogue set in the underworld featuring his now-dead mentor as a Socrates-in-hell character who still speaks to us from beyond the grave.[24] Like the foreknowing audience experiencing dramatic irony in classical tragedy,[25] we readers know that the real Socrates is already dead; and a similar ironic insight sets the scene for the ensuing dialogue with the near-dead Cephalus and his son Polemarchus, two money-makers in the commercial Pireaus who, at the time of Plato's writing, had been driven into exile and died.[26] We the audience members know that the version of justice that these two espouse is highly questionable, since we are privy to their eventual fates. Plato has cast an irony over the entire scene by presenting to us, without explicit commentary, a Socrates who similarly gives a show of taking seriously the account of one who is going (fearfully) to hell, though all the while Plato plays upon our privileged awareness of Cephalus's family's eventual demise.[27]

What does it mean, then, that this book is a book about death? How does that deathly casting affect our reading of the political vision that the book apparently promotes? What does it mean that all of Socrates' main illustrations are myths about death when, in the same text, all of the poetry banned in the *Republic* is poetry primarily about death and stories about Hades (386–388c)? I want to suggest that Plato is very much aware of his role as writer, as suggested in this passage from the *Phaedrus*, a writer who leaves his texts "behind" him: "Socrates: Then anyone who leaves behind him a written manual, and likewise anyone who takes it over from him, on the supposition that such writing will provide something reliable and permanent, must be exceedingly simple-minded; he must really be ignorant of Ammon's utterance, if he imagines that written words can do anything more than remind one who knows that which the writing is concerned with" (275d).

Writing, Socrates explains in the *Phaedrus*, is like painting: The product stands before us as if it is alive, and yet you can't carry on a dialogue with it. The problem is that most writers, and most readers of writing, presume that something necessarily important and permanent inheres in the words. Such is "dead" discourse (276b). Jacques Derrida interprets these written words of Plato's as a straightforward privileging of speech over writing.[28] On such a view (which Derrida wishes to challenge), writing is but a second-order image of speech; speech reveals more flexibility and give-and-take, but at the same the living presence of the author allegedly ensures the stability, integrity, and unity of the various utterances. On such a view, Plato as writer is self-loathing, admiring Socrates' dialogues more than he does his own literary compositions. On such a view, Plato is a Platonist, one who attempts to capture the (logocentric) spirit of Socrates in writing but who knows his efforts fall woefully short.

But then, how did Derrida arrive at this conclusion? Surely on the basis of reading Plato's text. That text, however, announces itself as inadequate, and Derrida simply assumes that Plato means by that announcement that his own writing will always fail to convey fully the living word of Socrates. Maybe Derrida should extend Plato a greater benefit of the doubt, granting some plausibility to the sneaking suspicion that Plato might be inviting his own reader to question his own texts—and not simply so that Plato's apparent self-hatred will serve as a launching pad toward communing with greater Platonic, Logos-dominated truths.[29] Rather, maybe Plato the writer is writing about dead writing so that we might start up with him, after his death, a dialogic engagement via the text, a deferred meaningfulness that doesn't simply erase the protracted presence of the author. "I have a suspicion," wrote Friedrich Schlegel, "that some of the most conscious artists of earlier times are still carrying on ironically, hundreds of years after their deaths, with their most faithful followers and admirers."[30] Writers such as Lysias and Homer, and writers of political compositions and laws such as Solon, are to be called "wise" rather than simply "literary," says Plato's character Socrates, if they can demonstrate "the inferiority of his writings out of his own mouth" (279d). So how should we read the political composition, the *Republic*, if we suppose instead that Plato isn't trying to leave behind him a manual that will provide something "reliable and permanent?"[31]

I want to suggest that we not bury our noses too closely in the book. In reading the *Republic*, we need to look up from the elenchic arguments and up from the drama as well.[32] The real dialogue and the greater drama of the work involve a subliminal, extratextual exchange between Plato as author and us as readers. Plato is trying to turn the dead letter of the written page into a living dialogue,[33] and he has a whole array of devices at his disposal to prompt us toward such an engagement. His tactics, I want to propose, are not meant to be manipulative or underhanded or self-concealing, but are the way they are, subtle and indirect, because he values our independent discovery of them and our considered participation in his project. He cannot simply tell us what he wants to tell us, we have to find out the point of it all by and for ourselves, and there is good reason for all of this circumlocution and subterfuge, as we shall see.

The *Republic* in various critical moments draws our attention to the activity of reading (and to the activity of writing).[34] Such sections should strike us as a little odd coming from the character Socrates, for nowhere are we told that Socrates writes anything, nor do we have a sense from the many Platonic dialogues that Socrates is as much a reader in life as he is a talker. In such passages, we might suspect that we are beginning to detect the self-conscious presence of Plato, who seems to drop clues that we are to read this text of his with a certain critical distance, for appearances can be deceiving.

One such clue seems to be dropped in the pivotal passage on the difference between reading the "letters of justice" in individuals or in polities (368d–e). Up to this point the characters in the dialogue have been grappling (for the most part unsuccessfully) with the question of the comparative rewards of justice versus injustice, and we readers, frankly, have been struggling along with them. When Socrates proposes that he and his auditors are rather "shortsighted fellows" who can't read very well the smaller letters of justice, and thus the group ought to pursue such letters writ large, we readers of this text begin or ought to begin to suspect that Plato, the author, seems to know that we have been squinting pretty intensely at this book of his, and the results thus far have been pretty hazy. The hint in effect doubles as a commentary upon the material to follow: We readers have been tipped off that the text is aware of itself as a text, and that we ought to be equally aware of ourselves as active readers. So what does this mean?

Cut to the most famous of all sections in the *Republic*, a section that is the climax of the "large-lettered" political section, a section that seems to hold the secret key to it all, namely the Allegory of the Cave in book 7. Socrates up to this point has deployed all sorts of ploys, arguments, images, illustrations, metaphors, and stratagems to try to convince Glaucon and company of the virtues of pursuing justice (*dikaiosyne*), and these pretty patterns have largely failed to convince. Now, as a last resort, Plato takes us deep into a cave, where we learn about some strange little stick figures who are chained in such a way that their heads cannot turn so that they must stare straight ahead at a wall in front of them, and some puppeteers behind them cast shadows on the wall, which constitute these stick figures' entire reality, or so they believe. At this point in the dialogue, someone (probably Glaucon) interrupts and remarks that this cave image depicts an "odd picture and an odd sort of prisoner." To make his point more directly, Plato might have substituted "shadow" for "picture" in this last remark. For surely this entire cave parable is an allegory about us, the earnest readers who are trying to make sense of this cave story. Socrates (or Plato, as it were) admits as much in the next line, when he says that these pictures are "like us."

Professional Platonic interpreters generally jump in at this point and explain that Plato's cave story reinforces the "divided line" analogy that immediately preceded it (509d–513e), the point of which is that we humans live in a world of mere appearances, that true reality lies in a world somehow beyond this one, that true philosophers in the know are aware of this great schism and that ordinary people allow their immediate surroundings to pass for ultimate reality. Certain philosophers, unchained, can ascend to the world of knowledge, bask in the bright lights of Logos; and then, if somehow they can compel themselves or allow themselves to be compelled to turn around and return to the land below full of chained stick figures, at least they, the philosophers, will know that the shadows are only shadows.

But I think Plato has perpetuated a little joke upon generations of all-too-earnest readers—though it was a joke that was probably intended to be an *inside* joke (we readers have let him down). Plato knows that the idea of a deep cave myth will sound mysterious and alluring to attentive readers. As they read, they will visually construct this odd picture, and their imaginations will run wild: What does it mean, what does it all mean, where is the answer? They will scour the details for deep hidden truths, and they will study these lines extremely carefully. A parallelism emerges: So enthralled as they read about these stick figure prisoners staring straight ahead at the wall in front of them, Plato's readers, he hopes, will eventually catch themselves staring ahead at the page in front of them. The

spell will be broken, and maybe they will laugh a little at themselves. If these words in front of us are like shadows on the wall,
then we must question even these words, these pages, this entire
book, now in front of us. Interpretation will not be easy.

Plato has dropped enough hints that we are to read this grand
myth with critical reserve, and the comic reflexivity of the prisoner
image should at least suggest that Plato doesn't want his readers to
stare at this myth with complete credulity. Still, subsequent generations of spellbound readers have mined this myth for only the most
straightforward of interpretations. Plato, they say, is extending to
us, in so many words, the saving vision of philosophic reason; he is
revealing an otherworldly source of knowledge and goodness; he is
explaining Socrates' death at the hands of the Athenians. Upon such
a reading, the myth suggests answers to many of the big questions
in life (i.e., truth with a capital T exists, go find it and bring it back).

Yet the myth is playful and admits itself as such, and I suspect
that Plato expected his immediate readers to recognize it as such
(and also to make the easy recognition that the myth is centrally
preoccupied with the already dead Socrates). Surely the Allegory of
the Cave—whatever else it is—is Plato's play upon Aeschylus's play
upon the Prometheus myth—though for some reason this not-so-
cryptic allusion is seldom mentioned in Platonic commentary.[35] The
imagery of chains, fire, caves, shadows, and a miserable humanity
would immediately recall the Prometheus story to a Greek audience. Prometheus, it should be recalled, was the one who discov-
ered mortals living "deep in sunless caves" (452). They were "confused and purposeless," passing like "shapes in dreams." And in
those days, humans "had eyes, but sight was meaningless" (447).
Out of good will to humans, Prometheus stole fire from the gods
and taught humans skills for practical living. He was the one, well
before Socrates or Plato, who gave humans mind and reason (444).
He was the one who invented numbers for humans and set words
down in writing. He taught them many useful skills which helped
them to attain wealth and greatness (463), and he showed them all
the treasures of the earth—bronze, iron, silver, and gold hidden
deep down. In addition to cunning and ability, Prometheus gave us
"blind hopefulness" (252) by turning our eyes away from death
(249).

That the Allegory of the Cave is an obvious play upon the Promethean myth should lead us in certain interpretive directions and
foreclose others. Prometheus helped to found cities, but Plato ap-

parently still finds humanity wanting. Such purely practical skills are insufficient. We are, the allegory seems to suggest, still residing in caves; we can't really see though we have eyes; Prometheus's fire didn't really liberate us, we are all chained as he.

But the point of this satiric commentary cannot be, as the traditional Platonic reading would have it, that Plato is making a pitch for greater reason, greater enlightenment, as the solution to our woes. Prometheus already gave us reason (*nous*). The shadows are still shadows, we have eyes but still do not really see; but the implication need not be that there is literally a greater reality behind the shadows. This allegory is not fundamentally about epistemology, it is not about the intellectual bankruptcy of the Athenians who tried Socrates, it is not just a dramatized justification for philosophers to rule.

The *Protagoras* dialogue gives us a clue as to Plato's ulterior point (not every Platonic dialogue need be consistent with every other, but these two, the *Protagoras* and the *Republic*, were probably written about the same time, most Plato scholars have agreed). In Socrates' version of the Prometheus story, Prometheus gave humans *techne* and fire, but he failed to grant them political wisdom (319d). Thanks to Prometheus, humans could fight off beasts for they knew the art of warfare, and such warlike tendencies eventually drew them together to form fortified cities. But because humans did not know how to conduct themselves politically, Socrates says, they would injure each other and scatter again, and thus their cities would self-destruct, and the human race itself would be put again in jeopardy. Zeus then sent them, by way of Hermes, the qualities of respect for others and a sense of justice, "so as to bring order into our cities and create a bond of friendship and union" (322c).

The allegory then, as an update to the Prometheus story, presents a roundabout claim about the need for political justice—which surely is a main theme of the *Republic* as a whole—but the pursuit of justice here cannot simply be a matter of beholding some new transcendental source of light (the usual reading): Plato cannot simply be calling for a second theft of fire from the gods! Rather, the play upon the Prometheus myth connects the allegory with another prominent theme, also recurrent throughout the *Republic*, of the relation between *sight* and the *consequences of justice*: What are the visible benefits, the visible consequences, attending to the pursuit of justice? The shadows in the allegory are mere shadows, mere appearances not in the sense that there is purported to be a greater reality in some world literally beyond this one but, rather, in the sense that such shadows are mere externalities, visible only, as it were, when one is blinded to the fact of human finitude. Prometheus teaches us all sorts of reasonable, practical skills—especially skills that can be quantified—but these skills altogether do not bind us together in cities. They are the kinds of skills and the kind of knowledge that provide purpose and hopefulness only when we turn a blind eye toward death, human mortality. They are the kinds of skills that produce visible consequences—in another dialogue Socrates names such tangible Promethean benefits as wealth, nobility, fine clothing, and healthy body[36]—but such externalities pale in importance in view of death. Utilitarianism and consequentialism— Prometheus is suggested here to have been the patron saint of Athenian sophists, Socrates' lifelong opponents—cannot bind us fully together. And, by contrastive implication, true political wisdom—whatever it is—must take death more fully into account. Doing right, pursuing justice in this political world, will defy utilitarian considerations, and the benefits of political wisdom may be visible, as it were, only from the perspective of death.

Of course Socrates' death provides the background for much of the cave allegory—this is no great secret nor any great insight into the hidden workings of the text. The underworldly imagery of the scene surely borrows from Orphic sources, including the Homeric *Nekyia*, and constitutes another of the many *katabaino* (descent) scenes that run from the beginning to the end of the *Republic*, providing the main dramatic motif for the book as a whole.[37] Once again (as with the opening dialogue in the Pireaus with the now-dead Cephalus) we find ourselves in Hades, and our cavelike existence can be so construed.[38] But the point of this deathly casting cannot be, as the Straussians have insisted, mainly to issue a warning to would-be Socratic philosophers that their lives may be imperiled if they attempt to bring justice down from the heavens.[39] Rather, the Promethean tenor of the allegory suggests that Socrates' accusers, Promethean-Pythagorean[40] prisoners all, were at the time more dead than Socrates. I do not believe Plato constructed that deathly irony simply to perpetrate an elaborate compensation fantasy or simply to enforce some invidious distinction between the prisoners' ignorance and Socrates' supposedly superior insights. There must be more to this complex story than assigning blame, issuing warnings, and privileging philosophy.

Indeed, the allegory invites us to look at all of human existence from the perspective of death (which, after all, is the only distinctly mortal perspective).[41] And from that vantage the question for the philosophically inclined becomes: Why pursue politics or justice or goodness when humans are, as it were, already dead?[42] In the allegory the one stick figure who breaks free and beholds the light outside the cave meditates on precisely this question (516c–517a). Such a person no longer covets the prizes and honor and power that humans confer upon themselves, and he would agree with Homer that it is better to follow the plow of an indigent serf "than be king over all of these exhausted dead" (*Odyssey* 11.489–90). At this point, such a person has not yet turned around and reentered the cave. But Socrates was a person who had, as it were, reentered the cave. He continued to engage his fellows though he strongly suspected them to be know-nothings, and he remained in Athens to the end, despite all. This, then, is the main question posed by the allegory: What is the nature of the vision, what kind of person is it who sees the shadows as shadows, who sees the rewards of this world as paltry, who is well aware that all human endeavor ends in death, and yet can nevertheless rededicate himself/herself to this cave of ours?

Visibility is a motif that recurs throughout the *Republic* but is most apparent in the two main allegories of enlightenment, the divided line and the cave scene.[43] If the light outside the cave is supposed to supplant the Promethean fires (517b), what is the nature of this light? I suggest that we readers have interpreted this light far too rigidly, gazing too uncritically at its image on the page in front of us while we search for some secret gnosis that holds the key to Plato's cryptic cosmos.[44] Such mesmerizing stares have yielded time and again the standard Platonic interpretation: that Plato literally believes in transcendental entities, "Forms," that somehow hover metaphysically above us and to which only a hyper-rationalism may gain epistemological access. Instead I want to propose that Plato invokes the vision of the essential *eidos* as a sustained play upon the theme of external (i.e., visible) consequences, which serves his overall project of begging the question of (and ever deferring any answer to) whether the pursuit of justice brings tangible rewards (especially in view of death).

Once alerted to this possibility—namely, that Plato's famous Forms are a literary device playing ironically upon the theme of consequentialism—then we start to notice textual evidence supporting such a view.[45] The term *eidos* itself, as Eva Brann has argued, apparently is ironic, for it combines in one term both the aspect of visibility and invisibility—an intelligible "look"—the "sight" of something that cannot, properly speaking, be seen.[46] The questions surrounding these two main allegories all involve the quandary of how one can "see" justice, though it eludes our normally short-sighted grasp. The text employs all sorts of visual devices to convey the difficulty involved in conceptualizing justice in a world in which the pursuit of injustice literally pays better. Socrates, for instance, tries to explain that the light of true justice, to those who have seen it, is "higher," "larger," "sharper," "brighter." In the cave section he remarks that it is very difficult for the ordinary person to see beyond the cavelike "shadows" of justice,[47] and by contrast the person who "sees" a different kind of justice will look ridiculous to the cave dweller (517e). I don't believe the main point of this invidious comparison is to enforce some ingrained, intractable distinction between those who see and those who can't or between sensible and essential realms; rather, the comparison emphasizes how difficult it tends to be to commit to seemingly remote notions of justice. Indeed Socrates insists in the cave allegory (518c) that the power of learning inheres in everyone's soul. But then he subtly upbraids those who choose in fact not to follow this vision: "It's as if," he says mockingly by way again of highly visual imagery, "we couldn't turn our eye from the dark to the bright without turning our whole body around" (518d).[48] Sight alone evidently will not suffice to convince most persons to dedicate their lives to the pursuit of justice. Therefore we must, as it were, try to turn the whole "soul" and the "eye of the soul" toward the vision of justice, and then back around toward the cave.[49]

Virtually every passage in cave allegory attests to the great difficulty inherent in the attempt to convince persons to commit themselves to the pursuit of justice. Leading persons up to the proverbial light is, Socrates quips, like trying to lead them out of Hades and up to the gods (521c). And in a second, equally lighthearted analogy, Socrates says that the turning of the soul toward the light is not like the chance spin of an oyster shell from the dark side to the light side (521d). (The choice rather is arduous, the result of human deliberation, not mere happenstance.) Moreover, even once they are turned toward the light, such enlightened figures often prefer to linger in these upper regions and are liable to refuse to return to the cave. Hence they must be compelled to return; otherwise justice might never rule, for no right-thinking philosopher, Socrates remonstrates, would ever willingly descend. The purpose of these barbs, I submit, is to sting *us* with a critical commentary about our common worldly practices, for we humans tend to resist "seeing" for ourselves the greater significance of the pursuit of a "common good" (520a). Those readers who peruse these passages in search of hidden metaphysical information—as if Plato's ulterior point is to lay out a textual obstacle course whose challenge is met only by those epic readers whose exegetical skills are truly heroic—are maybe missing the point (as it stares them right in the face, I want to add).

Socrates insists that the road to philosophy's perch is narrow and steep. People are so disinclined to walk this path by themselves, he ventures, that it's as if a winch (521d, 521e, 523a) is required to lift the soul up toward the light. Socrates then elaborates on the many steps along this difficult way. A would-be philosopher must be well trained in gymnastics and poetry (521e). He or she must be able to count and to calculate. In a series of exchanges with Glaucon—*all* of which play upon sight themes in describing the process of philosophic education[50]—Socrates defends calculation as a skill contributing to the faculty of perception, which involves judging distances and depths (523b). Glaucon eagerly jumps in to demonstrate his own spatial acuity: "You obviously mean things seen at a distance or drawn in perspective" (523b). Socrates rebuffs him mildly with a pun: "You haven't quite hit the mark."[51]

Socrates' attempt to explain the peculiar vision belonging properly to the "eye of the soul" continues. Ordinary sight and ordinary sense impressions do not order themselves into intelligible classifications such as "large" or "small" (523c–524d). The faculty of understanding,[52] which operates separately from, as it were, the realm of visible impressions, must supply these classifications. Certain studies, such as mathematics, geometry, and astronomy, help to train this faculty, which then helps turn the soul toward the higher regions. Plato not so subtly seems to remind us that he is again deliberately playing upon sight metaphors: "Each of us has in his soul an organ blinded and ruined by other pursuits, though more worth preserving than ten thousand eyes" (527e). Socrates shifts attention from two-dimensional plane geometry (528b) to the study of three-dimensional solids,[53] and a discussion about the particular relevance of astronomy follows. This discussion, I suggest, is crucial for the proper appreciation of the famous Forms.

Socrates earlier had passed over the discussion of solids—which

would have helped Glaucon's understanding of "depth" perception—and instead skipped directly to a discussion of astronomy,
which, he notes, is the study of solids in motion. Earlier Glaucon
had praised the study of astronomy on the grounds that it makes
the seasons, months, and years more perceptible, which benefits the
activities of farmers, sailors, and soldiers (527d). Socrates had gently
chided him for his "vulgar utilitarian" appreciation of astronomy,
and now Glaucon wants to make amends. In his new praise for
astronomy, Glaucon, evidently looking up in the air, remarks, "I
think anyone can see that astronomy forces the soul to look up and
leads it from things here to things there" (529a). Socrates expresses
his disapproval over this claim and adds that some earnest philosophers treat astronomy in a way that actually turns the soul's gaze
"downward." He rebukes Glaucon for his literalism: "How nobly
you seem to take the study of things above!"[54] He even mocks him:
"I'll bet if someone leaned back and tried to learn something by
staring at the patterns on the ceiling, you'd think he was contemplating with intellect instead of his eyes" (529b).

Look up, blink down, lie on your back, stare at a book—the
study of justice ultimately defies all of these shortsighted approaches.[55] The proper study of astronomy should treat the heavens
as an aesthetic model, and no more than that (529e). And the study
of music as a way of apprehending a greater sense of harmony
should be taken with great reserve. Socrates mocks the Pythag-
oreans who struggle endlessly to measure audible sounds as a way of
understanding greater harmony and justice (531c). None of these
people—astronomers, mathematicians, musicians—quite reaches
justice (531d). Even mathematicians aren't very "sharp" at dialectics
(531e). Plato's point in distinguishing so starkly in this section between the visible and the intelligible need not be that he wants to
privilege the latter as if such a realm literally exists. To jump to that
conclusion is to read the book in much the same way that Glaucon
stared up at the stars. To be sure, Plato wants us to disengage our
sensibilities from our immediate surroundings, and he lures us on
with the image of a higher, brighter, better, truer realm. But he
places so many qualifications around this upper realm and insists
that its apprehension is so extremely elusive that we must at least
call into question our own first assumptions about what he means.
He carries his exclusionary criteria, for those who can see properly,
to the point of parody. Dialectics should be a joy unto itself, but
very few humans will devote the necessary time and discipline to it

(535c). Older men, in fact, are no longer receptive to learning (536d), so Socrates will start with the young; though the youth aren't ready to appreciate dialectics either, and they must be trained for thirty years (readers often seem to take these passages about age merely as down-to-earth practical advice). At one point in this discussion (536b–c) Socrates breaks in and admits that he is making himself look ridiculous because he is speaking far too seriously about philosophy, having forgotten that they have been talking playfully all along.

Readers at this point should also take this reminder to heart. Many of our serious professional commentators today, however, simply look past these remarks about playfulness and dismiss the frequently sportive character of the dialogue as a whole. Philosophy, they seem to hold, ought to be grave and ponderous, and the point of Socrates' dissembling—if they detect it at all—supposedly must be to reinforce indirectly the supramundane essentiality of the Forms. Somehow, after all of these twists and turns, ups and downs, thrusts and parries, puns and jests, images and allegories, questions and more questions, Plato is made out to be a hyperrationalist and manic metaphysician. If you think hard enough and squint long enough at his book, you supposedly stand a chance of communing with the Forms. Maybe, however, such a reading represents not the ultimate faithfulness to Plato but the ultimate victimization, a result of Plato's extended ironization of those who abide by a consequentialist ethics, even those who take consequentialism to an otherworldly extreme.

I propose rather that the Forms function in the *Republic* as yet another visual device, albeit one that helps put our notions of visibility into perspective. This light supposedly outside the cave serves as an aid to the imagination and to the understanding, a heuristic device, a foil to our normal affairs that helps us get, as it were, an outside look at ourselves. But I want to insist that the *Republic* through and through is about politics, not metaphysics; that the main drama centers upon the act of returning to the cave, not the ascending out of it. The light is a ruse, a mere image, a setup, and Plato admits as much. The constant play upon visibility in the text certainly supports an antiutilitarian, anti-Promethean reading of the cave, but Plato's apparent insistence that the alternative source of light remains difficult if not impossible to grasp undercuts the standard "transcendentalist" view of the Forms. The notion of an elusive *eidos* somewhere heavenward continues to play upon our need for visible rewards; it keeps us enthralled and reading; it is ultimate extrapolation of the idea of consequentialism and yet at the same time contains a sustained spoof thereof. We in the cave require tangible rewards and visible benefits for our efforts, and we have a hard time imagining anything outside the cave. At numerous points in the *Republic* Plato equates the "shadows" in the cave with wealth (though the shadows also stand at times for honor, reputation, gain, and in general all of immediate reality). A commitment to politics and to political community, on the other hand, requires that one look beyond one's nose and beyond the concern for immediate payoffs; a commitment to such an elusive, seemingly abstract concept of political justice requires that one be able to entertain a "big picture" on worldly affairs. But such a vision is hard to grasp—which is a polite way of saying that people generally choose *not* to look this way (the point is not that they are inherently stupid). Plato's portrait of us humans here in the cave is indeed funny (and not just a little sad as well): little stick figures ever-resistant to an expansive outlook that suggests that there may be more to life than Prometheanism. Unwittingly, we live our lives now as if we were already in Hades, already dead, and the shortcoming of the Promethean ethic is that it must ignore the fact of our mortality. Plato wants to convince certain souls of the importance of reentering the cave, though such a life may well look like a living death. But note: He never proves the existence of the Good anywhere in the *Republic*; he continues to beg the question of the nature of the light at the end of the tunnel; he is reluctant to lay all of his cards on the table; he dodges, he hedges, he forwards deliberately specious or contradictory or fallacious arguments; he writes a thoroughly unconvincing book if the point of it all is to show that justice pays better than injustice. Maybe the commitment to political justice requires a supreme sense of irony, because—dare we say it point blank?—the Forms and particularly the Form of justice do not, and never will, exist as such. The light is *only* metaphorical.

The *Republic* overall is the story of a series of attempts to convince Socrates' interlocutors, Thrasymachus, Glaucon, and Adeimantus, about the importance of pursuing justice, put to Socrates in the form of the question, Does a life of justice pay better than a life of injustice? Socrates tailors his arguments to address the respective concerns of each of his three respondents. Thrasymachus early in the book, after taking up the discussion where old businessman Cephalus and his son Polemarchus leave off, demands in effect a quantifiable answer to the justice question—something like the number 12—and Socrates eventually in the dialogue supplies Thrasymachus with such a number: 729. The just man, Socrates computes, is 729 times happier than the unjust man. To the attentive reader it becomes clear that Socrates' mathematical arguments are mock (though it may well be that justice indeed delivers, as it were, a greater happiness).[56] Glaucon early on challenges Socrates with the dilemma of the ring of Gyges and the helmet of Hades, both of which evince his concern for visible consequences in general. Much of the *Republic*, including the central line and cave allegories, is pitched to Glaucon, though Plato repeatedly alerts us readers that such images are just that, images.

Adeimantus's query—overlooked in most of the secondary literature—represents the toughest nut to crack. He presents Socrates with the challenge of a true helmet of Hades, thus extending Glaucon's worldly concern for visible consequences into the realm of the invisible (*aides*), a veritable afterlife.[57] What if the gods don't exist or don't care, he asks—why, then, pursue justice in this world? What if there is no otherworldly benefit to seek or retribution to worry about? As I read it, the final allegory, the myth of Er, represents Socrates' response to Adeimantus (though the section is addressed explicitly to Glaucon). In this final Hades scene, Socrates seems to respond simply by denying the premises of Adeimantus's question. Essentially he contends that the gods do care. Socrates paints a big cosmological vision and weaves a fantastic tale of underworldly reward and retribution, involving an elaborate scheme of reincarnation. The bottom line in all of this: Good actions in this life will be rewarded in an afterlife, bad will be punished. And humans have the capacity to decide between the two and thus should seek the knowledge to be able to distinguish between good and bad (618c).

All but the most credulous readers scratch their heads after reading the fairy-tale-ish myth of Er. Can Plato really be serious? Has he gone off the deep end? Some commentators have contended that the ending is just plain bad, and they wish it away. A few diehard Platonists still insist that Plato means what he says here, but their numbers are diminishing. We might take a cue from the young Karl Marx, who was one of the first to contend that the myth of Er was a spoof of sorts.[58] Don't believe that Plato has gone evangelical, Marx proposes. Plato doesn't really believe in this eschatological scheme, nor has he betrayed the spirit of Socratism (not in the sense of rationalism but as open-ended inquiry). Like Socrates, Marx argues, Plato here is being ironic.

We can gather our own evidence insinuating that Plato is being something less than straightforwardly sincere in his presentation of the myth of Er, this Pythagorean phantasmagoria. A tip-off is that the entire section conspicuously contains self-referential contradictions, many of which call attention to the act of writing. The entire myth, for instance, is presented in an obvious mock-Homeric mode of writing—which is a bit unsettling especially since Socrates has just dismissed artistic representation as several removes from the truth, and Homer is named as the chief culprit of such a form of writing. Why admonish Homeric poetry and then pile on the allusions to the *Iliad* and the *Odyssey*? And, if one remembers, most of the poetic talk to be banished in the city involves talk about Hades—yet here in the myth of Er we descend once again into the nether regions.[59] Why, for that matter, end a book supposedly about a poetry-free philosophic education with a colossal superpoetic myth? Plato's coy presence seems to be with us.

The sight metaphors continue throughout the myth of Er—indeed the myth presents the biggest image of all. The myth retells the telling of a story about an infernal traveler—Er—who has returned to tell his tale about the whole cosmos, having witnessed in the underworld "a sight worth seeing" and "a spectacle."[60] One of the main reasons to descend into the underworld, we are told, is to learn that one must remain faithful to the pursuit of goodness, and even in Hades one shouldn't be "dazzled by riches" and other evils (619a). Er recounts the fates of souls that he saw in Hades, and two in particular—Orpheus and Odysseus—seem juxtaposed as polar examples. Orpheus and Odysseus were also infernal travelers, they both had seen death and then returned to the world. Orpheus descended to retrieve his lost love but he became embittered after his failure, and he forswore all love of women thereafter. Amazons tore him apart (according to several versions of the story), and his dismembered head floating on the water transformed into a singing swan. In the underworld Er sees that Orpheus, who chose first, chose the life of a swan, for he still hated women and wished not to be conceived and born of a woman (even though his original descent into death was out of love for a woman). The story suggests that he thus got what he deserved—a nonhuman life.

Odysseus drew the last lot, but it turns out that he would have picked the same soul had he chosen first—even though it was the least attractive life to the others. The significance of his choosing the life of "an ordinary citizen" has been interpreted by Straussian commentators to mean that one should avoid politics, but I don't believe that reading is textually justified. Instead, Odysseus was a person who, like Orpheus, suffered and knew death, but, unlike Orpheus, he still affirmed ordinary human life. The difference between Odysseus's past worldliness and his newfound worldliness is that, remembering his previous struggles, he is now cured of ambition and eschews the badges of honor. Odysseus had some difficulty finding this life (unglamorous as it appears), but once he sees it, he chooses it gladly.

Odysseus's ironic fate seems to accord with the anticonsequentialist, antiexternalist vision of happiness and reward that the book indirectly promotes all along. Such seemingly uneventful rewards will not be appreciated by others, and they bring happiness only to those who know suffering and death and yet are able to withstand the cynicism that death might otherwise counsel (whereas the embittered Orpheus becomes the victim of irony). Still, the myth ends on a grand flourish, an ostensible paean to consequentialism of a sort, stating that those who hold ever to the upward way and practice justice will indeed win "the prize for justice," like victorious athletes who collect their spoils.

What this mystifying finale means isn't obvious, though we at least know that Socrates has supplied Adeimantus with an otherworldly answer to his question concerning otherworldly matters. But the exact nature of this eternal reward ("both here and in the thousand-year journey we have gone through") isn't very clear, and actually Socrates has only begged Adeimantus's original question (if the gods don't care, then we don't know why the pursuit of justice is to be recommended). To the suspicious reader, I suggest, the ending—an underworldly extravaganza—looks inflated and contrived, and deliberately so. Just as Marx contended, it seems as if Plato wanted us, the readers, to see through the otherworldly designs that Socrates presented to his interlocutors. Plato subverts his own text (and we don't need a professional deconstructor to intervene and do it for us). Where does that leave us, then, if the myth of Er, as the kicker to this strange book, doesn't convince us about the relative benefits of pursuing justice—and in fact seems deliberately to fall short of any such proof? Maybe the answer is an answer left by default: From the perspective of death, perhaps there is no good answer, no good reason, to pursue justice (especially in light of the consequences and the paltry rewards).

That may be key: The book is supposed to fail to convince us on the level of argument—and shame on those generations of readers

who have chosen instead to flatter themselves by discovering "falla-
cies" in the arguments rather than crediting Plato with a slyly self-
deprecating pedagogy. Those who continue to quarrel about
whether philosophers should actually rule or not are missing the
magic of the book. Nor can the point be that the reader ought to
try to emulate or approximate the dramatic acceptances of the various characters, Thrasymachus, Glaucon, Adeimantus. Rather, the
book fails, and there is a lesson implicit in that failure. The images
of the book undermine themselves, so that we are invited or prod-
ded into questioning the visible designs of the book, seeing through
the arguments and allegories, identifying them as specious or mock
(though important lessons may still be conveyed via such designs).
Under the conditions sketched—namely, that human life ends in
death—no book can convince you to pursue justice in this world of
ours. Truly the visible sketch of political justice on the page in front
of you is preposterous—the Straussians are probably right about
that—and it is unlikely that even an elaborate scheme of otherworldly rewards and punishments will persuade you otherwise.

Still, the book leads us on. It cannot all be for naught. This dazzling book cannot be simply an esoteric mockery of the pursuit of
justice, a setup to ward off any effort in that direction. For instance,
despite our skepticism regarding the quasi-religious details that
make up story of the myth of Er, we nonetheless can appreciate the
idea behind Odysseus's homecoming.[61] We do, in reading this book,
get a glimpse of a bigger picture (as it were) about the importance
of justice, we do sense an oblique rationale for pursuing justice,
even though we've conceded that no concrete rewards may accrue
to us for our efforts. We want to continue. But once we have dismissed consequentialism as an admirable or persuasive grounding of
our pursuits, transcendentalism offers no viable alternative, either.
The ultimate secret revealed to the philosopher who ascends may
well be: There is no light outside the cave, the Forms don't exist,
there is no transcendental "reason" for seeking justice. The book
throws a bone to those readers who desperately crave such hard and
fast answers. The book in effect says: If you need arguments, here
they are. If you need numbers, designs, myths, fictions, lies, a theory of Forms, here they all are. If you need a self-help book convincing you about the importance of justice, here it is. But the book
is ultimately pitched to the reader who sees through such arguments, numbers, and myths, and who perversely presses on with the

interpretive challenge.[62] In the face of death, no arguments will suffice for convincing us to pursue justice in this world. In view of the nearly inescapable fact that the pursuit of injustice probably does pay better, there is no cute turn-of-the-intellectual screws that will automatically change your mind. In such a world, a world in which there is no good reply to give to the resident cynic-sophist, the dedicated individual will have to convince himself or herself about the benefits of pursuing justice. How is one to remain dedicated to this world if that is all there is? No one can tell you. You must turn yourself around; a book can't do it. And Forms won't suffice, either.

The *Republic* teaches us to look to ourselves, finally, for "reasons" or noble fictions to help convince us to continue seeking justice in this world—or, rather, to accept that no such discursive reasons are possible given the circumstances. I realize that some of my readers at this point might object, contending that my presentation resembles Tertullian or Sartrean existentialism: "I believe, *because* it is absurd." My answer to that charge is that the above ironic reading of the *Republic* departs from traditional existentialist accounts because it does not presuppose or offer or seek a new authenticity as a ground for existence. And the whole purpose of seeking to return to the cave is *intersubjective*: How is it that we might remain dedicated to a notion of the common good, to justice for the sake of others, in light of our radical skepticism, cynicism, and fatalism? The project is finally political, not strictly personal: For now we sense that what really holds a city together are these numerous acts of common striving. The book teaches aspiration (but without a clear end in sight). And the magic of the book is that the subliminal dialogue which Plato carries on with us readers helps to create this mutually reinforcing pose, of readers and writers engaging in a common pursuit toward the good. The odd result is that this book can create an ironic community (based on nothing more than a work of fiction): For a community of seekers *is* a community of sorts. That notion of community is, however, a far cry from the traditional reading of Plato according to which Plato allegedly seeks to impose uniform, universal standards upon a manipulated populace[63] (such a reading sadly caricatures the *Republic*, but generations of readers have accepted that read, which derives from Aristotle's original cheap-shot critique). Nor do I see that community as necessarily closed and invidious (for human mortality is a profoundly democratic condition). Instead, the book encourages a provisional embrace of the aspiration toward community by way of dialogue and questioning, ever mindful of death. Know thyself, and remember thy mortality.

Why dedicate yourself to others when that effort probably won't get you anywhere? Doesn't might make right? Why be good? The *Republic*, despite appearances, offers no real answer to these questions—at least not in the traditional sense of an answer. To the extent that he answers, Plato answers only by begging the questions, but in the process he helps disabuse the reader of his or her need for such answers. The *Republic*—to put it too programmatically—offers no program as such. It offers no set rationale. Throw away the image of philosopher-kings. Throw away the image of tripartite souls. Throw away the numbers game. There's no Form of the Good, no out there, no up there, no thereafter. We all live in a cave. We all shall die. Politics—if it is to work at all—requires irony.

This reading will be resisted. Much, so very much, has been invested in a literalist Plato through the ages. Entire books are still written today about the *Republic* in which irony is never mentioned or is even systematically denied (funny how irony unnerves some people). To be sure, a literalist read helps to allay our metaphysical anxieties. We can be comforted rather with our hopeful belief that rational self-interest is the very key to life and holds the modern secret to a viable politics. We can put Plato into a neat box. It throws us off, however, to think that the ancients might have been two steps ahead of us. Even the postmodern deconstructors, who sometimes present themselves as brokers in irony, can't quite seem to accept the idea that individuals such as Plato might already be complexly ironic in their writerly ways. That may be why Plato must be their fall guy, their straw man, Derrida's demon.

Imagine: Socrates says that he can't imagine any greater happiness than talking and associating with his fellows in Hades. If he does believe literally in a life-after-death and a scheme of rewards and consequences corresponding to one's actions in this world, then Socrates' activity in Athens will get him nothing more than more of the same—talk and more talk. Surely this noninstrumentalist stance directs a rebuke toward those Athenians who believe that money talks, or that you can take it with you. Remembering how the penurious Socrates eagerly matched wits with his money-grubbing opponents, Plato tries to find a way of continuing the dialogue after the death of his teacher, and he props up dead Socrates and tries to breathe life into him—for our sake. Therein lies the heart of Plato's politics, as founder of an entire tradition of writers, readers, and characters all confronting each other in the context of a fictive world of death, an extended community of dead poets speaking to one another from beyond the grave by dropping creative references to Orpheus, though all the while everyone involved in this protracted conspiracy knows that we are all subject to a literal death. Plato knows that Socrates died and died a failure in all conventional senses. But the point is to keep people talking. Plato is not offering us a system or a utopia; nor is he exhorting us toward us a pale asceticism, a grand metaphysics, a hyper-rationalism, an academic elitism. Instead he builds an ironic politics of the underworld, reminding us gently at every turn of our mortality and thereby prompting us toward asking each other what really matters in life. Who cares if we never find a final answer?

I hope that the above reconsideration of the Plato's deathly writings prompts a contemporary rethinking of the general relationship between irony and politics. Traditionally these two lives—the life of irony and the life of politics—have been regarded as opposites (Richard Rorty's voice is only the latest to make this claim). The ironist, it is said, defies all formula, deflates all good intentions, derides all noble purposes. He or she is a master of the noncommittal pose and delights in dashing all hopes for redemption. The politician (or the political philosopher), on the other hand, must be a believer in the cause. He or she must be earnest, must be resolute, must be committed—to humanity, to justice, to truth. These two lives are fundamentally at war with one another. Our contemporary postmodern pragmatists—such as Rorty—lately have been trying to teach us how to relinquish our cultural yearning for ultimate redemptions and justifications (Prometheanism more or less works, they say), and they view Plato—and the entire Western tradition—as the source of the problem. But perhaps Plato was well ahead of his time, and maybe his critics today might learn something from his efforts to build a politics out of death on the basis of irony. Even if objective dispensations of justice are not forthcoming, and political commitment does not in fact make sense in light of death, the alternative need not be simply to lower our sights, to abandon our vision, to stop telling inspiring stories. Under conditions such as these, it may well be that only an ironic return to the political world, in pursuit of justice, can bind us together and allow us to fare well in these strange lives of ours with each other.

For the life of irony having no reserve and weaving itself out of the flux of experience rather than out of eternal values has the broad, honest sympathy of democracy, that is impossible to any temperament with the aristocratic taint. One advantage the religious life has is a salvation in another world to which it can withdraw. The life of irony has laid up few treasures in heaven, but many in this world.

—Randolph Bourne, "The Life of Irony"

CHAPTER THREE

The Tomb

When Christianity left its native soil, the lowest classes, the *underworld* of the ancient world, when it began to seek power among barbarian peoples, it was no longer confronted with *weary* men but with inwardly brutalized, cruel people—strong but bungled men. . . . Christianity needed *barbaric* concepts and values to become master over barbarians; for example, the sacrifice of the first-born, the drinking of blood in the Lord's Supper, the contempt for the spirit and for culture, torture in all its forms, both sensuous and not sensuous, and the great pomp of the cult.

—Nietzsche, *The Antichrist*

This chapter offers a selective reading of the teachings of Jesus and the early development of Christianity, with the emphasis on the significance of Jesus' death. I would be remiss in attempting to write about the politics of death if I were to ignore or even to slight the tremendous historical influence of Christianity, especially in the Western world. At the least, Christianity makes a strong claim about its ability to conquer death, and faithful Christians through the ages have read various political lessons into that theology of an afterlife-to-come as well as on the basis of Jesus' exemplary ways while alive. Still, that small foot in the door provides but a thin justification for my reexamining this controversial, perhaps overworked terrain. Surely some readers will bristle at my contemporary effort to reread these religious texts, and they might well think the whole endeavor inappropriate. Such matters are best left (some might hold if only in secret) to religious venues, in churches, in theological journals, in private worship and prayer. Finally, it might be said, the integrity of religious faith rests not on human scrutiny and academic logic; Christian faith in particular reinvests the world with an unprecedented, unfounded hopefulness by way of the mysterious gift of Christ's coming—which by definition defies full human comprehension.

To my potential critics I say: Here I write, I can do no other. The questions I am asking I feel compelled to ask—and I can't imagine true believers not asking them as well or merely dismissing them on trivial, especially ad hominem, grounds. My purpose is not simply to debunk or demystify; nor have I forgotten that Christianity on the whole deserves immense respect, if only because it (to speak collectively) has provided profound consolation and meaning to centuries of humanity. Who am I to second-guess those believers? But it is also clear that Christianity, as an institution and cultural practice, is now a part of the public domain and thus cannot be exempted from serious critical review. After all, we in the West still follow a calendar that recognizes Christ's birth as the pivot point for all of history.[1] In politics as well, in America in particular, Christianity still wields an enormous influence (notwithstanding some disgruntled fundamentalists who claim otherwise)—the chances of a non-Christian, let alone an atheist, being elected to the U.S. presidency are extremely slim. Candidates aspiring to higher elected office in the United States know that Machiavelli's advice still holds in politics: "To those who see and hear him he [the prince] should seem all compassion, all faith, all honesty, all humanity, all religion. There is nothing more necessary to make a show of possessing than this last quality."[2]

It is also true that there exists on record a long and abiding tradition of Christian political theorizing and also much theological scholarship about Christian politics—so what I am doing is by no means altogether new; but that justificatory hook gives rise to another preliminary problem: What more can said, or needs to be said, about this tired topic?

Again I want to respond forthrightly to my own imaginary objectors. After much reading, of the Christian Bible, of much exegetical commentary—redactic, form, source—and of other scholarly criticism (including the unorthodox claims of Nietzsche, Max Weber, Mary Daly, Georges Bataille, René Girard, Julia Kristeva, Hannah Arendt, Norman O. Brown, and others), I am still wanting and dissatisfied. The usual so-called political readings of Jesus look at the Gospels and other supporting materials and typically attempt to extract a political lesson from Jesus' exemplary words and behavior.[3] He is labeled a pacifist, anarchist, subversive (or not); his attitudes toward the poor and the rich, the Roman authorities, the Pharisees, and the Sadduces are pored over; careful analysis is extended to his responses to Pilate's question, "Are you the King of the Jews?"; careful analysis is extended to the various meanings of "kingdom"; speculation is advanced regarding how many Zealots can be counted among his disciples; his apparent political motives are compared with John's; much ado is made of his notion of brotherly love; and finally, whereas some writers claim that Jesus' political stance is one of complete indifference toward all worldly attachments, others discern an outlook that invites individuals to withdraw allegiance from tyrannical governments on the basis of inner conscience. The possibilities are many, and many of these readings are extremely interesting and quite compelling; but characteristically these political readings draw almost exclusively upon Jesus' life and the circumstances leading up to his death, but not the idea of his death as such.

Much recent theological commentary displays a renewed effort, mainly but not exclusively Protestant in inspiration, to downplay the biblical Jesus in order to lay claim to a historical Jesus. The result, and probably the ulterior purpose behind many of these studies, is to demagnify Christian teaching, diminish the importance of sacramental ritual and instead place greater emphasis upon divine grace and individual faith. Most of these studies insist on a sharp historical distinction between Jesus' life and early Christian doctrine. Jesus, in this general view, was the divine Son of God who was sent to earth in order to teach humans how to live. He indeed led an exemplary life, sinless more or less, and along the way he compiled and left behind an oral record of miraculous events and a collection of parables and precepts. But he said little about his own death and nothing specific about how exactly his dying would save his followers. He was the Messiah whose coming was foretold in Hebraic scripture, but his life's teachings were not particularly eschatological in outlook; neither was his point simply to prepare his followers for an afterlife-to-come.[4]

Thus his death, the crucifixion on the cross at Calvary, left his followers in a lurch. Early writers had to fill in the blanks about how to follow an exemplary—but dead!—leader. Evangelists borrowed and culled from many cultural sources in order to make Christianity more appealing to unbelieving Gentile, Jewish, and Hellenistic peoples. Paul, in particular, developed a theory of the resurrection of Jesus' body; and he introduced other theological innovations, such as a stark spirit-flesh distinction; an ethic of agape; the notions of an apocalypse and second coming; and all of these innovations amounted to nothing less than an entirely new theological apparatus based on interpreting Jesus' death.[5] Although many latter-day revisionists regard some Pauline innovations as agreeable and helpful, they are quick to note that such deathly teachings may in critical moments stray from the teachings of Jesus' life. The point, then, is to recover the spirit of Jesus that is separable from the letter of scriptural mythologies.

My proposed intervention in these readings and disputes is to make a case for contesting that prevailing view that insists on a strong distinction between Jesus and Paul, that is to say, between the "life" teaching and the "death" teaching of early Christianity. I argue that, while it is of course abundantly evident that Paul was an ingenious and highly successful theological innovator, there is much underlying continuity between Jesus' teachings (based on the Gospels) and early Pauline doctrine; in other words, Paul was quite justified in doing what he did, namely, emphasizing the deathly aspects implicit in Christ's life. Moreover, I claim, Christianity as a theology does not make sense without this deathly dimension; and no methodological recourse to a reconstructed, extratextual historical Jesus produces a better case for Christianity. It follows, then, that my own interpretive method is to take the Gospels pretty much at their word (even though the various books by no means present a consistent portrait of the life and death of Jesus). In the following material I first draw upon many sources and rehearse several insights and arguments that have been published before—though my interpretive twists present a different composite; but my particular contribution turns on an interpretation of the idea of *sacrifice*, which I take to be central to Christology and thus irrevocable. Finally, my commentary upon the prospects and implications for a Christian politics, a renewable democratic theory, will follow from the analysis of sacrifice.

The Life Teachings

The reformist attempt to discount a trinitarian, polytheistic, and mostly Catholic reading of Christ and Christianity recalls the earliest theological debates out of which emerged the Christian Bible itself, as an effort to codify doctrine and stave off Gnostic and other heresies. These latter-day exegetes often assert that it is not necessary to understand Jesus as a literally divine presence living among and alongside other human beings. He was extraordinary and "blessed," and thus in a loose but not literal sense could be called the Son of God; the point is that above all his humanity is to be emphasized. As such, Jesus was an exemplary human being, sent by the divine creator in order to show the rest of us how to live; and in this sense he is indeed our savior. But the theology of resurrection is not crucial to the spiritual mechanics of salvation.[6]

But then, what were the lessons of his life? What were these exemplary teachings? I want to suggest that these parabolic lessons—and I base my claim on close and collated readings of the synoptic Gospels—were inconsistent, ambiguous, and if anything, extreme. The inherent ambiguity and extremism, moreover, provide threads of continuity with Paul's radical but not radically deviant thought.

First, it is likely that early Christians passed on many stories about the life and death of the figure known as Jesus; a number of oral traditions grew; starting about thirty or forty years after Jesus' death a number of these stories were written down. The oldest New Testament writings, most scholars agree, are the letters of Paul (1 Thessalonians). Paul did not know Jesus personally, and in his writings he shows scant interest in Jesus' biography. Many other stories, prayers, creeds, and tales were written down; and many of the early, evolving church creeds conflicted with each other. The theology of what we call Christianity wasn't clear from the outset, since, as already mentioned, Jesus died without leaving a coherent and fixed doctrine behind. He left rather a series of epigrams and parables, and on the whole he seemed to eschew doctrinal codification. He seemed to leave the burden of interpretation to his followers; and in particular he didn't tell his followers exactly how his death would save them. All of the details of what eventually became Christianity had to be negotiated and worked out.

Most of the doctrinal disputes surrounded Jesus' alleged status as the Son of God. In what sense is Jesus the Son of God, especially since his father-god is, presumably, the same creationist God of the Hebrew bible? In what sense is Jesus any more divine than the rest of us? How can that divinity be incorporated into human flesh? Is Jesus half-divine and half-human, and what would that mean? The prevailing heretics—the adoptionalists, the modalists, the subordinationalists, and the Gnostics—all provided answers to these questions, answers that in various ways attempted to solve the conceptual problem of divine identity by insisting upon Jesus' fundamentally separate, and thus very human, status. Christ was simply adopted by the divinity, or was a mode of divinity, or was the subordinated word of God acting in the world. Or, as with the Gnostics, whatever consubstantiality that Jesus-the-human might enjoy with his creator, his divine spirit had been imprisoned within the fallen body of a man.

One would presume that if the Gospels were accepted in large part to define early Christian orthodoxy against rival heresies, then we might find some clues as to the official (if evolving) position on Jesus' worldly status. Indeed, all of the four Gospels begin by wrestling with the question of Jesus' origins, but on balance they collectively beg the major conceptual question of the relative importance of prophetic versus biological beginnings. Matthew and Luke provide detailed human genealogies; Matthew, in fact, begins immediately with a genealogy. Matthew's genealogy traces Jesus back to David, which underscores the Jewish and messianic lineage; Luke traces Jesus' pedigree all the way back to Adam and names Adam as a son of God. Matthew's editorial juxtapositions are probably the most revealing. Right after establishing the direct Davidic lineage, the text moves to the question of Jesus' birth, which we learn was prescripted; and the messianic lines from Isaiah are quoted directly (Isa.7:14). Then the text moves immediately to recall the Hebraic prescripting of a savior birth in Bethlehem (most historical scholars insist that the Bethlehem birth site was a fabrication), and it foregrounds a coming confrontation between the current "King of the Jews" with this new potential rival on the scene, a rival at least in the sense that "a ruler shall come who will govern my people Israel." The text, however, seems maddeningly inscrutable on adjudicating the $64,000 question, namely whether Jesus' kingship is more "human" (and thus worldly) than "divine" (and thus otherworldly).

Much would seem to depend on the circumstances of Jesus' birth. Recent and not so recent so-called historical scholarship has advocated abandoning the Catholic interpretation of a miraculous virgin birth, even though this revision might jeopardize Jesus' human status as sinless. Most recently John Shelby Spong has insisted that Jesus was "born of a woman."[7] The Hebrew term for young woman (*almah*) in Isaiah 7:14, it is often pointed out, was probably misconstrued into "virgin." The idea of a miraculous birth probably borrowed as well from an older classical idea that larger-than-life heroes derive from the union of a deity and a human woman.[8] Contemporary feminists also want to expunge the idea of a divine impregnation, which, according to some theologians, left Mary a virgin before, during, and after Jesus' birth.[9] Moreover, Mary was informed of her pregnancy after the fact; she clearly didn't consent to it according to any contemporary liberal conception of consent. The entire episode, then, looks remarkably like religious rape.

Three of the four Gospels highlight dramatically the birth episode, and all three seem to favor the miraculousness of the affair.

Matthew specifies that Joseph did not know Mary until she had borne Jesus (Matt 1:25); Luke has an angel explaining to the incredulous Mary ("How can this be, since I have no husband?"—Luke 1:34); and John is more abstract in describing how Logos becomes flesh but does say that "children of God are born not of blood or of the flesh or of the will of man, but of God" and that Jesus is the "only Son from the Father." Still, if one abandons the notion of a miraculous birth and instead settles upon a particularly human, biological birthing (leaving the question of paternity aside), then it is hard to see why Jesus should be regarded as a special or holy human being at all. Let us perhaps grant, for the sake of argument, that the Gospels up to this point are equivocal about Jesus' worldly status as savior. The question of Jesus' special status would seem, then, to depend on his actions, about which the Gospels next elaborate.

Jesus, the stories tell us, at some point left John's desert ministry and started an independent, public ministry in the villages of his Galilean homeland and in the neighboring countryside—but not in the wilderness, as John did. He sought out persons living in settlements and in ordinary situations, as opposed to those scribes following more ascetic, or else scholarly, regimens. Jesus, then, took his ministry into areas with existing political and religious traditions and institutions. Moreover, these areas were internally ridden by all sorts of political, religious, and philosophical divisions. By the time of Jesus, the town of Galilee was known as a seat of Jewish resistance to Rome, and one of Herod's son regarded John the Baptist as politically dangerous. Other Jewish groups adopted various strategies of resistance and accommodation vis-à-vis Rome. But even today the question often arises, was Jesus political (and if so, in what sense)? And if Jesus was the king of the Jews in a political sense, how does that square with his spiritual mission as messiah, if at all? And does that political dimension of his activity reveal any insight into the question of his divine/human status on earth and thus into the purposes of his death?

We know that Jesus inspired a movement in his day and that he was condemned and executed under Roman law as a political rebel of sorts. But he actually broke no Roman laws. Others—Zealots and other religious figures—were more overtly political, acting as urban guerrilla fighters, dedicated to the ouster of occupying Roman forces. Jesus chose to teach in this setting, under these conditions; and he eventually was executed, for a charge for which stoning would have been at that time a more appropriate punishment, if we accept what scant evidence the Gospels provide us. What did he do to deserve the extreme punishment instead? Was the punishment of death completely unwarranted (thus underscoring his status as martyr)? Or did Jesus constitute a political threat, perhaps to several parties all at once?

The Gospels tease us with several possibilities. Jesus called on his disciples to follow him and become fishers of men. There actually were a few fishermen in the Galilean group, as well as a tax collector, surely a few Zealots (at least one, maybe eight[10]), a few craftsmen and peasants. He commissioned and authorized his disciples to preach and to drive out demons and unclean spirits. One of the main lessons of the preaching was that Jesus announced the approaching kingdom of God and called on people to repent. Sometimes the Gospels call this kingdom the "Kingdom of Heaven"— and it is hard to know exactly what this phrase means. Often the circumlocution is used in a spatial sense, as if one enters the kingdom of God, as if the kingdom has an immediate spatial dimension—a presence perhaps not in Roman, yet surely not far off. The language clearly seems to invoke the Hebraic messianic tradition; but then the question is whether this promise is worldly, political, and nationalistic, or whether it is apocalyptic, spiritual, and universalist. Is the kingdom of this world, or of the next? In other words, was Jesus openly confronting and defying the Roman authorities, attempting to usurp their power, or was he attempting an end-run, trying to get people to profess allegiance to a distant goal (which may also have constituted a threat to Rome, but surely a less urgent one)? Is he a literal king of the Jews in the here and now or is he just a prophet, albeit a very important prophet among prophets, who is trying to get persons to be good religious citizens as they bide their time waiting for the next world?

Dostoyevsky's reading of the three temptations in the desert in Matthew (presented in Luke also, in a different order) is extremely insightful for what the Gospels reveal about Jesus' politics. This dialogue between Alyosha and Ivan in the "Legend of the Grand Inquisitor" is not simply an indictment of the church or even simply of Russian socialism, as some commentators have claimed.[11] The reading poses vexing but important questions about Jesus' mission as depicted in the Gospels.

Without rehearsing all the details of this famous section of *The Brothers Karamazov*: Ivan mocks, in front of his novice monk brother, the idea of Christian brotherly love. Christ-love is impossible for humans on earth. We are sufferers, rather, and Christianity tries to rationalize our suffering or to make sport of it. It preaches, in essence, that *because* we suffer, we will be rewarded with eternal life. But Ivan will have none of this game. Like Job, he can't stand the idea that humans must suffer from physical infirmities or that we must suffer from the death penalty that hangs over our heads. He can't accept the idea that humans should be blamed somehow and held accountable for their condition, when they weren't the creators. The earth is soaked with the tears of humanity, and humans are basically innocent. He demands justice: "And not justice in some remote infinite time and space, but here on earth, and that I could see myself."

Ivan has the audacity to put God, the Creator, on trial. Somehow God has arranged the world so that millions suffer, including innocent children. And we are told that evil is essential somehow to this providential plan, a plan to which we are not even fully privy. So Ivan concludes that if evil is essential to divine creation (and Christian salvation), then creation itself is unacceptable, and the pursuit of worldly justice is more important than divine justice pursued through any sort of Christian strategy. If we must accept a theodicy of suffering children in order to defend God and his inscrutable scheme of things, or else must say that it's all too mysterious to understand, then God isn't worth it. In answer to the Pascalian argument, Ivan says that he would persist in his indignation against God even if he were ultimately wrong about all of this. It is too much to live under these unjust conditions.

He then tells his story about the Grand Inquisitor rebuking a returned Christ. It is here that commentators seem to confuse the purpose of the story with a singleminded attack against organized Christendom. The explicit point, instead, is to reveal the nature of spiritual freedom outlined in the Gospels. Ivan turns to the story about Jesus in the wilderness. The devil comes to Jesus and tempts him, and Jesus resists all three temptations. The first is to turn stones into bread; the second, the devil dares Jesus to throw himself off a cliff (and thus show that he is the Son of God and can perform miracles with his body); and the third, the devil shows Jesus the kingdoms of the world, true political power, the ability to use the sword of Caesar for the sake of goodness. Jesus spurns all three offers. Dostoyevsky asks why? What is the text attempting to teach?

Why did Jesus decide not to opt for universal food to feed humanity, a miraculous cure for the infirmities of the body, and for universal peace on earth? Christ rejected all that could have given him the power to make humans happy here on earth. Instead of ensuring our happiness, Christ evidently preferred to leave us free to respond to him or not as we choose. (The story is not simply about, as Wilson claims, Jesus' coyly refusing signs of divinity for the sake of ensuring human faith.) Apparently, a condition of that freedom is that we must be left in the dark, surrounded by ambiguity and evil, for only under such conditions is our choice to follow him truly free. Instead of following rules, laws, decrees, or miracles, we are free to decide good and evil, having only his image as our guide. But the Grand Inquisitor thinks this is a terrible burden, because it condemns us to lives of ignorance, poverty, suffering, injustice, and anarchy. Jesus evidently had more respect than compassion for us (to put it charitably); but if he had truly loved us (in another sense), perhaps he would have lightened our burden. So we live in perpetual confusion, subject to suffering and death—all so that an ambiguous and virtually unendurable freedom might be preserved? Is it worth the time and tears? Is this what Christianity is all about?

Dostoyevsky's legend attests to the logistical problem inherent in the very idea of having a savior in the world who won't save the world right now but instead attaches conditions to the salvation. Jesus promises salvation in a vaguely worded kingdom of heaven to come, but he coolly waits to deliver the goods. How, then, is he to keep his followers interested over an extended period of time, namely, as they live out their lives in the interim?

The very next section of Matthew's story, namely the Sermon on the Mount, seems to provide the clearest lessons that Jesus bequeathed to his followers—clearest because Jesus here puts forth his message in explicit assertion. He tells his followers who exactly on earth is blessed, what his plans are, and how his disciples are to carry out his plans. Interpreting the Sermon on the Mount is not like extrapolating a lesson from a story about Jesus' own actions, nor is it like reading a parable. The sermon is as close as one might get as to Christian doctrine according to Jesus himself (and claiming that the lessons apply only to disciples begs the question of why the sermon received the pride of place that it does in the Christian Bible).

The first lesson is that the poor are blessed and that the kingdom of heaven is theirs. If coupled with numerous other diatribes against the wealthy and digs against the pursuit of mammon (Matt. 7:19,

7:24, 10:9; Luke 18:22), Jesus' praise of poor people seems to produce a "proletarian" reading of his activity, as a rabble-rouser of the
economic underclass. According to this view, an "agitating" Jesus
hits the land-owning Romans and conservative Jewish factions
mainly in the pocketbook. His threat to officialdom is therefore not
simply theological, spiritual, and inward. Numerous interpreters,
however, insist on a crucial distinction between the versions in the
Sermon on the Mount in Matthew and Luke; in Matthew, the
"poor in spirit" are praised, in Luke, simply "the poor" are mentioned. Max Weber, for instance, offers such a reading[12]; and he
notes that in Matthew (Matt. 19:26; Luke 18:27) a legal loophole
exists so that even the rich might pass through the eye of a needle
("What is impossible with men is possible with God"). Although
this escape clause probably provides too much consolation for those
latter-day readers who, through contortionist exegesis, want to reconcile Christianity with capitalist fund-raising efforts, Weber's point
is that Jesus' general message—worldly indifference—should not be
equated too glibly with a politics of contemporary socialism. Jesus'
animus against wealth, which clearly is strong, is a function of his
desire to teach worldly disengagement. The point is not to organize
the poor and to redistribute wealth and to install a new economic
system.

Nor is indifference the same as asceticism, according to Weber,
who also challenges Nietzsche's reading of a Christian ascetic "slave
revolt in morals" as the motor logic behind Jesus' activity among
the downtrodden. Jesus organized a motley group of the poor, the
infirm, the outcast, and women, but the main motivation behind
this theodicy of disprivilege was not *ressentiment* and the need for
revenge. A degree of vengeance was involved, thinks Weber, but the
point of the early ethic of "acosmistic love" wasn't simply that the
tables of privilege will turn in the kingdom to come.[13] Jesus in the
Gospels does display some retributive tendencies, Weber claims,
but there is also counterevidence to undermine such a one-sided
reading. Moreover, the transformation of Christianity in the first
and second centuries from a warlike, reformist religion into an
"apolitical religion of love" was completed, he adds, not "by subju-
gated classes with their slave revolt *in ethicis*, but by educated strata
which had lost interest in politics because they had lost influence or
had become disgusted by politics."[14]

Weber sees the seeds of Pauline agape already at work in Jesus'
evangelical activity, and thus he minimizes the violence, vengeful-

ness, and invidiousness in the early works. He is probably right to dispute a simplistic Marxist/proletarian reading of Jesus as well as a Nietzschean slave revolt reading; but in doing so, Weber glosses over a more complicated story. His reading of Jesus' "charismatic" authority has carried a great deal of weight, but that reading of Jesus' almost magical personal gifts soft-pedals Jesus' tactical extremism. The biblical evidence presents a pretty clear picture of Jesus' forceful, uncompromising ways—an extremism that can be acknowledged without lapsing into a Marxist or Nietzschean interpretation.

Charismatic Authority

Weber used the term "charisma" to describe Jesus' apparently extraordinary ability to convince potential followers to drop everything and to dedicate their lives to him. Today charisma holds primarily positive connotations, referring to an individual's abundant, if indescribable, interpersonal gifts. But even for Weber, charismatic authority and the accompanying "virtuosity of faith" among followers went in hand with an antirational, unconditional reliance on one's god. It shouldn't be assumed automatically that this antirational dimension of Christian faith attests to the integrity or superiority of such faith. To be sure, early Christianity went to great lengths to distinguish itself from Jewish and Gnostic scholasticism—and Jesus was a non-scholar preaching mainly to the uneducated—but in common parlance today we might refer to such acts of inexplicable dedication as fanaticism. Surely the evidence shows that Jesus fanned the flames of fanatical devotion.

If we look at the Gospels, we notice a great number of inconsistencies in Jesus' admonitions to his disciples, many of which seem to defy logic. It is almost as if Jesus dares his disciples to follow his edicts because the demands are so extreme or absurd—as if meeting a test of faith is tantamount to faith itself. First, although Jesus attracted a great deal of attention for his miraculous healing powers and ability to drive out demons, he did not rely solely on some miraculous dimension of his charismatic person for organizing his movement. Rather, he was more practical and down-to-earth. As Jay Haley has argued,[15] Jesus was a skilled tactician in building a band of followers. The Gospels show him attending to both magical and worldly means of doing this. He drove out demons (though he was unable to do so in his own birthplace[16]), but he doesn't depend

solely on miracles for spreading the faith. Rather he starts an orga-
nization of twelve men (and Luke says that he then enlisted seventy
more), and he gives them clear instructions for spreading the word.
For a person who eschewed showing signs as a basis of faith (as in
the temptations-in-the-wilderness story), Jesus seems curiously selective, even arbitrary, in his employ of miracles. Why be miraculous on Monday and not on Tuesday? Why does he need others to
perform miracles on his behalf? Are his spiritual powers such that
there are limits to his miraculous abilities—that is, can he cure
bodily ailments but not change people's beliefs?

Other inconsistencies start to mount. In the Sermon on the
Mount, Jesus insists that he is not calling for change, but then he
proceeds immediately to call for changes in adultery laws, divorce
laws, oath-taking laws, and laws of revenge. He says that he is not
abolishing the law but, rather, fulfilling something like its true
spirit. Somehow he, an untutored scribe, is the heir to a Jewish legal
tradition about which all current Jewish experts are utterly mistaken. Only he apparently holds the key to the true spirit ("It is
written, but I say unto you"). It turns out that adhering to the true
spirit of the laws requires that one exceed the laws. Jesus is em-
phatic (if also sarcastic) about the need for excessive measures: "For
I tell you, unless your righteousness exceeds that of the scribes and
Pharisees, you will never enter the kingdom of heaven" (Matt.
5:20).

What, then, does Jesus mean by exceeding the law? Let us look
carefully at the examples. The prohibition against killing is replaced
by a prohibition against all anger and insults. Divesting oneself of
all anger would certainly be hard to do, and Jesus himself doesn't
seem so forgiving toward his own enemies (Matt. 23:13–36; 26:24).
The prohibition against adultery is replaced by a prohibition against
all lustful thoughts (yet consider that the power of suggestion is
strong and hard to repress). Some commentators review these first
two revisions as expressing the importance of a new faithfulness
based on interiority. What is important in upholding the law is supposedly not outward conformity to laws and correct worldly behavior but rather internal compliance. Jesus therefore teaches a virtue
ethics. Some Protestants take this point a step farther and construe
it as a statement against good works as the key to salvation. If we
look at the text of the Gospels, however, the point of exceeding the
law isn't simply to enforce internal compliance; rather, it seems that
Jesus is setting high, virtually impossible standards for humans—

internal and external standards alike. Perhaps he is really asking too much in legislating against, for instance, lustful ideas and anger. That these standards are nearly impossible to meet does not mean they are exalted. Rather, although the text does not say this explicitly, if we read Jesus as a tactician and organizer, then setting unreachable goals would be a good way of keeping potential followers psychologically dependent on his promise of eventual salvation.

He says in both Matthew and Luke that if your right eye causes you to sin, pluck it out; and if your right hand causes you to sin, cut it off; if any member causes you to sin, cut if off (remember that this section is about adultery and lust!). Also, don't swear at all. These admonitions, even if toned down through interpretive license, certainly are not simply about a new internal spirituality. Cutting off hands and plucking out eyes are also not simply benign disengagements from worldly involvement. (I don't mean to sound judgmental or sarcastic, but I do wonder whether any fundamentalist Christians today, those who claim to follow Scripture in a strict sense, ever engage in the practices of eye plucking or hand chopping.)

Jesus raises the stakes even higher. Do not resist evil; in fact, love your enemies. (Aside from the famous rhetorical appeal of the demand, how exactly is it possible for one to love an enemy? Do you begin by hating your own hatred?) Turn the other cheek. Walk the extra mile. In fact, he says in unequivocal terms: Be perfect. And this perfection is manifest not simply in solitude or silence (though Jesus doesn't want his followers to parade their piety in public) but, rather, in forsaking all worldly attachments—a demand that, again, isn't a call to internality but, to use Weber's language, represents an ethic of innerworldly renunciation. Give up all treasures. Accept no money. Don't be anxious about your life. Don't be anxious about food or clothing. Realize that others will hate you. Don't challenge Jesus' authority. Do not love your father, mother, son, or daughter more than you love Jesus; in fact, renounce all family ties. Is there any widely compelling way, to a modern sensibility, to avoid the conclusion that such excessive imperatives represent an attempt to encourage cultlike fanaticism? Latter-day readers often try to reconcile Christianity with a suburban, middle-of-the-road ethics, but the scriptural evidence simply doesn't sustain that reading.[17]

Some commentators claim that the point of Christianity isn't to be found in Jesus' charge to his disciples but rather in his parables (Matt. 13:1–52; Mark 4:1–34; Luke 8:4–18, 13:18–21). Jesus spoke to ordinary people, the poor, the sick, the uneducated. He taught not in synagogues but in the open air, on roads, in villages, on the shores of lakes. The strange people in his group—women, children, lepers—were often viewed as godless or unclean. He did not quote Scripture to make his point but instead used the language of the parable and the proverb. The parable, it is sometimes claimed, is radically democratic and inclusive. It appealed to the everyday experience of his ordinary listeners with a disarming simplicity; and yet it claimed a transcendental authority that abjured worldly classes and stations. Thus the parable speaks to one's interiority. Anyone can understand the message, and this accessibility provides a real source of energy for outcasts. The Romans may be in power now, but I am the salt of the earth and will receive even greater rewards in heaven!

Yet that reading of the parable isn't supported by scriptural evidence. The parables appear to be simple, but they mask a new kind of esotericism—the "secrets of the kingdom of heaven" (Matt 13:11). When Jesus starts talking in parables, he indeed astonishes the masses, but he leaves his own disciples scratching their heads in disbelief (Matt 13:36; also 15:15). They don't know what he's talking about, and they ask him why he speaks in parables (Matt 13:10). He answers by quoting the prophecy of Isaiah, which in effect says that the masses are dimwits and that they can't be reached through straightforward language. The best you can hope for is to get them to "understand with their heart" and then they will "turn for me to heal them." He then asks the disciples to hear a parable about sowing seeds, the point of which is that one hopes a few seeds land on good soil: Maybe a few listeners will understand Jesus' apparently cryptic lessons. Even after some parables about parables, the disciples ask Jesus to explain the meaning to them (in Mark, Jesus has to explain "everything to his disciples in private"—4:34). Jesus then describes the kingdom of heaven through various analogies: a grain of mustard seed, leaven in bread, a treasure in a field, a merchant in search of fine pearls, a fishing net. He says that at the closing of the age, evil people will be separated from the righteous, and in a furnace of fire men will weep and gnash their teeth—and then immediately he asks, "Have you understood all this?" The disciples, who likely are terrified after that fire imagery, answer without further question or elaboration, "Yes."

In brief: Those who look to the parables for a democratic teaching that isn't dependent on the logic of death and resurrection seem to elide the underlying esotericism that Jesus explicitly advances in explaining his use of parables. Indeed, later Paul will pride himself on his abilities at parabolic interpretation, as a kind of gnosis, the key to true spiritual knowledge.[18] Jesus hopes at best to find a few followers who truly understand his message; for the rest, it is enough that they remain dedicated to him as a healer or enraptured with the vague promises of a kingdom of heaven at hand. But to disassociate the parables from the logic of resurrection is to adopt a patronizing view of the ordinary Christian masses: It is to forward a reading of Jesus' attractiveness which asserts that his ways are illogical, mysterious, and *therefore* perhaps exalted. The illogic of his success supposedly attests to the possibility of providential supervision. But this so-called charismatic reading of Jesus does not satisfactorily explain his success among followers or why he constituted a threat to the Roman authorities who put him to death. We must push on with our midrash.

The Death Teachings

About the time Jesus wants to know what the people are saying about who Jesus is (Matt. 16:13), the Gospels become much more revealing about his worldly status. Peter tells him directly that he is the Son of the living God. From here on, the Gospels become more gory in their description of Jesus' mission. Jesus responds to Peter that "flesh and blood has not revealed this to you, but my Father who is in heaven." He starts talking about a church that can prevail against the powers of death (16:18). Matthew, Mark, and Luke all report that Jesus starts to foretell his own death at this point (Matt 16:21: Mark 10:32; Luke 18:31). He now intimates that the disciples might be mistaken about the distinction between life and death ("For whoever would save his life will lose it"), and he strongly insinuates that their dying might be part of the new bargain ("and whoever loses his life for my sake will find it"). Some of them, however, won't "taste death" before the coming kingdom—whatever that means.

He mentions the idea of a raising from the dead for the first time (Matt. 17:9) and foretells his own death again (17:22); finally he starts talking about torments in hell (18:9). Eventually Peter gets worried about the terms of the deal they have struck: "Lo, we have left everything and followed you. What then shall we have?" (19:27). Jesus gives him a few more parables about the abundance of heaven. But now Jesus has become pretty clear that the route to heaven will be circuitous—on the way to Jerusalem he tells the disciples for the third time that he's going to be condemned to death, mocked, and crucified, and then raised on the third day. The text is curiously silent about the disciples' response.

So Jesus goes to Jerusalem with his disciples for Passover.[19] He must have been aware of the heavy conflicts with Jewish leaders that lay ahead, and he seems deliberately confrontational. He's warned not to go, but he goes anyway. He goes into the temple and starts overturning tables. He tells the businessmen to get out, and he lets the beggars in. The priests ask him by what authority he does such things. He says that he won't tell them. The Pharisees and Sadduces start posing trick and loaded questions of Jesus. Is it lawful to pay taxes to Caesar? (It is a no-win question; he offends either Jews or Romans.) They mock the logistics of resurrection. They want to know the greatest commandment in the law. And they ask point-blank: Whose son is Christ and how does that lineage through David work, exactly?

Jesus gives them an extended tongue lashing ("Woe to you"), and after leaving the temple, his disciples want to know the signs of his coming. After an elaborate, colorful explanation, Jesus reminds them again of his pending death: "you know that after two days the Passover is coming, and the Son of man will be delivered up to be crucified" (26:2). The text next tells a story according to which Jesus reproaches a disciple for his miserly concern for the poor, especially considering that "you always have the poor with you, but you will not always have me."[20]

He then gathers his disciples together for a feast, and while they are eating, the first topic that he brings up is betrayal ("Truly, I say to you, one of you will betray me"). Then, again while they are eating,[21] Jesus informs them that they are eating his body and drinking his blood.[22] It is the blood of a new covenant, he says, and they won't be drinking together again until after his death. And after they sing a hymn together, they go to the Mount of Olives, and Jesus brings up the topic of betrayal yet again. All the disciples vow to the death not to deny Jesus.

Shortly I will return to an extended analysis of this Last Supper scene. For now I want to carry the story all the way to Jesus' death. Why was he killed? Many have asked this question, and I don't pretend to be able to offer a definitive answer. Clearly the Gospels seem to portray Jesus as knowing that he will be arrested by the time of the Passover dinner episode. The text then portrays events that seem to confirm this foreknowledge. He knows that he will be arrested, and then he is arrested. He is first condemned to death by a supreme Jewish tribunal, which condemns him as a blasphemer. He is handed over the next morning to Pontius Pilate, the Roman authority in the area. Pilate seems to question his guilt, and he asks, "Are you king of the Jews?" Matthew, Mark, and Luke show Jesus giving an ambiguous, elliptical answer ("You have said so"). John reports Jesus as saying, "My kingdom is not of this world." In Matthew and Mark, Jesus won't respond to the charges, so that Pilate "wonders greatly." In Luke, Pilate finds no crime. Pilate turns to the crowd, and they call for Jesus' death.

So, I repeat, why was he killed? Was it Pilate's brutality (surely underplayed in the text)? Or was it a pro-Roman Sadducean conspiracy? The Gospels, especially John, tendentiously depict the problem mainly as a theological confrontation between Jesus and the Jews, but that denouement flies in the face of other textual evidence. Clearly Jesus was a rabble-rouser of sorts in the temple, and he seems to have made many people nervous, not just aristocratic, priestly Jews. There is substantial evidence that he was confrontational rather than conflict-averse, and it is also clear that he was successful in organizing a loyal and growing group of dedicated followers. His band of followers surely seemed threatening to many people; indeed, they probably seemed like a crazed bunch of fanatics who had forsworn all possessions and family ties in order to follow him. These early Christians were probably regarded as excessive and uncompromising in their ways, and they probably attracted attention for engaging in bizarre, barbaric, and repulsive rituals. Maybe Jesus posed a threat not just as a new theological innovator, but because he was the leader of a cult (in the contemporary sense of the term)—a cult that increasingly preached deathliness.

Many latter-day Christians ignore or minimize Jesus' volunteerism in fulfilling his role as messiah. They see his crucifixion as separable from his life's teachings, and they focus on his suffering as unjustified, the result of human sinfulness. Or else, to the extent that they attach importance to the resurrection, they see him as victim but argue that his regrettable martyrdom is essential for a theology of salvation. Jesus is "the Lamb of God, who takes away the sin of the world" (John 1:29). He bore our sins, and thus washed away the sins of the world. But Nietzsche points out a complication in this scenario: How can you go out and intentionally try to be victimized and sinned against, in order to fulfill a messianic mission? Jesus can't be given credit for being a messiah if he is truly a victim. Nietzsche points to suicidal tendencies in Jesus' activities: Like the Socrates of the *Apology*, Jesus asked for it. He had to die, thus he knowingly traveled to Jerusalem, provoked a confrontation with his rivals, wasn't remorseful when Pilate gives him the chance. Maybe, as Haley argues, earlier in his career Jesus didn't emphasize death. Part of his lure to the poor and disenfranchised was that he seemed to promise them enormous riches, a wonderful paradise, a great power in compensation for their current sufferings. Indeed his talk of a kingdom of riches at hand seemed to support such fantasies. Maybe, however, he went too far in his promising, and when the authorities called his bluff, he had to equivocate or else produce the goods for his followers; and so maybe a suicide (masked as a crucifixion) was the only way to save face in the eyes of his followers.

In any event, his death must have left these disciples in a lurch: What were they to do now, now that their leader was dead? How were they to get to this supposed kingdom of heaven? How exactly were they to be redeemed and saved by his death?

At the time of Jesus' death, Christianity as a theology of redemption and salvation was not fully formed. Jesus' followers and later church writers had to fill in the gaps, to put on the finishing touches, to cobble together a theology of resurrection, a soteriology. Perhaps we can gather a sense of how they assembled this apparatus.

If we look again at Jesus' last days on the basis of the Gospels, Matthew and Luke especially, we see the following picture emerge. Toward the end of his days in Jerusalem, Jesus starts making a number of prophesies about the end of the world. He talks about earthquakes and judgment days, when nation rises up against nation, and all of his followers will be brought before governors and kings for his sake, and they will be hated for his name's sake. These will be the days of vengeance, to "fulfill all that is written"(Luke 21:22) Others will claim to be the Messiah, saying "I am he," but the disciples are not to be led astray. Anyway, after the crowd yells, "Crucify him, crucify him" and he is mocked through the streets as the "King of the Jews" who can't save himself, he prays, "Father, forgive them, for they know not what they do" (Luke 23: 34). In Matthew his last decipherable words are, "My God, my God, why hast thou forsaken me?" (27:46). He dies, his body is lain in a tomb. There's an earthquake, they find the tomb empty; Jesus eventually reappears to the disciples and tells them "that everything written about me in the law of Moses and the prophets and the psalms must be fulfilled" (Luke 24:44).

To readers of the Hebrew Bible, the above story should seem a little suspicious, a bit too coincidental. We might recall, for example, the words in Isaiah 53, where we find talk of a Lord who will be "despised and rejected by men," who has "borne our griefs and carried our sorrows," who was "wounded for our transgressions"; but it was this "chastisement that made us whole, and with his stripes we are healed." Yet all of this was the Lord's plan, when "he makes himself an offering for sin"—and this "servant"—the Lord's "offspring"—will "bear their iniquities" because "he poured out his soul to death."

In Jeremiah 31, we hear about a restoration of Israel out of a new covenant, which is no longer like the old covenant but is a covenant *within* the followers, written "upon their hearts"; and no longer will people have to learn about the Lord from scribes but will know the Lord directly.

In Psalm 22, a prayer for deliverance from mortal illness, we read the lines:

> My God, my God, why hast
> thou forsaken me? . . .
> But I am a worm, and no man;
> scorned by men, and despised
> by the people.
> All who see me mock at me . . .
> Yea, dogs are round about me;
> a company of evildoers encircle
> me;
> they have pierced my hands
> and feet— . . .
> Posterity shall serve him;
> men shall tell of the Lord to the
> coming generation,
> and proclaim his deliverance to a
> people yet unborn,
> that he has wrought it.

Clearly, the Christian Gospels borrow heavily—directly, word for word in many instances—from Hebrew Bible sources, in an obvious attempt to link Jesus with a messianic prophetic tradition. A number of explanations for this word-for-word intertextual continuity are possible: 1) Jesus was the divine Son of God, and he said the right thing at the right time because he was the Messiah and thus an uncanny correspondence occurred blessedly, and the divine words would help witnesses recall their own biblical studies; 2) Jesus himself was so versed in biblical sources that he said the right things at the right time (for instance, while hanging on the cross) so that people would link him with the messianic tradition; he was thus a bit calculating and humanly manipulative, not wholly or directly divinely inspired; 3) Christian writers went back to their bibles and deliberately invoked the messianic tradition in order to make retrospective sense of Jesus' death.

In all three cases, Jesus' complicity in his own death would be somehow overshadowed by the prophetic foregrounding to that event. But none adequately explains Nietzsche's problem of logistics: If Jesus did deliberately set out to get himself killed, how can that act be reconciled with being the Son of God who will wash away our transgressions? How can one go out and willfully become a martyr? Can one ask for suffering and still claim victimization?

Sacrifice

If we pursue the third option to its logical conclusion: Christian writers drew upon another Old Testament and classical motif—that of sacrifice. Herein (I want to suggest a bit grandiosely) lies the essence of Christology. The thematics of salvation provide undeniable textual continuities between the old and new testaments, and the whole inner logic of the Christian salvational system hangs on this notion applied to the life, and not just the death, of Jesus Christ.

God so loved a world, John 3:16 tells us, he gave his only Son. This lead maxim for many Christians requires the background belief that humans are basically fallen since the time of Adam and Eve. Despite the covenant, and the new covenant after Noah, no one, therefore, up to Christ's appearance, was able to enter the gates of heaven. God at some point evidently decided to rectify this sad state of affairs (though no one knows why it took him so long to build up a sufficient reservoir of superabundant love before he took decisive action). At any rate, he eventually sent his only Son as an emissary, whose death would wash away the sins of all humankind. The key to this scenario is that Jesus, in some important if unclear sense, is half-human and half-divine. Such an ambiguous, amalgamated nature allows him to enter the gates of heaven and to get the rest of us admitted as well. But underlying this scheme of things are some unspoken assumptions, which should be spelled out clearly but seldom are. There is indeed a logic to this narrative; the theology of salvation doesn't rest finally on a complete mystery.

First, God's sending his *only* son is meant to emphasize how dear that son is to him, and thus how much of a sacrifice he is making on our behalf, and thus how much he loves us (the transitive theorem). But according to the logic of that extended love, God's character must be chauvinistic and petty. Clearly this notion is a borrowing from the Old Testament sacrifice of Abram's only son Isaac, and thus a play upon the Jewish people as the favorite sons of God. But in this new version, God is willing to save *his* son, despite the fact that Jesus is half-human, because, after all, Jesus is God's son and thus half-divine. But this means that God loves his son more than he loves the rest of us (this invidiousness doesn't seem to bother Christian believers, because it is pretty much taken for granted that parents love their own children more than other children; and even though we are all God's creatures, divine blood in this case is apparently thicker than created blood).

Christ is our savior because he takes advantage of his ambiguous nature for our sake. Once he has his foot in the door of heaven, he sets a precedent for all humanoids. If God is going to save his own son, then he is going to need to lower his admission standards generally, allowing entrance in principle to almost any otherwise fallen human being. But the unspoken key to this scheme is that God is ambivalent, torn, at odds with himself over the whole affair. Part of him wants to save humans, but he feels he must go through a roundabout procedure, first sacrificing his beloved half-human son as a sort of guinea pig. Again, clearly this story borrows from and plays upon the old Hebraic theme of sacrifice.[23] But in the Old Testament, and in all other classical sources, a sacrifice is burned in order to make an appeal to God, to change his mind about some matter.[24] In the New Testament version of sacrifice, God, too, makes a sacrifice.[25] But the bizarre thing about the new version is that God, in sending his only son, is making a sacrifice—to himself.[26] God makes a sacrifice in order to change his own mind! One wonders why he, out of that same supposed love for us all, didn't just save us without all the hassle. Doesn't God have complete control over the gates of heaven?

In short, how could Jesus be both a sacrificial emissary of God and a human sufferer? We probably must conclude that this central narrative of Christology is a flawed reworking of older themes of sacrifice.[27] But it was extremely effective for the times, it pulled powerful cultural strings—and who can argue with success? We know of many other such transcultural borrowings that embroider this death motif. Surely Orphic-Pythagorean underworldly themes dovetailed with early Christian reinscriptions of sacrifice and apocalypse. The idea of Jesus as shepherd, Patricia Vicari contends, probably derives from a pagan icon showing Orpheus—the tamer of wild animals—among the animals, often sheep.[28] The Orpheus figure—a shepherd who magically experienced death and returns to tell about it—also apparently inspired the early Christian writers who were trying to connect Jesus with a Davidic-messianic tradition. Clement of Alexandria, the second-century apologist, tried to demonstrate Christ's musical aptitude by comparing and contrasting it to that of Orpheus. Orpheus's songs, for one thing, charmed only beasts instead of humans. Christian musicology, Clement argued further, can be traced back to the Hebrew Bible, with the young David as a lyre player.[29]

Still, even the possibility of an Orphic genealogy doesn't adequately account for the curious features of the Christian reinscription of the sacrifice motif. Let us return to the Eucharist scene of the Gospels. It is beside the point whether the account of the episode in the Gospels is historically accurate. We are rather interested in the text as representation, as the written basis for Christian belief through the ages. Surely there is sufficient textual evidence to conclude that early writers made a concerted effort to link Jesus with a Jewish tradition of Passover, and they reinforced that connection through the use of lamb analogies. The Jews ate lambs in celebration of their covenant; Christians, celebrating a new covenant, eat lamb as well. The logic of sacrifice dictates that Jesus be that lamb of God; hence the Christians eat Jesus' body and drink his blood.

But that train of thinking seems too neat in accounting for this festival of quasi cannibalism.[30] The event is shocking. Latter-day accounts that dismiss the literalness of the sacrament of transubstantiation trivialize the extent to which the event is supposed to be read as shocking and extreme, an event of actual, and not merely

symbolic, blood and guts.[31] The shock value is crucial to the theme
of betrayal—this is a litmus test for gauging the devotion of the
disciples.[32] Jesus worries about betrayal immediately before and after breaking bread and drinking wine.[33] If you so love him, then you
would be willing to eat his body and drink his blood. The new
covenant, a bond forged in anticipation of Jesus' impending death,
is supposed to be grave; and thus the act must be intense and morbid. Notice the extremely odd features of this scene: Jesus has announced that he is going to die. He invites his closest disciples to a
last dinner, halfway through which he announces that his own body
is the featured entrée that evening. We have, then, a dinner party of
thirteen men, men who have given up all possessions, men who
have renounced their families, men who likely are celibate, men
who worry about demons and hostile external forces, and they bond
together via Passover imagery in anticipation of their leader's death.
Paul will later write that Jesus' sacrifice is a better sacrifice than
older sacrifices because it features not the sacrifice of goats and
calves but his own blood (Heb. 9:17). What is going on in this
strange, cascading congeries of sacrificial motifs?

First of all, we cannot ignore that this party is an all-male event.
Mary Daly is one writer who confronts the conspicuous and undeniable masculinity of the whole affair.[34] She connects it with the
general all-male trinitarianism of Christianity, and she associates
that preoccupation of the relationships between fathers and son,
and the attendant male-to-male bondings, with necrophiliac tendencies: The only way men bond together successfully is through a
fantasy of apocalypse and destruction. But out of this celebration of
death must come rebirth—and then the logistical question is how
can men effect rebirthing without the presence of women? Daly's
answer at this point is unsatisfying: She claims (perhaps as a result
of her own tendency to believe that only women can be birthers)
that Jesus somehow becomes a goddess/mother; and likewise she
regards Jesus' earlier loving activities as exemplifying a spirit of an-
drogyny and cross-dressing. Unfortunately, Daly's intriguing narrative runs out of steam at this point.

Weber, too, examines the absence of women in Christian sacrament, but, contra Daly, he doesn't see the ethic of brotherly love
and love for one's enemy as necessarily revealing a hidden "feminist
character" to the religion.[35] In fact, many masculine cults effect that
magical transformation of rebirth without the influence, implicit or
otherwise, of women: "Wherever an ascetic training of warriors in-

volving the rebirth of the hero is or has been dominant, woman is regarded as lacking a higher heroic soul and is consequently assigned a secondary religious status."[36] The notion of sacrifice does not require a feminist contribution either. The orgiasticism of the Vedas in ancient India proves a counter case in point. The priestly soma sacrifice was originally a male intoxication orgy that probably dates farther back to "ritualistic copulation in the fields as a means of securing soil fertility . . . with its phallic hobgoblins."[37] Fertility sacrifices were paid to a god, Rudra, and at such sacrifices, only the (male) priest drank soma and ate sacrificial meat.[38]

In general, Weber sees the purposes of religious sacrifice as twofold: first, it is a "magical instrumentality" invoked to coerce the gods, the key to which is that "the gods also need the soma juice of the sorcerer-priests, the substance which engenders their ecstasy and enables them to perform their deeds"; second, "the sacrifice, especially of animals, is intended as a *communio*, a ceremony of eating together which serves to produce a fraternal community between the sacrificers and the god. This represents a transformation in the significance of the even older notion that to rend and consume a strong (and later a sacred) animal enables the eaters to absorb its potencies."[39] With respect to the Christian Eucharist in particular, Weber notes that the prospect of *communio* through eating has terrified many believers because of the doctrine that "whoever does not believe and yet eats, eats and drinks himself to judgment."[40] The Eucharist, then, sets the standards extremely high for ritual purity as a prerequisite for participation; and without the possibility for prior absolution through confession, Puritans would later abandon this sacrament.

Nietzsche helps us as well to think through the high stakes and the inner dynamics of Christian sacrifice. In the *Genealogy of Morals* he attempts to trace the murky origins of the idea of sacrifice. The need for sacrifice, he speculates, probably derives from a metaphysical anxiety concerning the origins of the tribal community, which raises the question of a tribe's obligation to its ancestors. "The conviction reigns that it is only through the sacrifices and accomplishments of the ancestors that the tribe *exists*—and that one has to *pay them back* with sacrifices and accomplishments: one thus recognizes a *debt* that constantly grows greater, since these forebears never cease, in their continued existence as powerful spirits, to accord the tribe new advantages and new strength."[41] Can one ever give one's ancestors enough in return for one's very existence? The problem of cross-generational obligation exacts a heavy price: it escalates to the conclusion that one can pay back the dead only with more death, and ultimately with one's own death: "This suspicion remains and increases; from time to time it leads to a wholesale sacrifice, something tremendous in the way of repayment to the 'creditor' (the notorious sacrifice of the firstborn, for example; in any case blood, human blood)."[42] The debt grows larger and larger, to the point that the ancestors of the most powerful tribes must grow more and more fearful and monstrous to the imagination, until they are transfigured into a god. Christianity, featuring a god of maximum indebtedness, turns the idea of sacrifice around, so that God becomes the only being who is pure and holy enough to discharge unredeemable man from his debts. In short, Christian sacrifice ultimately attempts to relieve man from the burden of existence itself; it is a death wish, an aversion to life itself. Yet elsewhere Nietzsche says that the Christian sacrifice only *seems* to be a sacrifice unto death; actually *Christo emulaia* conceals a strategy to transform oneself into a thought of a god.[43] The Passover lamb is not, in the end, devoured and destroyed but, rather, sits reconstituted at the right hand of the Lord.

For all of Daly's, Weber's, and Nietzsche's insights into the assumptions animating the thematics of Christian sacrifice, we still need to explain why *eating* the body at the Eucharist is so central to this male festival of transformation. On this point, we might borrow a few insights culled from other tales of heroic descent into underworldly death. The myths of Ianna and Tammuz, Isis and Osirus, Cybele and Attis, and Aphrodite and Adonis all feature the element of sacrifice and, more conspicuously than the Christian version, the element of dismemberment or immolation. Sacrifice goes hand in hand with dismemberment, and these elements are common to almost all myths of dying and resurrecting gods.[44] The reason is simple: If there is no dismemberment, there can be no radical reintegration. Dismembered separation surely heightens the dramatic sense of anguish and passion. But more, such resurrecting gods often follow a fertility cycle that requires a ritual of transformation: A new life pattern emerges only by feeding on the old one. Rites involving aspects of cannibalism surely represent the need for communion and ultimate friendship,[45] but even more they signify transformation, the attempt for the living to start anew by feeding on the dead.

Christianity as a religion represents a spirit of utter novelty; it proclaims a new hope for the world, an utterly new beginning for humanity. It is the ultimate religion of change—even more so than eastern religions that proclaim the transmigration of souls. The Christian God has changed his mind and has redirected his providential course of action—he will finally save fallen humanity and allow them entrance into heaven and eternal life. Therefore humans, too, may enter into a radically new conception of life. How then can sacrifice-through-eating contribute to the mechanisms of particularly all-male rebirthing?[46]

The trick is to find a bodily, biological function that can symbolize the possibility of male rebirthing. It must be a second miraculous birthing, one that doesn't require the intervention of women. Eating is indeed magically transformative, a mysterious method of reanimating the body; it can thus symbolize taking in the burden of the past, now consumed, hidden, digested, and thus transformed. It gives and sustains life, out of dead matter. "All sacrifice is eating," quips Norman O. Brown.[47] Men by themselves can be eaters and not simply destroyers of life. But there is a repressed, darker side to this all-too-human function: The processes of digestion and excretion are excruciatingly literal methods of transubstantiation. The Gospels feature Jesus and his disciples eating but never excreting; there is no sacrament of excretion, and the other end of this transformative process is conspicuously absent from the text. If Christ's body and blood becomes consubstantial with the bread and wine, as church doctrine eventually holds, and if the sacrament of Eucharist is not merely a *figurative* act of remembrance and thanksgiving but constitutes a worldly *communio*, then what is the theological status of apostolic shit?[48] How does the sacred turn into the profane, the highest into the lowest? The question should not be dismissed as cutely psychoanalytic. Christianity presents a particular theory of the body, and given its preoccupation with the body, it can hardly be ignored that the body excretes.[49] To be sure, later Christian scatologists become fascinated by the lower regions. The early iconography of hell almost always features a devil who shits sinners into hell.[50] And thanks to Erik Erikson, Brown, and others we are now privy to the excremental origins of Lutheran faith.[51] Rabelais begins heroic Gargantua's genealogy by describing a mock nativity featuring a miraculous excremental birthing due to Garamelle's eating far too much tripe (and the narrator points out that "I find nothing in the sacred Bible that is against it").[52] The Gospels do in fact seem curiously withholding on such down-to-earth matters. We are told that the apostles take a postprandial snooze in the garden of Gethsemane but other key metabolic functions are not described. Rather, the Gospels move on precipitously at this point to report the details of Jesus' death.

How, then, can eating, digesting, and excreting contribute to a theory of all-male rebirthing? Is there, in other words, a thematic continuity that ties together the sacrificial functions of the Eucharist with Paul's soteriology?

Before we put the pieces of the puzzle together, let us recollect some of the strands of the argument. The thesis I have been implicitly and explicitly working against is the claim that Paul is a radical innovator who develops *ex nihilo* a theory of resurrection and atonement. According to this view, Paul creatively resurrects Jesus' body and speaks of a second coming (*parousia*), a day of judgment at which time other dead souls will be raised and judged. Thus Christian followers, thanks to Paul, are not following a dead but, rather, an arisen spiritual leader, who will then come yet again. Moreover, all newfound spiritual purposefulness owing to Christ's resurrection turns on the mechanics of Jesus' death as atoning sacrifice. In short, Paul alone is responsible for the soteriology—and the entire (and probably misconceived) Christology of sacrifice.

Commentators today often attempt to assess the extent of Paul's innovation. Some try to trace his ideas of sacrifice back to Jewish, Hellenistic, or Gnostic roots, and the point of such an approach is to distill how much Paul borrows and how much he invents. Others take a different tack and insist that the Eucharistic dinner provides no sacrificial function whatsoever; thus, it is claimed, there can be no continuity between sacrificial eating and sacrificial death.[53] A recent anthology devoted to the idea of Christian sacrifice begins thus:

> It is characteristic of contemporary ecumenical theology to refer to the "sacrifice of Christ" without further elaboration. Doubtless the wholly understandable reason for this is the need to find a commonly agreed point of reference from which to tackle the hotly disputed question of the eucharistic sacrifice. All the major Christian traditions have affirmed that Christ's death is sacrificial in character. . . . But the truth of the matter is that in modern times there has been no agreement about the nature of sacrifice, and thus no agreement about the sense in which the interpretation of Christ's "sacrificial" death is to be understood.[54]

Indeed, much to my surprise I have found in the secondary literature nothing but confusion on this central tenet of Christian theology. For some reason theologians have focused exclusively on the various interpretations that Jesus' death might be understood as a human event; the sacrifice is thus a sacrifice from humans to God. But no one, as far as I know, has explored Nietzsche's brief remark that the Christian sacrifice is and depends upon a notion of a sacrifice from God to God.[55] My point is that, as a God-to-God sacrifice, it doesn't really matter what particular mode of divinity Jesus adopts or exemplifies. The narrative assumes only that Jesus be part-human and part-divine in some sense. But that general notion of sacrifice, from God to God, is implicitly required for any Gospel-based understanding of Jesus as savior, whether dead or alive. No coherent teaching of his life's work can be extracted otherwise (even if we grant Christianity wiggle room for a spiritual license that defies doctrinal ossification); nonetheless, the overarching messianic mission necessarily implicates God as prime mover and instigator. Christian churches are probably right to insist on John 3:16 as the central basis for faith: God so loved a world, he sacrificed his only son—a sacrifice that doesn't make Jesus a bit player in the affair but does decenter the importance of his life's teachings (most of which in any event beg the question of, and thereby attest to, Jesus' ambiguously divine/human status).

Working toward the culminating sacrifice, emplotted from the outset as if divinely prescripted, the Gospels are extremist, violent, and bloody—in short, deathly—from the beginning to the end. As Albert Schweitzer argued some time ago, the apocalyptic motif runs throughout the Christian corpus, from start to finish.[56] Those deathly concerns were perhaps exploited, elaborated, and extended by Paul, but they were there all along for the plucking; and thus, in light of Jesus' missionary motives, it is extremely difficult to view Paul's theory of bodily resurrection as representing a radical theological departure or innovation.

Paul's Passion

It is true, as Hannah Arendt remarked, that wherever he went, Paul preached death and resurrection of the dead.[57] Clearly Paul was preoccupied with the idea that human bodies die, and he was obsessed with the question, How can the dead be raised? (1 Cor. 15:35). But contemporary theologians, in discussing his theories of salvation, tend to underplay the bloodiness of Paul's preaching in favor of a bloodless version of faithful agape. Thus even the death teachings become whitewashed, and all bloody connections to the synoptic Gospels are wiped clean. If we survey Paul's writings on sacrifice, however, a much more sanguine picture emerges. First, we notice that Paul's soteriology quite evidently depends on the background logic of a God-to-God sacrifice, with Jesus as the trigger mechanism that trips opens the gates of heaven for all other humans. Jesus suffered death, Paul explains, and thus tastes death for all humans (Heb. 2:9). Acting in that capacity, Jesus is a "mediator" of a new covenant (Heb. 9:15), a "ransom" for all (1 Tim. 2:6). He is indeed a sacrifice, who is slaughtered like a "paschal lamb" (1 Cor. 5:7). His death is therefore like other sacrificial "first-fruits" (Rom. 8:23; 1 Cor. 15:20, 23); he is the "first-born" among the dead (Col. 1:18; Acts 26:23). Paul emphasizes that Jesus' blood is necessary to purify this new covenant (Heb. 9:22; Rom. 3:25; 1 Cor. 11:25; Acts 20:28). In fact, Paul insists that without actual blood shed, there can be no atonement (Heb. 9:18, 22). Moreover, Paul states clearly that he thinks this bloody human sacrifice is far more profound than the older rituals involving merely animal sacrifice (Heb. 9:12). This new version puts an end to such petty sacrifices. He then calls upon followers to "present your bodies as living sacrifices" (Rom. 12:1).

Although Paul spends a great deal of time writing about Jesus in deathly, bloody, and bodily terms, reformist theologians notice instead his emphasis on sanctification through grace. What counts, finally, is the interior spirit (as it were), not the bodily exterior (thus such graceful sanctification is sanitary, the logic seems to go). Paul makes this point, however, in connection with two very bloody matters. He raises the issue in one place with respect to eating idol meat (one can eat such meat as long as one doesn't know where it was killed [1 Cor. 8:4] which means that the external body can eat as long as the internal spirit is left unawares). Second and more prominent, Paul invokes the spirit-flesh distinction very graphically in connection with his discussions of circumcision. But commentators tend to leave dangling Paul's preoccupation with the penis, and they seldom make an attempt to link it with his general soteriology—though the two are obviously connected, at least through a blood motif. Can we, however, draw a more direct connection between Paul's two great, supposedly innovative concerns, namely the resurrection of dead bodies and the prohibition against bloody rites of penile mutilation?

First, it is no extravagant hyperbole to say that Paul is obsessed with the penis, at least in his letter to the Romans. Of course he is making the point that Christians ought to follow an inner faithfulness rather than rely upon old rituals and legalisms. In faith, God makes no distinction between Jew and Gentile, circumcised and uncircumcised. The new covenant is "written on their hearts" (Rom. 2:15), not on their penises. "True circumcision" is not "external and physical" (Rom. 2:28). But Paul's discussion of the penis clearly dovetails into other discussions about the death of flesh and, therewith, into his prohibitions against sexuality. The section on penises in Romans is preceded immediately by Paul's diatribe against persons who follow "lusts of their hearts" and engage in practices "dishonoring bodies" (1:24). He expresses concern about women who exchange "natural relations for unnatural" (1:26) and men who commit "shameless acts with other men" (1:27). Circumcision, he explains further, is of no help to the Jew who commits adultery (2:23, 25). One's "members" are at war with one's mind and thus make one captive to the "law of sin" (7:23). All of this obsession with sexuality causes death, until one screams, "Who will deliver me from this body of death?" (2:24). The reason for eschewing circumcision and sexuality is the same: The flesh of the body dies. But if one follows the new covenant, one's spirit can live on (8:10). So one shouldn't take too much pride in one's bodily circumcision (3:27). One should avoid the penis, if one wants the rest of the body to rise after death. Put to death all fornication (Col. 3:18). It is good to be chaste (1 Thes. 4:3), and best to be celibate altogether (1 Cor. 7:8–9).

Exercising sexual self-control, then, is somehow loosely connected to the resurrection of the dead.[58] But commentators do not connect Paul's lowering of the penis with the raising of the dead.[59] To be sure, the discussion of circumcision allows Paul to make his point about a new spiritual covenant. Surely as well, the letter to the Romans expresses a practical innovation that he devised in his evangelical campaigns on the road. Rewriting the rites of circumcision allowed Paul to overcome a major obstacle in selling his new version of Judaism to a Hellenized, phallophilic people. If conversion to Christianity were to require a two-step process, in which a man must first become a Jew (as an adult) before he reaps the benefits of the kingdom at hand, then he must be not just baptized (a symbolic circumcision) but actually circumcised. As a child, circumcision presents a small problem, which can be resolved into the general traumata of early childhood. But as an adult, circumcision usually presents a larger problem. If following this strange savior requires putting one's member on the chopping block, then who needs it? Paul's abstract discussion of circumcision surely reflects an evangelical innovation that was born of experience in the trenches.[60] Salvation would indeed require bloodletting but not the blood of one's penis.[61] Christ's blood, therefore, could serve that function once and for all. Now potential believers were off the hook.

Commentators who do probe deeper into Paul's remarks on circumcision often make a point of insisting that circumcision contains no sacrificial overtones, and thus there is no remote tie-in to the Eucharist.[62] Yet Paul himself directly links the language of circumcision to Christ's sacrificial function: "In him also you were circumcised with a circumcision made without hands, by putting off the body of flesh in the circumcision of Christ" (Col. 2:11). In other words, Christ's sacrificial circumcision saved all of us, so that, for one thing, we no longer need to be circumcised in the flesh (Gal. 5:6; Phil. 3:3). But there's more. Robert J. Daly contends that postexilic Judaism expressed a strongly sacrificial element in the rite of circumcision, especially by associating Passover blood with the blood of circumcision:

> The words of Moses' wife Zipporah in Exod 4:25: "You are a bridegroom of blood to me," become in the Septuagint: "Behold the blood of the circumcision of my child." This suggests that Moses was delivered from death by the (sacrificial) expiatory power of the blood of circumcision, an interpretation supported by the *Palestinian Targums*: on Exod 4:25, "Now may the blood of this circumcision atone for the guilt of my husband"; on Exod 4:26, "How beloved is the blood of [this] circumcision which has saved my husband from the hand of the Angel of Death [Destroying Angel]." This interpretation can be dated as early as the second century BC.[63]

Daly adds that the blood of circumcision held considerable theological significance by being connected to notions of sacrifice, Passover, and covenant. He says that the rabbinical insistence that at least one drop of blood must flow in circumcision seems to have been the background sentiment informing Paul's claim that "without the shedding of blood there is no forgiveness of sin" (Heb. 9:22). Moreover, Paul's theology of baptism as participation in the sacrificial death and resurrection of Christ appears linked in the texts to his discussions of circumcision (Rom. 6:3–4, Col. 2:11–12).[64]

I realize some of my readers might be thinking at this point that I have taken Paul's penis out of context, giving it undue emphasis. But I turn this question back upon such readers: How can one possibly read Romans without focusing on Paul's obsession? Moreover, how does this bodily concern contribute, if at all, to Paul's theory of bodily resurrection? That line of questioning does indeed lead us back to the Eucharist. In a grand leap of associative logic, I now pose the question: Is there any way to connect the Eucharistic concern with all-male birthing to Paul's penile soteriology?

Here Norman O. Brown provides a brilliant key, or else a dirty little secret, drawing on Freud's famous essays on anal eroticism as well as Freud's notion of a death instinct.[65] In *Life against Death* Brown pursues a sweepingly grand thesis that repositions the death instinct as central to human psychology. Death is an integral part of life for humans, according to Brown's Freud, and yet there is a peculiar morbidity in the human attitude toward death.[66] Humans—or at least many of those living in the West—are characterized by the incapacity to accept death, and thus try to flee from death, to deny it, repress it, overcome it. For civilized Western man, the main defense mechanism against the idea of death is sublimation.[67] Death sublimation takes the forms of monument building, city building, wealth accumulation, and the pursuit of spiritual immortality. Brown sees the revolt against bodily death and its various sublimations as a manifestation of male aggression: "This human posture of life at war with death is epitomized in the fantasy—originating in infancy but energizing all human history—the wish to become the father of oneself."[68] Moreover, there is a special psychoanalytic connection between (male) sublimation and anality.[69] In a tightly worded explication (the dazzling details of which I will skip over), Brown repeats Freud's claim that an integral part of an anal symbolic complex is to equate the feces with the penis, an equation that reveals a recurring fantasy of giving birth to oneself, of becoming one's own father.[70]

> Thus the morbid attempt to get away from the body can only result in a morbid fascination (erotic cathexis) in the death of the body. In the simple and true, because bodily, language of the

unconscious, Eros can be deflected from the life of the body only by being deflected onto the excremental function. In the true life of the body (which is also the life of the id) value can be detached from the body only by attaching value to the non-bodily excreta of the body, which are at the same time the dead matter produced by the body, and which incorporate the body's daily dying. In more technical terms, sublimated anality presup-posed the castration complex, the decisive death of the body which according to Freud desexualizes and paralyzes the penis. With the death of the penis the center of erotic attention is transferred to the dead body par excellence, the feces.[71]

For Brown, the "excremental vision" is integral to the Christian (albeit mainly male) concern with bodily resurrection, featuring a miraculous male rebirthing out of an episode of eating and shitting. If Brown's sudden sweeps of logic seem facile, it might be because Freud and Brown attempt to retrace the elusive, far-fetched train of Christian logic that, on the one hand, purports to accept the exis-tence of bodily death while, on the other hand, resurrecting a trans-figured body, a body that supposedly no longer dies.[72] "The time has come to ask Christian theologians, especially the neo-orthodox, what they mean by the resurrection of the body and by eternal life . . . For we have seen that the perfect body, promised by Christian theology, enjoying that perfect felicity promised by Christian theol-ogy, is a body reconciled with death."[73]

Toward a New Democratic Theory

My point in pursuing these netherworldly trains of logic wherever they may lead me is not to suggest that the Christian death-rebirth narrative ought to be rewritten in order to accommodate a more feminist-inspired view of spiritual rebirthing (more on that in the next chapter). Nor am I obliquely endorsing Brown's orgiastic the-ory of Dionysian renewal, a return to the body. Nor is my task, finally, to second-guess the beliefs of practicing Christians. Rather, I hope that the above focus on the deathly preoccupation of the Gospels helps to illuminate the particular vision of death that the Christian Bible, as I read it, implicitly but necessarily promotes. Once we put that death vision into perspective, we can then assess the political implications, the damage and the fallout. I am inter-ested in the extent to which the general Christian narrative, based on a new covenant written in blood and ever posed toward death, has been used as the background universalist sentiment for a particular version of modern democratic politics (but the point I want to highlight isn't simply the crude claim that death is a great equalizer). Most modern democratic theory departs from the Greek concept of democracy, namely as a humanly constructed equality before the law, *isonomia*. Humanly conferred equality is, rather, replaced with a far wider, potentially more inclusive concept, the idea of a naturalized, pre- and post-political equality before the Christian God, a god who makes no distinctions based on nature, a god therefore who is evangelical and cross-national (the prophet Mohammed was not the first to happen upon this idea), a god who believes in the equality of all human beings not just at birth but at death: We shall all stand in judgment at death before this just Creator.[74] These are powerful notions, very inspirational, almost indispensable because they now envelope much of Western culture. My interest is not in the literal truth or falsity of the Christian afterlife but rather in the way the Christian specter of death can mobilize people politically in a particular way, fashioning them into a community, a community posed toward death in the here and now.

Which is to say: I want to take issue with a particular conception of democratic politics for which Christian deathliness provides the background ideological support. My challenge isn't with the obvious patriarchy apparently built into the system—the preoccupation with father-son relationships, cannibalism, homoeroticism,[75] necrophilia, male-rebirthing, and anal complexes—hence hypocrisy isn't the final charge. Nor is my main point here to insist that men should stop attempting to usurp from women the functions of cultural and psychological rebirthing, thus rendering women secondorder spiritual, and therewith civil, agents (that task I leave to others). Rather, I return to my main theme above, taking issue with the central Christian motif of sacrifice, namely, as a uniquely Godto-God sacrifice. Such a sacrifice, I submit, does a great disservice to the idea of democracy now deployed in most democratic models.

The sheer concept of Jesus as an inexplicable gift who in some important if ambiguous sense is half-human and half-divine contains an idea that could be of tremendous benefit to democratic theory and politics: Here is a figure who in his person deconstructs (as it were) the age-old sacred/secular distinction and who, acting as representative Everyman, could thus reinvest human affairs with a kind of sacred integrity. Instead of denigrating the importance of life in this world, instead of inducing a call for ultimate salvation from human affairs in general, Jesus' worldly presence could serve an antirationalist, antiutilitarian, antieschatological democratic agenda. Democratic affirmation of other peoples and persons would not be staked on a clever contract; human dignity wouldn't require an argument or foundation but would be firmly rooted and respected nonetheless. Democratic inclusion wouldn't require or mask secret economies of exclusion, invidiousness, or judgmentalism. Democracy would be the noblest of virtues, not a second-best compromise, a calculated risk.

But alas, Jesus' creolized, mongrel nature could not be separated from his mission as messiah. His ambiguous nature as half-human/half-divine hero was too attached to his ambiguous, double-agent role as sacrificial priest and victim.[76] God was too much in charge of the whole show. The God-to-God sacrifice introduced a tremendous providential instrumentalism into the Christian narrative that overshadowed any possible countervailing message regarding humanity's on-the-ground, unconditional dignity or any chance for a veritable kingdom at hand, a notion of heaven on earth. The character of the sacrifice; the fact that God was the instigator, that his purposes were primary; the idea that changing his mind about humanity would become the main plot twist, that his agenda should be foremost, that he should be the final transcendental arbiter of taste concerning human dignity; all preordained that whatever significance Jesus' life might hold on its own terms would be eclipsed by his death. How could it not follow that humans in general would become more valuable dead than alive, and that any ensuing democratic politics would become at best a second-order value, an afterthought? Eternal life, sitting next to the father-creator, would become the highest, the only real goal. Instead of the deification of man, says Nietzsche, his "undeification, the digging of the deepest chasm, which only a miracle, only prostration in deepest self-contempt can bridge."[77] The God-to-God sacrifice is the origin of an instrumentalist democratic sentiment, a point that is occluded by the fact that God himself is the leading instrumentalist in the story and by the fact that humans seem to be beneficiaries of that divine intervention.

"Democracy is Christianity made natural" (p. 126). Nietzsche provides a trenchant critique of democracy (on slightly different grounds from the above argument, via the analysis of *ressentiment*), but too many democratic theorists ignore him or miss the main point, or at any rate what I take to be the main point. In calling for an ennobling of virtues, a proactive rather than reactive morality, a life-affirming rather than death-affirming ethos, Nietzsche inspires some, rankles many others; but his detractors jump too quickly to the conclusion that his critique of democracy entails in turn an elitist, aristocratic, class-based, domineering, ultimately antidemocratic stance. That reading, however, need not be the only reading. In fact, Nietzsche's critique can be used to provide an alternative democratic vision: "In Christianity, three elements must be distinguished: (a) the oppressed of all kinds, (b) the mediocre of all kinds, (c) the discontented and sick of all kinds. With the first element Christianity fights against the political nobility and its ideal; with the second element, against the exceptional and privileged (spiritual, physically—) of all kinds; with the third element, against the natural instinct of the healthy and happy" (p. 126).

Christian thought, for Nietzsche, destroys the possibility of an unconditional and humanly-generated affirmation. It sacrifices human self-valuation to God's transcendental authority. Applied to democracy, Christianity exalts the hostility and resentment of an underclass. It takes the "stored-up antipathy" toward the masters and channels it into a sense of happiness that "could lie, after such long oppression, simply in feeling oneself free" (pp. 123–124). It then preaches "petty people's morality as the measure of things" (p. 117). It demands that all people conform to such leveling standards, the result of which is that mediocrity becomes, by default, the prevailing value. "This mediocre nature at last grows so conscious of itself (—acquires courage for itself—) that it arrogates even *political* power to itself" (p. 126)—hence the call for democratic politics everywhere.

Again, the real point need not be that a nostalgic Nietzsche is lamenting the toppling of a class of aristocratic warrior blond beasts and is advocating their restoration to power. Rather, I might suggest that he is worried about the general and potentially dangerous conditions of democratic valuation—borne of reactive hostility and of the thirst for deathly revenge, such democrats are virtually incapable of affirming something in its own right or for some humanly derived, life-promotional purpose. Democrats are not democrats because they really believe in democracy as a positive value. The turn toward democracy, its real motivational force, is to strike a preemptive blow against others; it is a leveling strategy designed to prevent a hostile takeover by anyone else. Such democracy demands that all be in charge, precisely so that no one can be in charge. Although certain modern libertarians might endorse such a political platform, such a grounding for democracy provides scant reason, nor any moral standpoint, for affirming others, for valuing various peoples and persons, in their own right. If anything, Christianized democracy is too logical, too calculating. It wants to subsume all worldly endeavors under one theocentric metanarrative: The first and great commandment is, Love God with all your heart, and the second (similar to the first and yet definitely distinct) is, You shall love your neighbor as yourself (Matt. 22:36–39). Humans are to love God first and each other next, only therefore as a function of their common status as creatures of God, as fellow players on his providential stage. Although many cynics might think it best to subordinate human purposes to divine purposes, divine instrumentalism has a hard time generating any attachment to worldliness per se, worldliness as a first-order priority, as an end and not a mere means; and a democratic politics issuing from such overarching instrumentalism has a hard time providing reasons for itself, especially when the system experiences strain, when push comes to shove, when humans see each other not as angels or neighbors but as adversaries. That was Hobbes's realization: Christianity doesn't ultimately provide a very good basis for conflict-mediation and conflict-management. In many cases, the Christian will prefer death to life, a vision of eternal bliss rather than a life of democratic contestation. Even Christian religiosity, as utilitarian as it is, ultimately cannot provide a compelling theological case for itself, even through a last-ditch appeal to the "mystery" of faith: One wonders how many practicing Christians would still be faithful—Job-like— remaining ever devoted to their god and to their neighbors should the promise of heaven and the threat of hell be somehow revoked, written out of the new covenant.

Likewise, there gapes a huge hole, a big bunch of begged questions, in democratic theory today: Why should we respect others widely, why should we recognize and affirm their civil existence, why should we pursue a life in common with those so different from us, why should we engage in the often arduous process of agonistic negotiation, especially when so many of us are dubious about the proposition that death will somehow dispense justice? Nietzsche says that Jesus died too early and suggests charitably that if Jesus had lived longer, he would have recanted his own teachings about death.[78] So, too, might we agree with Ivan's unspoken conclusion in the analysis of the three temptations: Jesus made a mistake. But, as his political heirs, maybe we can forgive him. The true spirit of Jesus, relieved of his messianic duties, suggests that Jesus would probably have accepted the devil's offers, even if the letter of the Gospels suggests otherwise. Like the Grand Inquisitor (and like some of the reformist theologians mentioned above), we must recover Jesus' spirit and correct Christianity, but now for the sake of a new democratic justice—

And not justice in some remote infinite time and space, but here on earth, and that I could see myself.

CHAPTER FOUR

The Womb

For Death must be somewhere in a society; if it is no longer (or less intensely) in religion, it must be elsewhere; perhaps in this image which produces Death while trying to preserve life. . . . One day, leaving one of my classes, someone said to me with disdain: "You talk about Death very flatly."—As if the horror of Death were not precisely its platitude! The horror is this: nothing to say about the death of one whom I love most, nothing to say about her photograph, which I contemplate without ever being able to get to the heart of it, to transform it. The only "thought" I can have is that at the end of this first death, my own death is inscribed; between the two, nothing more than waiting; I have no other resource than this *irony*: to speak of the "nothing to say."

—Roland Barthes, *Camera Lucida*

ontemporary feminist theory—to speak generally and surely too sweepingly about a group of investigations whose approaches and concerns are quite disparate—is, on the whole, impressively adept at challenging binary oppositions and at upsetting accepted essentialisms. But at least one very rough-hewn male-female opposition still abides, if surreptitiously, in much of the literature, a set of underlying assumptions that loosely but resolutely identifies the signifier "man" with matters relating to death, while the signifier "woman" relates more intimately with matters relating to life. Preoccupation with death, on this reading, is a "male" problem.[1] Philosophers who prime themselves as "beings-for-death"—Plato, Hobbes, Hegel, Heidegger, Sartre—are overwhelmingly male.[2] The key players of the foregoing chapters—Socrates, Christ, Nietzsche, Foucault—are conspicuously all men. Theorizing about politics from a standpoint of death could be said, I suspect, to be a male approach, even if it might engage more fruitfully issues of gender than prior attempts at contractarian modeling. Men bond with each other only or mainly through images of death, destruction, and apocalypse;[3] men are closet necrophiliacs.[4] Feminist theory, on the other hand, with its attention fixed on the mortal but still-breathing "body," holds better potential for generating a viable life-affirming politics.

Yet this impressionistic scheme of things doesn't simply encode man as death, and woman as life. Actually it proclaims for woman a closer association with *both* death and life, while it ascribes to masculinity a deep-seated psycho-socio-cultural aversion to both categories. The entire analysis turns on an imaging of and discourse about nature. Woman is natured; man is denatured. Woman, of course, is better attuned to the rhythms of life. She gives birth. She listens to the body. She attends to the needs of other bodies. She is relational. She is supremely biological. She is connected organically to nature, at home in her earthiness and proud of it. And there's more. Since she's more attuned to natural biological processes, the rhythms of birthing and caring but also of decline and decay, she is ultimately more accepting of human finitude, of mortal death.[5] Woman allows the symbolics of birth and death, the womb and the tomb, to collapse into one another.[6] Women are bleeders. Blood returns to the earth, giving it new life. From dead bodies, life regenerates. Women understand these fertility cycles.[7] They accept death, but, more aware of finitude as such, they also make better mourners.[8]

Men, however, deny natural death. Ever since man left the garden, he has been out of step with nature and has sought to give meaning to his life by becoming the subject of his own story, a linear narrative that reaches beyond, escapes, and maybe conquers nature. He wishes to separate himself, distinguish himself, individuate and attain autonomy, take flight from connection and embodiedness. He is disgusted with (and therefore perversely and hostilely attracted to) all things biological: pregnancy, birth, weaning, menstruation, death.[9] Part of his disgust is, no doubt, due to his worry that he, as procreator, may be incidental to the birthing and life-giving process.[10] His fragile ego so threatened, he seeks compensation through other body-denying pursuits. He is also dimly aware that the phallus decomposes along with the death of the body; hence he must find some way to prop up the phallus after death.[11] The result of so many insecurities is that man ventures after immortality, he attempts to build everlasting monuments to himself, he constructs elaborate fictions about the presence of a pure soul that is imprisoned in the body and lives on after bodily death.[12] He believes in extended linearity over ongoing regenerative cycles. Escalating his undeclared war with woman, he even tries to arrogate to himself her procreative function by attributing generative powers to his destructive tendencies. He starts building weapons and bombs shaped like phalluses.[13] His denial of death doesn't mean that he avoids all confrontations with death; rather, he risks it, mocks it, longs for it. He engages in competitive death-defying but therefore death-erotic games with other men, as if the winners might live on forever in heroic remembrance (in a rewriting of naturalist discourse). Such male attempts at self-rebirthing are ultimately silly (from biological standpoint) and maybe even apocalyptic. Man flees from death but desires it as well.[14] In short: Men, especially Western men, are relentlessly engaged in an ambivalent and therefore dangerous cat-and-mouse game with death, a sport that may well eventually spell an unnatural doom for all beings on the planet.

Hegel is, in the terms presented above, the male theorist par excellence. He is the theorist who views history as a spiritual march toward death, who tells individuals and communities that their ultimate freedom resides in understanding that death looms ever on the horizon.[15] At critical moments he reveals that the "beings-for-death" in his account are mainly men.[16] When he mentions womankind explicitly, he writes that woman impedes this spiritual overcoming of natural death; she is an obstacle to the manly march toward resolution; she is an "everlasting irony in the life of the community" who "changes by intrigue the universal end of the government into a private end."[17] She represents the ties of "hearth and blood" over and against the polis, and thus will be swept away in the progression toward more rational, public, and mature forms of human self-organization.[18]

Although many feminist theorists challenge in various ways Hegel's priorities, others continue to accept, more or less, his gendered categories with respect to death; and a great number, apparently not wanting to follow his negative lead, have resisted recuperating an alternative feminist political theory on the basis of irony. Donna Haraway is an exception on both counts. Drawing on her background in the Western natural sciences, Haraway confronts openly the prevailing biological and naturalist discourses that focus on the body.[19] At the same time she was one of the earliest brokers in irony as a feminist strategy for theory and practice. Much of her energy, quite clearly, has been devoted to finding ways of staving off a male-induced nuclear oblivion. Her work, on these and other scores, inspires. So inspired, I devote the better part of this chapter to her work. As a fellow traveler along the same crooked path marked by the hard-to-read signs of irony, death, and politics, I wish to direct my own ironic and admiring gaze upon her most influential book, *Primate Visions*.

Gorilla My Dreams

Donna Haraway's *Primate Visions* is a book about monkeys and apes but also about the feminist politics of irony.[20] It is a book that should be taken seriously by all political theorists, feminist or not, ironic or not. Haraway is a splendid storyteller, and one can learn a great deal from her about the history of Western primatology—as storytelling. She is also a daring and creative thinker whose grand theses and breathtaking insights can dazzle, befuddle, provoke, and inspire. The book convincingly reveals many of the racist, gendered (and classist and colonialist) assumptions informing the practice of modern Western science, primatology in particular—and as if that weren't enough, the book additionally sends one into bouts of brooding about the fate of the species (a loaded term, we learn).

Haraway is also a keen reader, attentive especially to politics. We professional political theorists owe her a great debt for her cross-disciplinary forays. The book ought to be read in our classes. Our field is so filled with primatological images—origin stories, notions of man as a *zoon politikon*, state-of-nature accounts, noble savages, blond beasts, species-beings, claims to natural law and natural rights—that after reading the book one wonders why it has taken us so long to recognize formally the so-called natural affinities and traffic between the disciplines of primatology and political theory. Should I dare let my enthusiasm for this book gush toward the hyperbolic, I would recommend that theorists of politics spend at least as much time with this book as they might with recent "naturalist" political accounts, to wit, Roger D. Masters's *The Nature of Politics* or Ian Shapiro's *Political Criticism*.

More, Haraway attempts to combine irony and politics in a way never thought possible by liberal-pragmatist Richard Rorty. *Primate Visions* sparkles with ironic moments and ironic moves, which build upon Haraway's earlier affirmation of irony developed in the now-famous cyborgs essay.[21] In that piece, Haraway puts feminist political irony front and center ("This chapter is an effort to build an ironic political myth faithful to feminism, socialism, and materialism"[22]); and although irony enjoys a less prominent role in *Primate Visions*, it also recurs conspicuously. Haraway writes about early primatologists in "an ironic mode" (p. 35); later she sees ironies in a story about post-colonial primates in India (p. 263); she "piles irony upon bitter irony" in retelling another chimp story (p. 267); she claims boldly that irony is basic to feminist reinscriptions (p. 280); she remarks that reading feminism into sociobiology is fraught with irony (p. 359); she suggests that most sociobiologists have lacked a sense of irony (p. 366); and she ends the book on an ironic vision (p. 378). Notwithstanding Hegel's view of irony as a primarily feminine tropological strategy, many or most theorists have had a hard time reconciling feminist theory and practice with irony, and Haraway stands out as a clear exception to this general rule.

For Haraway, I want to claim, irony is not merely a way of holding heterogeneous material together, though at times it serves this purpose in her writing.[23] Irony is not simply the juggling of diverse perspectives, just as Haraway is not merely a word spinner and yet another storyteller. She wants to claim that "one story is not as good as another" (p. 331). She wants to avoid the infinitely regressive and relativist claim that we can discern no foundation or referent or standard for any position because all accounts are based on stories, signs, fictions, and perspectives; and although she adopts poststructuralist language, she clearly wants to avoid certain temptations of poststructuralism (p. 6). One danger, I take it, is that rampant poststructuralism tends to lead to political paralysis. Her book is not just an exposé, not just an exercise in debunking and demystification. Rather, her irony and storytelling reveal a political stance or ethics, and I want to develop that ethics in the pages to follow.

Here is my critical/imaginary take on *Primate Visions*: Donna Haraway, the author of this text, is part Mary Shelley and part pop star Madonna. She is a new composite, a hybrid, a construct, a freak. By naming her Shelley Madonna (Madonna Shelley sounds better), I do not mean to trivialize; I mean it as no cheap shot. I realize that such interpretive claims are potentially double-edged, that they probably say more about the analyst than the analysand, that they contain my projections, condensations, repressions, and transferences, that they are Procrustean stretches or crude reductions that can never reanimate the richness and detail of this book project. Nevertheless, the Madonna Shelley figure is the one that I happen to want to pursue, it is a heuristic device that helps make the points I want to make; and I draw on Shelley and Madonna in order to highlight and explore Haraway's own claim about the shift in SF (scientific fact/speculative fiction) from organicism to cybernetics in the late twentieth century.

Haraway as Mary Shelley

I base this association mainly on Haraway's magnificent chapter on Carl Akeley ("Teddy Bear Patriarchy: Taxidermy in the Garden of Eden, New York City, 1908–1936"). Indeed, Haraway invites an association between Shelley's character Victor Frankenstein and Akeley as a character who similarly encounters gorillas on mountaintops (p. 31), but she also recognizes a great difference between these two tales as tales. Shelley wrote a jeremiad, a nightmare about "the crushing failure of the project of man," but the Akeley tale, at least as told by Akeley and as sacralized in the American Museum of Natural History, presents a chapter in salvation history and the happy-ever-after triumphs of science. But Haraway doesn't seem to exploit fully the parallels between Shelley's tale and Haraway's own act of rewriting and redescribing Akeley's story. I want to say: Haraway has written a horror story very much along the lines of Shelley's *Frankenstein*. Her chapter on Akeley is downright deathly. It reeks of death (which is no criticism, in my book).

Both Shelley's *Frankenstein* and Haraway's "Teddy Bear Patriarchy" raise questions of self-reference and authorial purpose. Shelley associates her own act of writing with monster production ("hideous progeny") in which birthing and death are grossly intermixed, very much like Frankenstein's "workshop of filthy production." (With a little contextualist background, most readers also learn that Shelley was her dead mother's little monster and was writing this tale amidst her own dead babies.) Like Haraway's chapter, *Frankenstein* all at once mingles issues of birthing, death, politics, science, and gender. *Frankenstein*, which is subtitled *The Modern Prometheus*, is about the mythic ambitious/rebellious titan male life-bringer, who symbolizes in one figure both science and politics. It is also a story about education and gender (especially if one knows about the male Prometheans, Byron and Shelley, in Mary Shelley's life, and about Wollstonecraft's coupling of educational and gender issues). Like Haraway's chapter, *Frankenstein* is a book that presents its story from multiple perspectives, through various eyes: Shelley, Walton, Victor, the monster. Finally, again like Haraway's chapter, *Frankenstein* is a story about nature-culture disputes, about origins, about falls from Eden, about noble savages turning vicious, about Milton and Rousseau, about property, about couples, about maleness and femaleness and biological ambiguities. They are also stories about Pandora's box of evils, about the threat of apocalypse.

"Teddy Bear Patriarchy" is a delightful piece of writing, and Haraway is very conscious of her own act of storytelling qua storytelling. Although she wants to expose the patriarchal anxieties and decadence informing late capitalism, she does not affect the pose of disinterested observer or omniscient narrator, though frequently her language is critically distancing.[24] She sometimes mocks and sometimes rebukes Akeley, but she doesn't divorce herself completely from her subject matter: there are many moments of sympathy and identification. Still, Haraway insists on a fundamental difference between her own taletelling and Akeley's: hers she casts in the "ironic mode," and that is the register, she tells us, "most avoided by Akeley" (p. 35). Here, claims Haraway, Akeley and Haraway part ways, whereas Mary Shelley from the outset invited her readers to see a parallel between her bookish progeny and her character Frankenstein's monstrous progeny. Although Haraway likens her project to Mary Shelley's (both tales are "dissections"—pp. 31, 35), my sense is that Haraway doesn't see her project and her own relationship with Akeley in quite so hideous and parallel terms as Mary Shelley regards her own book (though I still want to claim that their projects resonate, with or without Haraway's explicit acknowledgment).

Political theory has always belonged to the genre of travel literature. Starting, to name a start, with the ancient Greek *theoros*, who traveled to neighboring *poleis*, theorists have always viewed themselves as wayfarers and tour guides, those who have undergone odysseys and witnessed spectacles from other worlds; and these heroic visions have traditionally helped cultivate epic individuals and purposive missionaries, mostly male. Haraway identifies primatology as a species of travel literature (e.g., p. 251), and she tells us all about Akeley's toils, tales, and travels. Haraway acts as *our* tour guide into the wilds of Akeley's bizarre world. She apes her subject. But this self-referential aspect of her work, while conspicuous,[25] isn't thematized as especially grotesque or even integral to the narrative. Haraway just doesn't do much with it, and the reader is left wondering what to make of it.

Akeley, she tells us, was a New Yorker who, evidently operating according to nature/culture, mind/body, male/female, white/nonwhite, human/animal binaries, went out into the so-called wilds on a primatological mission. Apes represented a possible Ur truth about humanity, divested of "culture." They were exotic, dark, untutored, sweaty, sexy. Akeley shoots gorillas (reluctantly, he claims) with cameras and guns, for their own sake and ours. He takes these dead gorillas, now stuffed, back to New York, or else he takes his snapshots of gorillas (another form of disembodiment), and thus dead gorillas become enshrined in the museum, there spiritualizing the values of patriarchy, capitalism, democracy. Ordinary people enter the museum and gaze at these dead, stuffed animals (captured timelessly in "live poses"), and they are transported to another time and place.

But Haraway, like Dante, plays both pilgrim and poet in telling her tale; although, unlike Shelley and Dante, she talks mostly about her role as poet-scribe and less about her *own* pilgrimage and ours with her. She follows her guide Virgil-Akeley into the wilds on her mission, capturing him with her pen and her gaze. Somehow in reading her story, unlike my reading of Dante's *Inferno* or Shelley's *Frankenstein*, I just didn't get the sense that Haraway is playfully conscious of the irony of *her* following Akeley and her leading us into his wilds after him. She knows that her own writing is another exercise in travel literature (e.g., p. 14). Surely she knows that the story of wild man Akeley is exotic, or so it will seem to us, an audience primed for primatological insights. But sometimes I felt that she was so mesmerized with her man that she forgot her reader. I was being taken on a tour, and somewhere along the way that tour became more engrossingly literal than figurative, more factual than fantastic. I felt as if I should don a safari hat while I was reading, while my hand clutched a butterfly net propped next to my Lazy Boy recliner.

She takes us to New York (in a brilliant, if intentionalist read of the signs in the museum, her own gaze at the gaze), then she takes us out into the wilds. She re-creates for us Akeley's (Haraway's?) captivating moment of fascination and terror in speculating the distance at which he must put down the camera and pick up the gun while his fantasy adult male gorilla charges at him. She shows us these noble brothers in death, bonded males. In eloquent prose she reanimates the body of this taxidermist and stuffs it for all time— only then to dissect it for us. She tells us great stories about Akeley's great storytelling feats. She even lets us listen in with the stenographer who listens in on wild man Akeley while he tells his wild stories (p. 46). What a wild story Haraway tells! Then she resurrects Carl's "resurrection" (p. 47) in the vicarious writings of his (second) wife. She then raises questions of authorship, and in particular Haraway questions Mary Jobe Akeley's right to claim Carl's body and his words. What's going on here?

Themes and issues emerge in this chapter reminiscent of the now famous Heidegger-Schapiro-Derrida series of essays on Vincent van Gogh's painting(s) of old shoes.[26] Heidegger, in brief, interprets van Gogh's shoe painting as revealing the plain truth of a pair of peasant woman's shoes. Schapiro responds that Heidegger misses the artist's presence in the work, an important aspect of the painting, he claims. Van Gogh actually painted the series of shoe pictures while he was in Paris, and they are clearly the artist's own shoes, not the shoes of a peasant. Heidegger has deceived himself, projecting into the painting his own associations with peasants and the soil. He has engaged in a series of substitution: rural for city, female for male, low culture for high culture, text for context.

Derrida takes issues with Schapiro's scholarly exposition, and he restores some validity to Heidegger's reading. But he ingeniously plays the two readings off one another to reveal their joint short-comings and oversights. Much is excluded in each reading. Why assume that the pair is a pair at all? Why assume that these are even shoes? Why must Schapiro insist that the shoes reflect a given time and place? Why insist on a final reading at all, as if the canvas is self-policing? Derrida suggests that both Heidegger and Schapiro have repressed the diabolic in their readings, they have both been "laced" to a "foot-fetishism" in looking at this painting. The paint-ing could, for instance, be a painting (if you want to see the artist's presence in it) of Vincent imagining himself in a peasant woman's shoes. Or Vincent as a peasant woman in Vincent's shoes. And so on. Both Heidegger and Schapiro lay claims to irony, but such claims are difficult to sustain:

> Just like Heidegger, whom he quotes with irony on this point, Schapiro rules out the possibility that there might be the slight-est "projection" on his own side. Sure of having scientifically determined the content and the origin of the painting (town shoes as the personal object of the painter), Schapiro has an easy time denouncing Heidegger's identificatory projection: Heideg-ger has annexed the shoes to his social landscape and hyper-cathected them with his "heavy pathos of the native and the countryman." He was doing the very thing he was guarding against: he has "imagined everything and projected it into the painting."[27]

The painting is, as it were, spooked, says Derrida, it is haunted with "ghosts." We reanimate the painting with van Gogh's presence, and then we kill him off: "And I know of no apocalyptic, hieroglyphic, phantomatic or pathetic painting which could give me this sensa-tion of occult strangeness, of the corpse of a useless hermeticism, its head open, rendering up its secret on the executioner's block."[28]

Derrida, for his part, knows himself to be caught in a trap of interpretation. We could always respond to him, for instance, that he is only assuming that (dead) Schapiro never considered the diabolic, though Schapiro's text shows no explicit authorization of that possibility. Presumably, Derrida's lesson is that we should avoid the presumption that a stable reality lurks behind the play of signs. Derrida's mission is to restore self-enclosed validity to the written text, which is always potentially unbound from context. His hostility is directed toward the (phonocentric) assumption that the spoken word is always more immediate, more real, more true, more natural than the written word.

My point is *not* that Haraway is engaging in straight "ideology critique." She knows that such interpretive strategies are "temptations" (p. 6). At times she *does* seem to suggest, Schapiro-like, that Akeley's activity in Africa is but a meditation on New York and New York's immigrant influx (pp. 29, 42, 55), that the major motivation behind modern primatology in general is to respond to stress in the postwar, anxiety-ridden city. Haraway saves herself from straight substitutions by showing us the "traffic" between nature-culture conceptions in these "border zone" areas of contestation. My point is rather that, despite claims to irony in her exposition, there is not a privileging of her read vis-à-vis Akeley's but a phonocentric bias that allegedly saves her writing from problems of self-referentiality, implicitly rendering it a second-order enterprise, a fantastic, removed reconstruction and not the real McCoy. Her tour is supposedly less real than Akeley's. Akeley shot real gorillas. Haraway only *writes* about these shootings. She is ironic. He is not.

Doubling is a prominent theme in *Frankenstein*. In fact, it would be fair to say that doubling is *the* major theme and plot contrivance throughout the book. The story is replete with doubles, couples, and twins—binaries who mirror one another, bound (or laced) together as pairs: Walton-Victor, Victor-Elizabeth, Victor–Henry Clerval, Henry Clerval–Don Quixote, William–William Godwin, William–baby William, Victor-God, Victor-Prometheus, Victor-Satan, Victor-Monster, Adam-Monster, Victor-Rousseau, Rousseau's noble savage–Monster, Rousseau's Emile–Monster, De Lacey–Monster, Male Monster–Female Monster. And of course, the meta-double, as I've been claiming, is that of Shelley with her own book, and that double invites the reader to engage with the book as yet another metadouble. The doubling technique invites us to compare characters one-on-one and to see a character through the eyes of another. Such an exercise tends to emphasize that the twins are closer than one (usually the reader) might otherwise realize. Ironies hence abound: Societies become more monstrous than monsters, monsters become more humane than humans, creators become victims of their creatures, men become mothers, domestic tranquility becomes a nightmare, and so on. The text doesn't simply deconstruct these terms; *Frankenstein* isn't a gender-balanced or neutral account. Rather, it is a story whose horrors emanate, via insinuation, largely from the release of male (homophobic) repressions: This is a story of a male shadowed and tailed by a threatening male whose anatomical proportions, Shelley informs us, are gigantic. To be sure, the book is about (the standard interpretation) the terrors of overambitious male self-birthing; but it is also a story (Shelley's compensation fantasy?) turning on the fascinating fear of male-on-male rape.

As in Rousseau's "Second Discourse," the key to Shelley's doubling technique is an explicit setting aside of all "facts."[29] Her horror story requires that we take imaginary leave of civilized society and enter the wilds of "fiction." She announces from the outset that her tale is a tale.[30] She opens the book with an author's preface, a confessional act which ostensibly establishes verisimilitude, grounds her own voice, and thus puts into motion a fact versus fiction writerly conceit. In the preface she tells a mini tale about how the subsequent big tale came to be, and this layered foregrounding of the so-called real story reinforces the alleged fictionality of the fiction. Later, of course, her general fiction will prey upon us, will play with our minds, will become a very real horror. Eventually we realize that Shelley's opening disclaimer is a disingenuous setup, a mere conceit. Nightmares are nightmares because the opposition between fact and fiction is blurred and everything is thrown into question. Monsters are larger than life—or are they?

Haraway doesn't make the same move at the outset of *Primate Visions*. She announces that her work is a work of storytelling, and she deconstructs the distinction between fact and fiction, encouraging the use of the term SF. But most of that blurring, she suggests, should be applied to the practitioners of primatology about whom she writes, such as Akeley. She doesn't announce her own work to be a work of fiction per se. Rather, she claims to work with real facts and real stories. Everything in her book really happened, and the names haven't been changed. The American Museum of Natural History in New York is real. Central Park, across the street, is

real. Akeley shot gorillas (in an attempt to craft a "true" life [p. 35]).
Such stories are engaging precisely because they are grounded in
realism; they are stranger than fiction, because they really, really
happened. Isn't science odd?

The doubling theme occurs throughout "Teddy Bear Patriarchy,"
but Haraway doesn't seem to highlight her own metadoubling vis-
à-vis Akeley. Akeley, she tells us, recast the African wilds in terms of
New York and vice versa, and he especially was confronting his own
(male) demons in confronting and shooting the gorillas. But where
is Haraway, our tour guide, when all of this action-packed drama is
taking place on the page in front of us?

Let us review the chapter, retracing our steps. Haraway begins by
reproducing the experience of a typical visitor to the American Museum of Natural History. She gives us a superb reading of the si-
multaneous "strangeness" and "ordinariness" of a visit to the African Hall, and her words attempt to replicate the transformative
effects that such displays have upon their witnesses, while she also
intervenes and skillfully interjects her commentary, breaking the
spell of the gaze. Tour guides describe, but they also guide. They
are mediators. She shows us the hall, and then she tells us that the
stuffed dead animals, caught forever in "live poses," afford a "spiritual vision made possible only by their death and literal re-presenta-
tion" (p. 30). Of course she had to restuff these animals in order to
make this re-re-presentation, but that's not her point. Rather, she
wants to remain faithful to the museum's claim to literalness and
address it on "literalist" terms.

The gorilla diorama stands out from all others, she says, and that
is because the painting in the display depicts the place where Carl
Akeley, taxidermist to these star gorillas, died. Haraway then asks,
Why gorillas? (p. 31). Her answer draws on *Frankenstein*: "One answer is similarity to man, the ultimate quarry, a worthy opponent.
The ideal quarry is the 'other,' the natural self. That is one reason
Frankenstein needed to hunt down his creature" (p. 31). Haraway
then takes us into the wilds, herself hunting the hunter Akeley
hunting gorillas. She sneaks up on Carl and imagines Victor Frankenstein occupying the body of Akeley; she even puts Victor's imaginary words in Carl's mouth (even though her somewhat contorted
narrative logic requires that she imagine a counterfactual/counter-
fictional situation): "If he had succeeded in his aborted hunt, Victor
Frankenstein could have spoken those lines" (p. 34). (Three pages
earlier Haraway makes a special effort to note that all of Carl's

words were written by an invisible ghostwriter, and now Haraway
plays ghostwriter to the ghost of Shelley playing ghostwriter to the
ghost of Akeley!) At the end of this first brief introduction to Carl
Akeley, Haraway kills him off, describing in some detail his burial
vault (p. 35). Immediately after this (fictive?) death, Haraway takes
us back to Carl's life. She brings the taxidermist back to life, starting
her biography with his birth and proceeding through boyhood into
his later, taxidermist years. Taxidermy is about "the politics of reproduction," she warned us a few pages back (p. 30), and now she
reproduces the reproducer Carl. She restuffs him in order to show
how intent Akeley reproduced realism. He worried about fakes and
frauds, and yet she reveals how much fakery was left unacknowledged in his allegedly improved taxidermic practices. She
shows us the realities behind Akeley's claims to realism. "Realism
was a supreme achievement of the artifactual art of memory, a rhetorical achievement crucial to the foundations of Western science"
(p. 41).

Realistic, essential, "typical" gorilla specimens (here one hears
echoes of Haraway's own imaginary account of the "typical" visitor
to the American Museum) had to be male for Akeley (p. 41). The
"tone of perfection" could be heard only in the male mode. It is
about measurement, she tells us, it is about virility. She tells us
more and more about his masculinity and its discontents. Akeley,
apparently, was at odds with himself, profoundly ambivalent. His
civilization was diseased by the same technology and wealth that
funded his excursions into the wilds and backed the African Hall (p.
42). But his efforts to bring the dangerous lessons of jungle peace
back to the wilds of civilization weren't simply manly; rather, he was
a transitional figure, one whose relation to nature required both
guns and cameras, at various times. "Camera hunting takes twice
the man that gun hunting takes," Haraway re-reports (p. 43). Both
gun and camera put a woman to shame reproductively, she adds.
But hyperliteralism is Akeley's tragic flaw in this account. His fear
of fraudulence, his insistence on realism, on the naked eye of science, on the independent man's honest (albeit ocularcentric) vision
all betray the "endangered self" (p. 45) and conceal a timeless death
wish, a hint of "an apocalyptic future" (p. 45). Death of gorillas,
death of Carl, stuffed bodies, death masks, museums, sepulchers:
death is everywhere in this chapter (though "fear of decadence"
may be even worse for white male capitalists than death). For males,
life is constructed through the craft of killing (pp. 28–29), and Ha-

raway evidently feels compelled to recraft Carl's life in a so-called male mode of representation (monkey see, monkey do). Indeed, her own text is as haunted by ghosts as are Carl's pictures about which she writes ("To make an exact image is to insure against disappearance, to cannibalize life until it is safely and permanently a specular image, a ghost" [p. 45]).

From here on out in the chapter Haraway tells us stories (all true, of course, though one is "apocryphal" [p. 43], and another story, Haraway points out, lacks all mention of Carl's first wife, Delia [p. 49]): stories about Carl staring into the "eyes of the plaster death mask of the first gorilla he ever saw" (p. 47); about Carl's resurrection through his second wife's authorship; about Carl's mock death incident involving elephants; about the treatment of blacks;[31] and then back to memorialization in the museum and the capitalist-male-patriarchal forces behind it. The chapter ends thus: "The surrealists knew that behind the day lay the night of sexual terror, disembodiment, failure of order; in short, castration and impotence of the seminal body which had spoken all the important words for centuries, the great white father, the white hunter in the heart of Africa" (p. 58). In the very last sentence, Haraway draws close to her subject: "Their practice (presumably that of the American Museum of Natural History) and mine have been literal, dead literal."

I would have preferred that Haraway not end her wonderful chapter on such a somber, apparently literalist note. The ironist in me would have suggested a little more explicit ambiguity, something like: "I changed a few of the preceding details and faked some of the above stories, but not many." Instead, Haraway underscores her own realism and comes out dead-set against the never-admitted fakeries of Akeley's form of science, thus becoming Akeley's spiritual ally, bound together with him in sincerity, in the need to purge science of hypocrisies, in the mission of bringing to light that which has been left in the dark. The book thus implicitly ends—despite all the apocalyptic allusions—on a sanguine outlook: We are all better off with such corrective accounts, especially with a scientific storytelling or storytelling about science that humbly admits its storytelling origins (a new and improved form of taxidermy).[32] Haraway is as much the SF storyteller as Akeley. I just wish she would have attended to her own horrors,[33] or at least offered us clothespins for our noses as we tour her own rag-and-bone shop.[34]

The doubling theme certainly runs throughout "Teddy Bear Patriarchy." Haraway reanimates Akeley, follows him into the wilds,

hunts him down, re-creates his shootings, kills him off, re-resur-
rects him, rebirths him, dissects him, stuffs him and restuffs his
gorillas, and rememorializes him in her own half-admiring, half-
contemptuous, museumlike, "dead-literal" chapter. But where is
Haraway? How did her ironic account become dead literal by the
end? My view is that she walks only two steps behind Akeley
(though I fear that she presumes that textual walking is more removed, less disembodying, than real walking; or that textual vision
is less disciplinary than the visionary storytelling tools—sculpture,
taxidermy, photography—used by Akeley). She is in love—an ambivalent love—with Akeley's manhood, preoccupied with his preoc-
cupations, she shares his well-intentioned concern for the fate of
the gorillas, humankind, and the earth.[35] She probably even shares
his reluctance over shooting gorillas: Somebody had to write this
dirty chapter, and it might as well have been she. The doubling
technique works to good effect, for we readers learn a great deal
about ourselves from reading these paralleled wild accounts (both
Akeley's and Haraway's), and thus Haraway's format resembles that
of Mary Shelley's. But again, in a key regard Haraway parts ways
with Shelley. Shelley ends her book by pointing out the veritable
evils of science; truly science doesn't have a happy ending at the end
of *Frankenstein*. Humanity now has at best a negative purposive-
ness—to try to kill one's monster, to put the genie back into the
bottle, to stave off apocalypse. Though Haraway mentions many of
these themes—science as a dubiously progressivist practice anxiously attempting to subdue an ominous nature and deny its own
decadence—I suspect that she regards her own task as accomplish-
ing something more than mere negativity. She is not simply hunting
down Akeley, as *her* monster (indeed, she rewrites the ending to
Frankenstein, imagining Victor as having successfully killed his monster[36]). Rather, she evidently believes that we can distill, and take
back to the city, lessons as a result of our readerly hunt in the wilds.
She has successfully fixed our gaze on dead Carl Akeley.[37] Hers is a
big book, a tour de force, the beginning of something new, a new
and improved form of taxidermy. Far from horrible and terrifying,
never just a little work of fiction, *Primate Visions* reads as the latest
installment in the science of primatology, virtually as sanguine as
past efforts regarding the ability of primatology to teach us about
ourselves so as to avoid self-destruction.

What to make of this? We might look to the classic theorist of
textual doubling, René Girard, whose notion of "mimetic desire"

illuminates many of the themes recurring in *Primate Visions*. Mimetic desire for Girard is the structuralist basis for many of our origin stories, the narrative foundation of political order.[38] Mimesis issues from and masks an originary act of violence, a scapegoating allegedly at the base of all political orders, which has the effect of sacralizing the perpetrators of the violence as heroic victims. In Girard's scheme of things, it should be no surprise that Shelley reveals the threat of male-to-male rape as the violent scapegoating mechanism animating the contemporary political order, our modern Promethean politics, or that Haraway points to similar mimetic frenzies in her synecdochic figure for late capitalism, Carl Akeley's male bonding/shooting of gorillas. The difference is that Haraway seems at least implicitly to hold (which I surmise by detecting self-referential omissions) that we can learn somehow to avoid trying to kill our monsters. Here Girard helps as well. He attends to the overwhelming use of mimetic doubles in Christology, the Christian narrative. Christ resembles God the Father, resembles flesh-and-blood humans, Christians are to imitate Christ. Of course violence undergirds this entire story: Christian redemption borrows heavily upon Hebraic notions of deathly sacrifice, and the entire Christian account is oriented toward ultimate apocalypse in the future. Christ, far from bringing peace to the earth, wants to hasten apocalypse. The Gerasenes, whose demons Christ tried to exorcise, knew this, that Christ was trying to upset the equilibrium that they had achieved with their demons, and thus they asked him to leave.[39]

Christ, that mythic missionary, the ultimate wayfarer, a tour guide between life and death, might be viewed for present purposes as an early primatologist (after Orpheus, of course). Haraway, for all of her evident disdain for Christianized primatological campaigns,[40] goes on such a mission herself (and takes us along with her). She showcases that dead guy Akeley, kills him off, resurrects him, memorializes him, all for the purpose of purging us of demons that lurk in us and our political order—demons responsible for making monsters out of others by way of demonology. Her act of violence (mixed with love and identification) provides a new foundation story, the sacralized basis of her new SF. Her readers will be disciplined into a new order by gazing at Akeley's body in her text.[41] Her work is deathly, which is why it is so strong, so impressive, so monumental. She is saving the world, following Akeley, following Christ, supposedly staving off apocalypse, providing us with a vision of a better, less horrible world. My question: Can First World Survival Literature (her coinage for primatology, from which her own writing cannot be exempted) really be *ironic*?

Haraway as Madonna

I shall not argue for this association along standard, discursive lines. Rather, I'll present a pastiche of images and connections, a format that best accords with my subject matter: the politics of the postmodern self. Virtually anyone occasionally hooked into the ubiquitous cable communications network of America should be able to follow a good number of my references to the multimedia pop star icon, Madonna.

Madonna's corpus of songs, videos, and films presents numerous themes that, with but a little effort and only slight manipulation, can be intertextually related to many of the motifs recurring throughout *Primate Visions*. Some of these common melodies are: boundary crossing, zones of meaning contestation, especially gender traffic (e.g., "Borderline"); shifting images of women ("Madonna," "Like a Virgin," "Who's That Girl?" "Angel," "Blonde Ambition Tour"); resistances to Christianity ("Madonna," "Like a Prayer," "The Immaculate Collection," "Act of Contrition"); resistances to patriarchy ("Madonna," "Papa Don't Preach," "Oh Father"); spoofs on capitalist consumption habits ("Material Girl"); explorations of assertive female sexuality, inquiries into the female orgasm, affirmations of the body ("Give It to Me," "Express Yourself," "Vogue," "Into the Groove," "Crazy for You," "Hanky Panky"); images of fun, festival, carnival ("Holiday," "Where's the Party?"); challenges to heterosexual, monoracial norms ("Justify My Love"); flirtations with danger, decadence, death ("Rescue Me," "Live to Tell," "Till Death Do Us Part"); disciplines of the gaze ("Physical Attraction," "The Look of Love," "Spanish Eyes," "Spotlight," "Strike a Pose"); and finally, even primatological images ("Wild Dancing," "I'm Going Bananas").

We could even say that Madonna, with her "Express Yourself" video splicing together images of machines with images of sex, and with her steel brassieres and high-tech synthesized stage performances, and with her general knack of keeping the communications system transfixed and attuned to her every move, represents the ultimate cyborg of late twentieth-century America.[42] To be sure, the Madonna-Haraway association may be a stretch and a projection on my part, but it is not simply a projection. Again, I want to say that

Primate Visions invites such a structural comparison. For instance, like Madonna's work, Haraway's work is based on strong visuals (p. 2). Haraway, like Madonna, draws extensively on filmic and popular literatures (pp. 3, 14, 67, 377), even cartoons (p. 212). Haraway, like Madonna, attempts to appeal to multiple and cross-over audiences (p. 15), and they both experiment with genre shifts (p. 377) and appeals to fantasy. They both entertain "temptations" in their work (p. 6). Moreover, Haraway is not afraid to depart from the standard, staid, scholarly mode of exposition, and she invites her reader to have fun (even though she also wants to provoke, shock, and disturb). Her book is meant to be accessible, inclusive of those "intrigued by popular culture" (p. 14). Finally, Haraway even ends the book with a song!

That song ("Mira's Morning Song") ends with the lines: "That science tells us of our worth / Welcome to culture / My dear daughter / It's the greatest show on earth," which reiterates *Primate Vision's* thesis that science, culture, feminism, and stage performance are all interrelated. We might further extend the Madonna theme by mentioning that both Haraway and Madonna are white women who address centrally in their work the cultural politics of sex. Haraway explains that primatology is sexual discourse (p. 11), and she devotes the latter part of her book to examining the work of four women primatologists who, says Haraway, become dancers in their work and see their dancing as political: "All four primate women scientists engage in a complicated dance in their textual and professional politics around constructing isomorphisms or non-congruences among the potent entities that emerge as actors in their accounts, called female, woman, and scientist. All four engage in problematizing *gender* by contesting for what can count as *sex*; that is, their reinventions of nature are part of their cultural politics. And all four set on stage a different kind of female primate self or subject to enact the crucial dramas" (p. 350).

In fact, much of the intervening material between "Teddy Bear Patriarchy" and "The Politics of Being Female: Primatology Is a Genre of Feminist Theory" can be read as an investigation of the traditional madonna image—the view of woman as natural mother—that persisted in the development of primatology, especially as women attempted to negotiate their stance toward and within the field. Haraway investigates Robert Yerkes' clinical fascination with "female receptivity" and his foundational insistence on the biopolitics of reproduction; she moves to Jane Goodall's "like a virgin" mothering of orphan chimps, as if women are some-how closer to "Nature"; she exposes the stressful, post-war, family-centered assumptions implicit in Sherwood Washburn's Woman-as-Gatherer rehabilitant humanism; she exposes the sadistic joking of Harry Harlow's surrogate mothering; for cross-cultural comparative purposes she takes a look at Japanese "matrilineal" studies; and at the end of this narrative she examines late eighteenth- to late twen-tieth-century feminist doctrines of social motherhood, contending that women have had few avenues to public speech other than "ma-ternalist discourse" (p. 357). And along the way she adds a reading of a Hallmark greeting card that features Fay Ray's revenge on King Kong executed by "a Marilyn Monroe sex goddess" (p. 161). The Madonna image once again captivates.

Madonna the pop star is a blonde (albeit unnatural blonde) white woman who crafts her public image as a woman who lets her sexual passions run wild. Yet Madonna plays on the Marilyn Monroe leg-acy of female objectification by refusing to be typecast as simply sex-body-woman. By ironizing her self-construction as a "boy-toy," she keeps her audience off-guard and guessing. Haraway teaches a similar lesson in sexual politics: "White women mediate between 'man' and 'animal' in power-charged historical fields" (p. 154). Jane Goodall, we can see in hindsight, virtually had to be white to medi-ate between white-male America and black-female (naturalized, sex-ualized, exotic) Africa. But this encoded mediation reinforces the general code that the "body in western political theory is not capa-ble of citizenship (rational speech and action); the body is merely particular, not general, not mindful, not light. It is sex (woman) to mind (man); dark (colored) to light (white). The body is nature to the mind of culture; in primate narratives, white women negotiate the chasm" (p.154). Madonna as white woman, femme fatale, can take advantage of the cultural codes inscribed in her color in order to challenge and subvert dualisms, between passive female recep-tivity and aggressive sexuality; she can change the color of her hair; she can cross-dress and grab her crotch; she can flirt with bisex-uality and lesbianism; she can kiss blacks on screen.[43] In Madonna's spoofing of her namesake, apparently rejecting the sacred notion of natural motherhood, Madonna joins Haraway in a dance about cul-tural/sexual politics. Indeed, Haraway's words about the primatolo-gist Sarah Blaffer Hrdy could well apply to Madonna:

> Hrdy's naturalized postmodern females emerge full of resources
> for exploring many interesting topics: female complicity and

collusion in male dominance, female agency of many kinds, the potency of sexual discourse in narratives of agency and of mind, the limits of functionalist principles of complementarity and difference, the power of narratives about competition, the logical errors involved in leaving the male an unmarked category in evolutionary models, ways of describing females as sites of internal difference that allow meditation on both bonding and competition, and the deep saliency of reproductive politics semiotically and materially in contemporary U.S. and multinational society. (p. 366)

But I imagine my associating Madonna with Haraway might cause some unease, especially among those readers sympathetic to Haraway who might regard Madonna as a tawdry textual referent and questionable ally. Madonna's critics are many, and some of the critical issues regarding her particular self-styled postmodern poses are as follows: She is a pop star who appeals to teenyboppers (read: youthful girls = pop culture = low culture = closer to nature). She is not to be taken seriously. She may attract a few trendy attention-seeking academics who want to jump on her bandwagon of media appeal, but she is, at bottom, a joke, a vulgar reflection of gimmicky American consumerist culture at its worst (P. T. Barnum lives on!). What's political about that? Even if she shocks a few Victorian sensibilities, how can that bounded subversion, situated as it is not far from her complicit self-objectification, be construed as progressively feminist at all? More generally, if this is postmodern feminism, how can that slippery strategy hope to effect *political* change?

We can well imagine the Frankfurt school's answer to Madonna, especially Max Horkheimer and T. W. Adorno's: Madonna is no progressive politico and certainly no revolutionary. She is a product of, and reproducer for, the culture industry;[44] and for all of her "cultural" flairs, hip contestations, and pop provocations, her activity remains only cultural and may even reinforce the norms of the society that it purports to spoof and subvert. Real change is material. Madonna's "material girl" commercially successful feminism—if that is what it is—will hardly topple or even threaten white capitalist patriarchy.

Haraway is no pop star or media maven, but her vision of strategic feminist politics—which I cull from various moments throughout the book—can perhaps help save Madonna from her critics; and pursuing this angle can help illuminate Haraway's own politics. She occasionally draws upon the Bakhtinian term *heteroglossia*.[45] Mikhail Bakhtin's carnivalesque Marxism, a materialism played out on the plane of ("low") culture and in the realm of language, provides a response to the Frankfurt critique. Rather than insisting upon a sharp either/or dualism between base and superstructure, the postmodern critics who have assimilated Bakhtin reclaim the importance of culture as the site of struggle. Haraway throws into further relief this very notion of culture—as that mediating site supposedly removed from "nature."[46] In any event, we see in *Primate Visions* her reworking and reaffirming culture and language and communications as a late-modern road to real political mobilization and change. Though Marx railed against young Hegelians as "mere" phrase fighters and inveighed against "mere" Feuerbachian interpretation as something categorically opposed to "worldly" change, Haraway simply relaxes these dualisms and in the process reveals underlying assumptions and metaphors—and thus the politics—that animate much of modern science and the politics that modern science in turn supports and animates. Such insights are, indeed, revolutionary in many ways, and not simply because they help enlighten a liberal voluntarist agency. If, as Lyotard contends, science is a narrative that must deny its own narratological origins,[47] then Haraway's complexly interwoven redescriptions of primatology, her stories about its storytelling, force changes in practice, for the stories *are* the practice, and that practice is a struggle over stories. "To contest for origin stories is a form of social action," Haraway declares (p. 289).

The Madonna connection to "cultural" feminist politics also prompts a rethinking of the relation between "center" and "periphery" in conceptions of political agency and change, a rethinking of the politics of "pop" feminism. Many theorists—Bakhtin, Jean Baudrillard, and Pierre Bourdieu come to mind—contest the distinction between low and high culture, and they read a gender code corresponding to these binaries, a code that accords with Haraway's contesting of female = nature and male = culture (also: low culture = female; high culture = male). Baudrillard, despite a somewhat patronizing manner, offers helpful suggestions for rethinking the traditional notion of political agency as a concerted effort to reclaim and occupy the "center" or to open "public" space.[48] A disaffected Marxist himself, he no longer finds credible a series of associations in the old revolutionary agenda that reads: Marxism = revolution = active = male = center. Subversion and change, he suggests, can occupy the regions formerly associated with "passive," "unintended," "marginalized," "multiple," "understated," "ironic"—in short, "female."[49] Some multicultural theorists have called,[50] in musical fashion, for "polyphonic"[51] heteroglossic resistances,[52] strategies that operate in the nooks and crannies of culture, high, low, whatever, whenever. Such strategies need not operate according to an overall blueprint or vision or dream of utopia, they look to no grand, overarching program, no metanarrative, no ultimate foundation, no final wellspring of legitimacy (or we should say, rather, they have disabused themselves of the need for such grounds of ultimate author-ity, a bible or script for action). They are animated in multiple ways, in pursuit of various questions, and they find compelling a plethora of reasons for and modalities of action. According to this loose vision, women (or better, feminists) as instigators and purveyors of social and political change, whether that change be broad or incremental, act however they can to resist, challenge, and alter hegemonic practices. They become opportunists. Madonna's opportunism may well be, politically speaking, no postmodern character defect. "Popular doctrines," Haraway observes, can be "profoundly political" (p. 67).

Haraway similarly reveals a feminist opportunism in her embrace of Hrdy's (and others') opportunism. She starts off her chapter on Hrdy with a note emphasizing that contemporary feminist discourse is marked by "tensions, oppositions, exclusions, complicities with the structures it seeks to deconstruct" (p. 349). Postmodern feminism is essentially no longer essentialist in its ways; it looks with suspicion upon appeals to organicism or biologism; it is characterized, if anything, by its collective refusal to be guided or grounded by one vision or one overarching narrative: "The discourse is not a series of doctrines, but a web of intersecting and frequently contradictory inquiries and commitments, where gender is inescapably salient and where personal and collective dreams of fundamental change and of bridging the gap between theory and other forms of action remain alive" (p. 349). Haraway herself picks and chooses from various primatological feminisms: Adrienne Zihlman's universalizing sisterhood subdues the heteroglossia of women's differentiated lives, she says, but nonetheless may be usefully deconstructed and rewritten, whereas Hrdy's map of proliferating differences might indicate directions for a postmodernist, decolonizing biopolitics; yet Hrdy's differences, contends Haraway, probably reveal more about the logic of late capitalism than about the possibilities for a new set of fictions/practices for international multicultural feminisms (pp. 350–351).

Haraway asks the half-charitable, half-calculating question: What can sociobiology do for us? She applies her own cost/benefit analysis to Hrdy's primatology in particular. Sociobiology started off as masculinist discourse but now has been partially coopted by feminists. Sociobiological feminist arguments can enable deconstructions of masculinist systems of representation, but Haraway cautions us about jumping to the conclusion that sociobiological feminism completely liberates us from the masculinist discourse that it seeks to challenge. In particular, sociobiological feminism draws our attention in rich ways to the tensions between postmodern discourse and feminist discourse.

Although the postmodernist and poststructuralist movements have afforded many new reading technologies to feminists and the gains have been significant, the famous "death of the subject" threatens to rob women of the identity for which they have been struggling, silencing them once again, and oddly puts feminists in the awkward position of arguing *for* the unmarked liberal self that earlier had been identified as a source of oppression. Foucault revealed his unmarked maleness in calling for the death of the author, at the very time that women's voices were starting to emerge.[53] Still, the death of the subject explodes the liberal dualism that implicitly codes potentially pregnant women-bodies as compromised citizens because they do not fully possess their own bodies. Postmodernism breaks down the western self, says Haraway, which entails a breakdown of coherence between subject and object for *both* men and women: "All subjects and objects seem nothing but strategic assemblages, proximate means to some ultimate game theoretic end achieved by replicating, copying, and simulating—in short, by the means of postmodern reproduction" (p. 353). So understood, the postmodern (dead) self accords well with the investment metaphors prevalent in sociobiology. Hrdy's feminism reclaims the female orgasm as a key player in genetic investment strategies, and in a way this move recovers the possibility that women can have orgasms on their own terms. But Haraway importantly challenges some of Hrdy's feminist triumphs in sociobiology. Hrdy's understanding of the unmarked, universal female orgasm probably betrays racial and racist assumptions: "Orgasms and female genital anatomy have vastly different racial semiotic fields. Middle-class and white 'politics of the female orgasm' can risk privileging women's sexual pleasure in reconstructing notions of agency and property-in-the-self within liberal discourse. Black feminists confront a different history, where black women's putative sexual pleasure connoted closeness to an animal world of insatiable sensuality and black men's sexuality connoted animal aggression and the rape of white women" (pp. 354–355).

Hrdy recovers a version of female agency, now rewritten and reconceived in terms of orgasmic investment strategies, but that image of investment remains indebted to the liberalism that it claims to dissolve; in fact, it becomes "hyper-liberalism". Writes Haraway:

> The promise of the self-contained and self-transcendent subject, which has historically been the fantastic longing embedded in liberalism, seems even more fraudulent in the postmodern landscape of disaggregating subjects and units powdered into impossible fragments in a vast simulated world ruled by strategic maneuvers. Both evoked and blocked earlier within bourgeois liberalism, female individualism in the postmodern landscape threatens to be a pyrrhic victory. To escape the rule of biological sexual difference, with its patriarchal moral discourse on the normal and the pathological, only to play the board game of reproductive politics, as replication of the self within sociobiological narratives, seems a parody of feminist critiques of gender. . . . Sociobiological females/women are cast again as mothers with a vengeance, this time in the problematic guise of the rational genetic investor, a kind of genetic receptacle, holding company, or trust, not so much for the spermatic word [*sic?*] of the male as for the contentious ultimate elements of code that assemble to make up the postmodern organism itself. (p. 359)

Haraway closes her exposition on Hrdy by observing that the very attempt "to locate the reconstruction of the biopolitics of being female in sociobiology is fraught with irony." Yet if we accept this ironic perspective rather than allow ourselves to be victimized by it, we might be able to look for "hints of a radical future" even within "hyper-liberal feminism" (p. 359).

Haraway expands upon such hints as follows. Hrdy's genetic investment models yield a "full array of sexualized agonistic strategic possibilities in hyper-liberalism" (p. 365): Not all women are alike, and Hrdy's universalizing discourse can accommodate notions of difference and specificity and identity. Yet it also can yield an image of females "committed to reproduction, but not within a maternalist discourse." That insight is to be valued. Haraway appreciates Hrdy's attempt to depict females as actors, heroes (sheroes), universalized yet differentiated. And Haraway wants to insist that despite all of its problems—including vestiges of liberal racism and liberal militancy—sociobiology should not be dismissed out of hand as a tool for feminists. In general Haraway wants to claim, in another ironic mediation, that deconstruction need not be hostile to science, or vice versa, that they are not mutually exclusive discourses (even if their mutual contradictions cannot be reconciled), though she does encourage sociobiologists to become more ironic about their own narrative resources (p. 366).

Hence Haraway's own opportunism shines through. In another Madonna-like dance step, Haraway insists that "boundary crossing and redrawing is a major feminist pleasure" (p. 366). We should learn to discover enjoyment and pleasure in heterogeneity and contradiction. "Complemented by a ready suspicion for the flaw in apparent natural truths, laughter is an indispensable tool in deconstructions of the bio-politics of being female" (p. 280). There is no good reason to lament the condition that stories are built upon other stories, that science is essentially a storytelling, story-laden, second-order, parasitic enterprise. Madonna obviously relishes her self-parody of and parasitism upon the memory of Marilyn Monroe. Deconstruction will not undo the work of science. Scientists, however, must learn to admit and indulge in the quixotic, mimetic nature of their work. Scientists—or, better, "scientists-errant"—go about the job of "doing" science precisely by following a story from a book; "science" is their authorizing activity (p. 346). In that spirit I sometimes point out to my students that they have never seen or observed infinity though they have been led to believe in this invisible concept. Their calculus teachers have taught them that they are all able to divide a line into an infinite number of points as they approach a given point—even though those students might go to chemistry class and learn that there exist indivisible subatomic particles; or in physics class they might learn that all space is curved, and thus a line cannot in fact be extended out infinitely into space. They've been told a tale, and they believe in it, and it works, for the most part, though contradictions between and among tales can emerge. Take infinity with a grain of salt. Spatial and temporal constructions are far too important to be entrusted entirely to scientific storytellers.

Haraway's postmodern feminist politics are, Madonna-like, affirmative, opportunistic, eclectic, offbeat, parasitic, self-parodying, contradictory, provisional, exploratory, ironic. "The U.N. Decade for Women perhaps should be read as a 'post-modern' phenomenon, offering a vision of possible connection and hope for global futures only on condition of accepting the permanent refusals of closure of identities, adequacy of descriptions, and master narratives about what it means to be female, woman, and human" (p. 286).

Post-Coital Visions

I've tried to retrace *Primate Vision's* majestic arc reaching from organicism to cybernetic communication, and to replot that trajectory as a shift from Mary Shelley's organicist horrors to Madonna's cyborgian celebrations. The idea of a shift masks, however, an important underlying continuity: Both sections are about death, death of Carl Akeley and death of the subject. We are back to death, Haraway's favorite subject. And in both sections, deathly themes are coupled with issues of birthing.[54] Haraway ends her book by noting that "running through the weave of these themes has been the thread of preoccupation with biological and political questions of survival, catastrophe, and extinction" (p. 369). Big death. She revisits the oldest issue in political theory, taking us right back to Plato's one-and-the-many quagmire: "reproductive bio-politics are the paradigmatic, iconic condensation of the whole set of narratives about same and different, self and other, one and many" (p. 373). She ends her book drawing on a myth of Er-ish story about earthly return, though she claims that the account is "ironic" salvation history and is even better described as "survivalist history." In that rejuvenating myth, "the aliens live in the post modern geometries of vast webs and networks, in which the nodal points of individuals are still intensely important" (p. 379). What can this mean? "In the narrative of *Primate Visions*, the terms for gestating the germ of future worlds constitute a defining dilemma of reproductive politics" (p. 381). Finally we learn: survival of the world means reproduction of the world. Reproduction means doubling without sameness. Politics means reproduction, divested now of maternalist *and* masculinist discourses. It is a grand vision: Haraway plays Madonna to the world, a new self-spoofing savior-birther, albeit acting now in the name of survival, not salvation (cyborg sex = reproduction by communications and information exchange = the Word made flesh = immaculate conception = Madonna). The show must go on. Human/cyborgs might just become immune to death itself. But I repeat myself: Is this ironic? Can First World Survival Literature really be ironic? I am unsure whether survivalist politics, however modestly proposed, can square with my particular understanding of irony: For Haraway, irony is but a tool, not an entire way of life.[55]

Haraway takes others to task for their feel-good stories and naive claims to realism which typically mask, she claims, an underlying violence culminating in a cultural death wish. Yet Haraway seems at times to forget or downplay the level of violence and claims to (re-constructed) realism that permeate her own narratives. That apparent contradiction can hardly be credited to a deliciously complex self-irony. Rather, it strikes me as an old-fashioned, straight contradiction that unfortunately detracts from Haraway's noble attempt to reconcile irony with politics and with a feminist politics in particular.

Those of us fascinated by the prospects of an ironic politics tend to look back to Plato for occasional instruction. In book 10 of the *Republic*, in the myth of Er, Socrates recounts a story about the fate of the soul of Thersites. Thersites, as Homer presents him, was a populist orator in the Greek army who mocked the patriarchy of his day—he was a "thrower of words" who would "quarrel with the princes with any word he thought might be amusing to the Argives." In book 2 of the *Iliad* (lines 212–277), Thersites scolds Agamemnon for his greed and sexism. Odysseus steps in to rebuke Thersites, claiming that he argues "nothing but scandal"; and Odysseus tells Thersites to quit "playing the fool" (and then beats him). The crowd turns on Thersites and now regards him, not Agamemnon, as the buffoon. Recalling this incident, Socrates in the *Gorgias* (525e) notes that Homer never condemns Thersites to eternal punishment in Hades (though Homer so condemns several princes and kings). His fate is reported, however, in the *Republic* (620c): In the myth of Er we read that Odysseus, in his otherworldly homecoming, chooses to return to the world in the form of an ordinary human being, whereas the well-spoken but ridiculous Thersites chooses to return, alas, in the body of a monkey.

Leviathan Meets Cyborg

> Nature (the Art whereby God hath made and governes the World) is by the *Art* of man, as in many other things, so in this also imitated, that it can make an Artificial Animal. For seeing life is but a motion of Limbs,

the beginning whereof is in some principall part within; why may we
not say, that all *Automata* (Engines that move themselves by springs and
wheeles as doth a watch) have an artificial life? For what is the *Heart*,
but a *Spring*; and the *Nerves*, but so many *Strings*; and the *Joynts*, but so
many *Wheeles*, giving motion to the whole Body, such as was intended
by the Artificer?

—Thomas Hobbes, *Leviathan*

In relation to objects like biotic components and codes, one must think,
not in terms of laws of growth and essential properties, but rather in
terms of strategies of design, boundary constraints, rates of flows, system logics, and costs of lowering constraints. Sexual reproduction becomes one possible strategy among many, with costs and benefits theorized as a function of the system environment. Disease is a subspecies of
information malfunction or communications pathology; disease is a process of misrecognition or transgression of the boundaries of a strategic
assemblage called self. . . . Race and sex, like individuals, are artefacts
sustained or undermined by the discursive nexus of knowledge and
power. Any objects or persons can be reasonably thought of in terms of
disassembly and reassembly; no "natural" architectures constrain system
design. . . . Bodies have become cyborgs—cybernetic organisms—com-
pounds of hybrid techno-organic embodiment and textuality. The cyborg is text, machine, body, and metaphor—all theorized and engaged
in practice in terms of communications.

—Donna Haraway, *Simians, Cyborgs, and Women*

Donna Haraway's captivating and elaborate storytelling doesn't end
with the gorillas depicted in her *Primate Visions*. In a later text she
explains that "primate vision is not immediately a very powerful
metaphor or technology for feminist political-epistemological clari-
fication."[56] Feminist visualisation must look beyond gorillas and create a new agonal site, a new iconic image, a new inspirational standpoint, a new techno-political myth, for contemporary practice. Her
answer is the cyborg.

Cyborg theorizing recognizes and reflects the late twentieth-century paradigmatic shift from state-of-nature organicism to state-of-
the-art communications technicism. Her new mode of cybernetic
storytelling borrows from and builds upon older Western traditions:
She plays upon, for instance, Platonic "one-and-the-many" problems;[57] and she rewrites Christian heroism and eschatology to cyborgian advantage. The cyborg condenses many influences into one

image, working like a modern trash compactor: "I am making an argument for the cyborg as a fiction mapping our social and bodily reality and as an imaginative resource suggesting some very fruitful couplings."[58] Foucault has influenced her, but his biopolitics are a "flaccid premonition of cyborg politics."[59] The cyborg offers feminists a more user-friendly technology. So powerful and promising that image, Haraway proclaimed in a carefully crafted manifesto, that the cyborg ought to be the political trope for feminists in the nineteen eighties. She backed her bravado with brilliance, imagination, and good humor: "Behold, *Cyborg*!"

I want to try to understand this turn in her thinking by attempting another comparative coupling, namely between Hobbes and Haraway. Obvious parallels between the two can be quickly noted: The common attention to textuality, nominalism, wordplay, rhetoric, as integral to politics; to scripts and scriptures that animate our world; the ironical invoking of monstrous imagery,[60] along with the joint writing of politics and the drawing of community limits by way of monsters; the fascination with artificiality as an inexorable aspect of human enterprise, therewith the use of the respective scientific languages of their day. To be sure, differences abound: Hobbes draws upon mostly geometry and physics; Haraway, biology, genetics, and electronics. Still, differences of time, place, and orientation notwithstanding, Hobbes and Haraway share an enthusiasm over a common insight: the lessons of science can inform politics to good effect.

Neither sketches an account that simply reduces man to machine; that caveat is necessary to mention because misunderstandings of Hobbes and Haraway along these lines are tempting. Both are quick to reassure that they have not ignored "human" desires, feelings, emotions, frailties, interests, and excesses along the way. Conjoining the natural and the artificial, disrupting such binary oppositions, they are acutely aware that they are offering their readers odd combinations, oxymorons, and ironical juxtapositions: Leviathan is a "mortal God"; cyborg is "resolutely committed" to irony.[61]

The source, the wellspring for irony in both, I want to suggest, lies in their joint fascination with death and their similar attempts to address death politically. Irony represents that sense of reversal, a turning-of-the-tables upon death, an attempt to eke an affirmative ethos out of once-desperate circumstances, to hold those fears and countervailing hopes together in unreconcilable tension. Hobbes's fears of death are well documented. Less noticed, perhaps, is that Haraway describes and induces very similar globalized fears. Her texts could be described, with little need for qualification, as Hobbesian. As argued above, death is a worry throughout *Primate Visions*. But the later writings are equally focused upon death and destruction. Her prose is embattled, her discursive world is threatened on numerous fronts: The talk throughout is about apocalypse, AIDS, nuclear war, deforestation, toxic pollution, environmental rampage. Hostile forces loom on the horizon; she writes of struggles, threats, diseases, violence, exploitations, dominations, deadly games, competition, resistances, and geometries of difference. Installing the cyborg as a "world-changing fiction," as a "political construction" leading toward "liberation" is nothing less than "a struggle over life and death."[62]

Like Hobbes, Haraway foregrounds her political project with a tale of threat and woe. As a writer, she provides an alternative, namely, the cyborg.[63] She doesn't offer a Hollywood ending to her essays, and she explicitly avoids writing in a "salvationist" genre ("the cyborg incarnation is outside salvation history"[64]); nonetheless, the cyborg is offered as a response of sorts to these background threats. The cyborg, she says, is not an innocently utopic image, though it may well stir joyful fantasies. It produces certain pleasures, but it also may provoke, disturb, and unsettle. As the illegitimate offspring of violent western tendencies, the cyborg might just be able to provide a counternarrative that subverts the coming apocalypse. The cyborg accomplishes this daunting task largely through irony—it is the "final irony" of the West's apocalyptic telos[65]—a mutant product of science that, short of shutting Pandora's box or putting the genie back into the bottle, might just redirect science's violence into less lethal activities. "Ironies abound" therefore in this story of scientific ju-jitsu.[66]

Cyborgs might just help stave off an apocalypse or two. Cyborgs use irony to that end, but evidently they are anything but ironic, Socratic-like, about the need for clinging to life, for avoiding violent death at virtually all costs, by any means necessary. Death for Haraway, as for Hobbes, is no joking matter. It is to be feared and combated. Throughout her later writings, the word Haraway uses most, next to *domination* and *apocalypse*, is *survival*. Haraway begins her "Manifesto for Cyborgs" with an emphasis on (instrumental) irony but ends with a deadly serious focus on basic survivalism.

"Releasing the play of writing is deadly serious. . . . Cyborg writing is about the power to survive."[67] Cyborg authors retell and thus subvert origin stories that long for fulfillment in apocalypse. "Survival is the stakes in this play of readings."[68] Certain matters, even for cyborgs, are not to be spoofed: "Discursive constructions are no joke."[69]

Hobbes's ironical insight is that the fear of death can be pitted against itself, for the sake of preserving life. Leviathan can scare some sense into us. Haraway similarly sees unexpected consequences to "taking seriously the imagery of cyborgs as other than our enemies."[70] She likewise invokes death as a dark threat in order to prompt us toward survival, though in places she suggests that she is post-Hobbesian in her effort to replace "masculinist fear" with some, presumably less fearful feminist disposition.[71] Yet she ends the manifesto imagining a feminist discourse that can "strike fear" into opponents.[72] She fuels such fears and fantasies, escalates such tensions, and finally claims to withstand somehow such deathly tendencies. Despite numerous and obvious dissimilarities in their projects, Haraway and Hobbes share similar fears, positioned rationalities, possible sci-fi futures.

As argued in chapter 1, Hobbes's globalized aversion toward death leads to messy problems; his model can't support the variety of empirical detail in front of him, and he starts having to make exceptions and amendments to his geometric designs. Whereas Hobbes invokes the threat of death but doesn't quite face those fears, so does Haraway invoke survival as a necessary and necessarily admirable goal but doesn't argue explicitly for her sweeping cyborgian survivalism. Oversights, conflicts, and excesses thus creep in; and irony can't really account for these pesky omissions (the cyborg even starts "taking irony for granted"[73]). It is hard to ignore that the cyborg genre in science fiction and film is one of the most violent forms of storytelling imaginable. Under Haraway's direction the cyborg provides an emplotment that might turn western violence upon itself and derail apocalyptic aspirations. Still, surprisingly, she never addresses the cyborg's own frighteningly violent tendencies.[74] While cyborgs may well avoid narratives of organicism, naturalism, and holism, they characteristically engage in violence with bodily immunity. Cyborgs don't bleed, cyborgs don't die. They are terminated or decommissioned or disassembled. If maimed, they can regenerate limbs or can clone themselves.[75] Machines and stories survive; human bodies don't. Is this cyborg stuff really as auspicious a model for discouraging murder and promoting life as Haraway purports? Perhaps she is not sufficiently fearful about the deathly potential of her *own* visualizations.

Elisabeth Bronfen has written splendidly on the close association between women and death as double-coded, cross-referencing tropes of liminality: "Death and femininity are culturally positioned as the two central enigmas of western discourse."[76] Such enigmas typically give rise to narrative expression; they insinuate one in the (deathly) enterprise of writing. But trying to express the inexpressible and enigmatic, to represent that which seems beyond representation, all but forces one into a self-ironizing mode. This is doubly true for women writers, who already are writing from the discursive margins. For Bronfen, death, women, and (ironic) writing are a "triangulation." Critical feminist writers must write in a way that self-consciously acknowledges the limitations of their activity, which thus "changes the representation into a performance which exceeds the text."[77]

To repeat, Haraway has marvelously led the way in bringing together feminist politics and irony. I would add that she has only implicitly and therefore as yet inadequately theorized those aspects of her own writing that draw precarious connections between feminism and death. In my humble opinion, I would say she has been insufficiently ironic about her own investment in matters of survival, too faithful perhaps to the vestigial piety that women are somehow the primary peacemakers and life-nurturers in this still gendered world of ours.[78] In attempting to diminish (masculine) violence, if Hobbes conjures up a "mortal God," Haraway smartly declines the easy temptation to offer in its stead a "mortal Goddess"— but her preferred notion of the invincible, strong-bodied, survivable cyborg errs too far on the side of indestructibility. She ends her manifesto thus: "I would rather be a cyborg than a goddess." For my part, although I respect tremendously her inspired attempt to lead us away from ugly humanisms and to enjoin us in refusing an antiscience metaphysics, I would nevertheless rather be a Socrates conversing in hell than a cyborg dancing in cyberspace.

CHAPTER FIVE

The Agora

You gods who hold dominion over spirits;
you voiceless Shades; you, Phlegethon and Chaos,
immense and soundless regions of the night:
allow me to retell what I was told;
allow me by your power to disclose
things buried in the dark and deep of earth!
—*The Aeneid*

In book 6 of Virgil's *The Aeneid*, Aeneas descends into the underworld, a no-man's land inhabited by bloodless "Shades," the lifeless but reactivated ghosts of departed human beings. On his way into the nether regions Aeneas first passes many monsters—Old Age, Fear, Hunger, Poverty—and, shaken with terror, he foolishly grips his sword as if cold steel might ward off these terrible forms. Learning that his efforts would be in vain and moving on, he passes multitudes of swarming spirits—the reawakened bodies of formerly heroic men and mothers and unwed girls, all of whom remained unburied after their deaths and thus now must wait one hundred years for Charon to ferry them across the Styx, the river of death, over to the banks of lower world. Persuaded by the accompanying sibyl and offered a peek at the golden bough, Charon reluctantly agrees to transport the not-dead Aeneas across to black Tartarus. Once on the riverbank, Aeneas and the sybil make their way past the snake-necked, triple-throated Cerberus; and then Aeneas enters a field where infants, innocents, suicides, and jilted lovers lie in mourning, many of them crying and screaming. In the surrounding woods Aeneas encounters, without warning, the dim shade of his past lover, Queen Dido. Realizing her fate (and his complicity in her death), he weeps and implores,

> Unhappy Dido, then the word I had
> was true? That you were dead? That you pursued
> your final moment with the sword? Did I

bring only death to you? Queen, I swear by
the stars, the gods above, and any trust
that may be in this underearth, I was
unwilling when I had to leave your shores.[1]

Aeneas tries to explain why he left her, namely, on the orders of
gods, supposedly to fulfill a higher political mission; and he adds,
surely a little too late, that he never expected that his going would
bring so great a grief to her. Should she accept the explanation?
What do you say to a dead lover under those circumstances—her
"wound still fresh?" Aeneas's words don't in fact "soothe the burning, fierce-eyed Shade." She isn't moved by his speech, she turns
her eyes to the ground, she tears herself away, fleeing into the forest of shadows into the arms of her former husband (who himself
was never altogether loyal). At least he now gives her "love for
love," whereas the earnest Aeneas is still her "enemy."

Aeneas moves on, as is his wont, and sees many sights in this land
of the dead. He finds the shade of his father, Anchises, from whom
he learns the spectacular time-defying secret that future Romans
will one day inhabit the souls of dead Trojans (who now anxiously
await rebirth); but they will be reborn only if Aeneas actually fights
the necessary battles to come (visions of John Conner in Terminator movies to come) and thus fulfills his destiny of founding Rome.
Along the way the miserable Phlegyas warns all the souls of the
underworld: "Be warned, learn justice, do not scorn the gods!"

It is a wonderful exercise for readers of *The Aeneid* to debate
whether Aeneas is by the end of the tale an object lesson in missionary insincerity or a reluctant but evolving exemplar of a perverse
nationalist piety—but whatever one's view of him, cad or captain,
the pivotal underworldly scene in book 6 sets the terms for the
debate. The descent is of course a clear play upon the Homeric
Nekyia of book 11 of the *Odyssey*, and it provides a turning point for
reversing the Homeric progression (Iliadic to Odyssean) that, for
Homer's heroes, transformed wartime wrath into political foundings characterized by the rule of law. Aeneas's particular descent will
eventually inspire other descents, most famously Dante's; but it also
invokes and draws upon a long tradition of earlier poetic descents
into the nether regions for the purpose of consulting with the dead,
usually about some feature of, or version or vision of justice.

Contemporary political theorists who fail to consult with the
dead, as it were, are missing out on a great panoply of insights

proffered by the *katabatic* 'descent' tradition—a tradition that requires a mix of literary and analytic skills. Such contemporary theory also elides, to its peril, possible artistic linkages among past and present and future which such imaginative descents commonly confer. If one is serious about justice and wants to give considerations of justice full weight and historical depth, certainly a consultation with the dead, whether by way of poetry or revelation, is called for.

Yet as mentioned above, liberal political theory evidently feels that it must refrain from endorsing or employing particular religious commentaries on the good life, and likewise on death. If not religion, then perhaps a poetic, literary embrace of the dead may be the only acceptable option left to us. A knowingly fictional flight of the imagination into the underworld has the benefit of sidestepping the charge that any politics built upon such insights smacks of metaphysics. Metaphysical speculations rightly must be disallowed in liberal political theorizing, if only because they introduce a form of discourse that defies public scrutiny and widespread rational debate. Still, if we want to explore death, and if death studies elude most positivist, physicalist forms of verification and falsification, then we have a serious methodological problem on our hands if we foreclose everything that looks remotely metaphysical.

But descents downward traditionally announce themselves as clinging closer to the ground than more literalist, pie-in-the-sky forms of metaphysical pondering. The Orphic tradition especially affords us a way to think about the mysteries of death while avoiding most metaphysical excrescences. The North American Orphics, for instance, commonly depicted the land of the shades as residing just beyond the horizon, remote and yet somehow proximate to the land of the living.[2] The *katabatic* tradition can productively serve liberal political theory, combining the analytic, literary, and what John Rawls calls the "substantive," without becoming metaphysical in a literal sense. Or perhaps we might say that it allows us a *political* metaphysics, an imaginary metaphysical politics, a way for some political accounting of death that doesn't excessively irritate liberal sensitivities over substantive claims about the nature of the good.

In this chapter I shall provide a social contract based on a death account, one that can serve liberal political purposes. While the account deftly dodges or disarms the charge of metaphysics, I must issue a second preliminary disclaimer. My social contract of death is not meant to crowd out religious conceptions of the afterlife. It is a thought-experiment, a standpoint, a uniquely political construction about death, and as such it is not meant to usurp or preempt or outstrip apparently competing religious claims. The objection might well be raised that I am requesting too much from religious believers in requesting, in effect, that they put their particular religious conceptions of death in temporary abeyance; or that I am rigging the liberal game at this outset by proposing a procedure over substance. But I believe that once stated, my social contract of death can dispel such objections, since the conception of death presented is admittedly thin and purely imaginative. The conception doesn't assign judgments, nor necessary rewards and punishments, to particular actions; rather, it throws such actions into question and permits many responses, including religious responses, to those questions. Moreover, it tries to retain a strong appearance of neutrality among rival religious conceptions since it avoids presenting a competing god or gods as the ultimate arbiters of morality and value. It is thus a secularist version of the afterlife that, to the extent humanly possible, tries not to offend or exclude the voices of religion.

Here goes my description of a political conception of death. I propose the writing of a social contract, to be debated and negotiated, written and performed *among the dead*, in the land of the shades. It is therefore a social contract unlike previous social contracts. Rather than written from the state of nature, it is written from the land of Hades; rather than an origin myth, it might be called a terminus myth; rather than starting from an Original Position, it imagines and anticipates a Final Position.

The Final Position

Think of oneself as a traveler to the world of the shades, or as a shade among shades. The land of the shades in this depiction is not a land of hellish torments or heavenly ecstasies bestowed by a judgmental divinity. It is, rather, a place of little more than discussion and debate, or silence, among the reawakened forms of the departed. The shades can talk, think, reflect, evaluate, and brood, but they don't act beyond thinking and talking. There's no place to go. Their former bodies are distinct and recognizable but, as shades, their physical selves have been rendered useless. They neither inflict bodily harm on one another through physical blows, nor put their ideas into subsequent action. Nor can they avoid one another, since, again, there's no place to go, and time has caught up with all of them.

Shades can recognize other shades in their former personhood—or at least their former gender and racial attributes are discernible—since their former bodies have not been abstracted into lifeless souls but rather, as shades, bear the accumulated marks of past lives. Shades do not operate under a veil of ignorance; they have not sipped from the river of Lethe. Instead, they retain knowledge of the former workings of society and nature; they understand the general idea of interest and desire; and furthermore, they retain awareness of their past particular interests and desires, as individuals and as corporate members. They also have an awareness, profound to say the least, that they are now dead. Hence they have the additional ability to put their past lives, interests and desires, into a larger context—the span of an entire life, whatever length it turned out to have been.

Their conversations, when they happen upon contentious subjects, do not necessarily degenerate into a mere clash of wills, because, for one reason, they no longer have as much of a vested interest in these past interests. Their self-awareness of death tends to put these particular interests into perspective, though it would be premature to conclude that the Final Position provides a vantage of absolute disinterest ex post facto. Still, it is hard for shades to ignore that these former interests won't get them anywhere or do them any more good. Shades have been divested of all power, all trappings of office and station. The Final Position in this sense is a position of near-complete equality of condition; it is no longer a meritocracy, since there is no longer anything to gain or anything to do really, except talk. The memories and vestiges of former talents, aptitudes, faculties, levels of intelligence fail to impress. Disparities in levels of knowledge in past lives tend to be leavened among the dead since information is freely passed among shades, and past lives are necessarily implicated with other past lives.

The Final Position is also a position of near-perfect freedom, since the shades can finally be forthcoming with one another; they can put all of their cards on the table. They are free to discuss everything and anything without consequence—at least no consequence in the sense that a superintending providence will weigh their words and reckon their deeds. History, for them, is over. Their only real constraint is that they must now coexist with one another. The past becomes the basis for discussion. Hence they tend to hold each other, and themselves, accountable for actions in their past lives. A god does not judge them; no votes are taken. But the shades are not divested of all decency and responsibility simply because they are dead. They are capable of feeling emotions, they are capable of evolving in their understanding of the past, they make gains in knowledge, insight, and emotional maturity. This is not to say that the Final Position is a position of omniscience providing a freakishly inhuman perspective. If that were so, there would be no need to talk or to try to learn through discussion. But the shades now have the time for, and expanded access to more information; they have a somewhat bigger picture on things as they reflect back on their lives. In addition, they are, in a way, ever watchful of human history as it unfolds, since new shades are always dying and thus providing new sources of information, new perspectives, fresh reports from the world above. They thus become aware of possible consequences to their former actions about which they knew little or nothing at the time of death.

So they talk. They exchange ideas, they try to persuade each other on points of difference, they try to justify and explain past actions that are in dispute. (They also reflect fondly upon actions that stir joyful memories, and these are shared, relived, and celebrated as well.) Differences in past lives eventually provoke confrontations; shades require of one another an explanation and accounting for all sorts of erstwhile events and social arrangements. Whatever persuades, persuades (some shades, for instance, might want to make recourse to Rawls's *Theory of Justice* in attempting to explain disparities in income). The Final Position affords a wonderful opportunity to say what hasn't yet been said or said sufficiently, to air points of difference, and perhaps to look for areas of reconciliation.

The Final Position is not one of perfect transparency, a collapse of all boundaries between public and private. Just as shades may retain their distinct and separate forms, so can particular boundaries between public and private goods be presented as distinct and defensible. The point, however, is that such boundaries are now subject to questioning and further review. Individual rights are not necessarily accepted on faith or on principle; theories of natural or civil rights are now reexamined from the perspective of death. Everything is thrown into relief.

Nor should the Final Position evoke a nightmare of majoritarianism, a mob mentality. The dignity of past lives can be well articulated; in fact, such dignity can probably now be more poignantly appreciated, at least in certain cases. Debates can take place among different associations and configurations of shades, on various scales. There can be one-on-one discussions, or within families, or even—and here is one true luxury of the Final Position—among all members of an entire nation. The benefit of the Final Position is that each person (or group) is given sufficient time to speak. There is simply more time to sift and sort through information, to exchange notes, to reflect upon ideas, to hear many points of view. Some shades simply require more time to tell their particular stories. The point isn't that the discussion necessarily goes on ad infinitum, to the point of boredom or nausea. The point isn't to see whether one can stand to bear others as they recur eternally; rather, the Final Position is a conception of a space for expanded and protracted discussion that permits more than sufficient time to present one's case and to hear others and to accept or to work through differences, if possible.

The shades, in sum, are accountable only to each other. Who knows how long their conversations and debates will go on? There is no enforcement mechanism to ensure that they must ultimately satisfy each other (but because they are captive to death and must continue to coexist, and because there's no place to run and hide, they probably will continue to talk). The Final Position provides, then, a basis for a social contract—both for and among the shades and for and among shades-to-be. The basic ethical stance evoked by the Final Position is this: What do you say to your other should you meet up with that person in the nether regions? Justice in the Final Position, should it obtain, is based purely on discussion, exchange, and persuasion. The Final Position allows for a semidisinterested retrospective on past interests and desires, but its underlying notion of justice is not based on an originary (and therefore blindly binding) adherence to a divinity or set of a priori principles or actual consequences or common sense of fair gamesmanship. Justice in the Final Position can't be prescripted. Rather, it is enacted through discursive accountability to other, once-finite human beings.

Advantages over Origin Accounts

Social contracts written from a putative state of nature might concentrate the mind as a useful thought-experiment, but they can no longer adequately serve as the arena for pure theory, a point even contemporary proponents often concede. State-of-nature accounts are hopelessly contaminated by their close association with Western biblical narratives, and few state-of-nature contract theorists work assiduously to disentangle these separate registers. The state of nature evokes a garden of Eden, a place of pastoral innocence before the fall; civil society represents human awakening, knowledge of good and evil and sexuality and death. The crude distinction between natural and civil worlds is meant to recapture a kind of sacred integrity that supposedly ought not be left to human hands; respect for human beings in their own right, or respect for property, ought to be removed from sinful political wrangling and reserved for a prepolitical, naturalized venue of valuation. The problem is that such a form of discourse is hardly compelling to the modern skeptic. As an argument today, naturalism isn't widely credible. Theorizing on the alleged basis of nature (as if the theorist enjoys privileged access to such a realm) loads the dice in favor of the conclusions the theorist wants to advance; hence it is no argument as such. It is a way of smuggling in prefixed distinctions between the essential and the contingent, and the whole point of distinguishing so starkly between the natural and the political is precisely to put certain things beyond, or rather before, the political pale; to put them beyond contestation; to render them out of argumentative bounds. Too often naturalism, in its attempt to restore notions of sacred dignity, tries to foist on unsuspecting readers a universalism that is not to be questioned. The state of nature provides a wonderful fantasy of prepolitical spatiality, a once-upon-a-time world that is inhumanly divine and sacred, or inhumanly organic and materialist, a transcendental place that is out of time but is also somehow strongly influential over, if not determinant of subsequent human space and time. (As mentioned in the last chapter, Donna Haraway has also implicated the state-of-nature tradition with all sorts of assumptions about biological imperatives and primatological codings, many of which reveal gendered, sexed, racist, classist, and colonialist biases.)

John Rawls, of course, knows the problems in reviving a credible natural rights tradition, and yet he believes that a kind of original state naturalism provides the best prospects for theoretical relief to rampant utilitarianism. Although borrowing from a state-of-nature tradition, and from Kantian transcendentalism, Rawls wants to position his Original Position somehow closer to the ground. He wants to locate his principles neither upwards in a metaphysical sky, nor in any figurative state of nature. Rather, he wants to draw attention to principles that are supposedly accessible and acceptable to all rational persons if only they think hard about them. While admiring deontology in comparison with utilitarianism, Rawls in his Original Position really doesn't deploy deontology as such. It turns out that his principle of justice as fairness, operating under the famous veil of ignorance, turns on a procedural notion of prudential self-interest. Persons in the Original Position, ever hedging their bets about their real flesh-and-blood lives-to-come, agree to the disinterested fairness of a system that permits freedom for all within certain bounds and yet permits differences to the extent that they benefit those who end up "least-advantaged" through quirks of fate and circumstance.

Most of the usual knocks on Rawls's Original Position don't apply to the above version of the Final Position. Critics complain that Rawls mobilizes an idealized, tendentious version of personhood, or that the theory abstracts the individual into a hopelessly disencumbered self, or that his theory of justice is overly regulative, too crude and clumsy to respect persons and society in their full diversity and complexity. Shades in the Final Position, by contrast, retain knowledge of their past lives in their full former colorings. Hence there arises in the Final Position none of the problems associated with the veil of ignorance.

To be sure, the notion of the Final Position sacrifices the blind, disinterested integrity of justice as procedural fairness; and since it doesn't offer in return a similar all-embracing principle of justice that applies universally, some might reason that the Final Position runs the risk of degenerating into a Hobbesian nightmare minus the prospect of physical death as a relief. Rawls's Original Position staves off the infinite collision of competing wills and desires. Hence, it might be argued, the Final Position sacrifices the very notion of justice and thus throws the dignity of individuals to the wind.

At stake in these conflicting theories of position, I would respond, is the very notion of justice. Rawls in his later formulation contends that his notion of justice is "political not metaphysical,"[3] but this slogan seems to betray a woefully inadequate conception of politics. Rawls admirably wants to take rights out of the metaphysical heavens and even retrieve them from a remote state of nature; but he has not yet located the political realm. In fact he takes politics completely out of the picture in his magisterial *A Theory of Jus-*

tice. Justice isn't something accomplished or enacted or exemplified by the imaginary participants in his volume, except to the degree that they accede to the logic of his notion of justice as fairness in the Original Position. But that form of consensual participation is extremely thin and decidedly prepolitical. Justice for Rawls is just precisely because it isn't a function of politics. Politics produces, he fears, a mere clash of wills; politics won't respect rights; justice must not be left to political "bargaining."[4] Rawls instead entertains the philosopher's fantasy of arriving upon first principles the compelling beauty of which naturally harmonizes society and eliminates the need for ongoing political negotiation. Rawls reveals that this is his not-so-secret wish when he refers, without a hint of irony, to the "well-ordered" just society,[5] a society that achieves "equilibrium" and "stability."[6] As we learned in Socrates' first sketch of a simple society in the *Republic*,[7] well-ordered societies do not need a principle or practice of justice; the need for justice arises out of conflict and difference. Rawls, to his credit, has achieved too much; he has founded a city in words that leaves nothing more to do by the participants themselves except to live out their lives according to the philosophical script of justice.

Another way of putting this comparative criticism: Rawls's evident fear of politics (as the wrangling of messy utilitarian wills) produces a vision of society that is overly benign in its depiction of conflict. Rawls produces a neat logical trick that writes conflict out of the resultant picture. In advance of the actual functioning of "non-ideal" society he finds a formula to distribute resources, to mitigate class differences, to alleviate envy, to stabilize "partial compliance" problems, to make disobedience "civil." But he seems a bit naive in assuming that a clash of warring gods, competing notions of the good, won't result in killing and warfare. Where is the killing and warfare, that is to say, the extreme cases of conflict, in *A Theory of Justice*? Could Rawls possibly respond to a potential combatant that killing would violate the notion of justice as fairness? Where for that matter is a word in *A Theory of Justice* about death, especially unnatural death at the hands of other humans? (At least Hobbes's discussion of death provided a motivational theory for the evolution between natural and civil society; which raises the question: Why would anyone want to leave the Original Position?) Rawls's vision of a well-ordered just society is coolly deathless, as if death simply doesn't matter to philosophical calculations about justice. We never learn whether death is necessarily to be feared:

somehow Hobbes's fundamental question simply disappears under the veil of ignorance in the Original Position. In fact, we know nothing about death, and thus very little about the priorities of life. We don't know whether it is best to live a long life or to die young; we don't know whether death in battle is honorable or despicable; we don't know whether wars can settle scores and thus serve justice.

The Final Position, by contrast, doesn't ignore the possibility of extreme cases of conflict arising in any society or among societies. It is capable of examining such conflict, putting it to the test, by offering a forum of discussion for former arch rivals, now that their positions have softened a bit, as it were. Although the shades aren't fully disinterested with respect to their past positions, and thus the Final Position sacrifices the Rawlsian gambit of wholly disinterested universalism, the Final Position compensates by offering for just review full human beings and full lives and a full spectrum of human desire and action. What this means is that the notion of justice animating the Final Position sacrifices the elegance and simplicity of Rawls's tidy formulations, but the resulting messiness—and complexity and agonizing difficulty—involved in such discussions among the shades might produce, in the end, a version of justice that is truer to and more respectful of human dignity.

Of course, contemporary conceptions of social contract, Original or Final positions, are ruses. Rawls and other such theorists know that their words barely conceal a performative agenda. The real test of a theory of justice is whether the reading of the theory inculcates in the reader the same or similar virtues that the theory preaches. On this score, I submit, the theory of the Final Position, with its notion of justice as talk among the shades, fares much better, is more internally consistent, than Rawls's theory. Rawls wants to teach people to respect persons as such, but instead his theory exhibits respect for logical consistency—which might or might not translate into respect for persons. The Original Position cultivates respect for adherence to one's earlier commitments, even if those commitments were blind or impersonal. Rawls wants to say that such commitments can produce social cohesion—and the design may look promising on paper—but I submit that he teaches a retrospective respect for rules and thus teaches conformity to rule-governed behavior—rather than accountability to persons as such.[8] Persons do not commit to persons in the Original Position; they commit to a game of logic. The resultant justice excludes real accountability; it excludes discussion, flexibility, moderation, negotiation, participation, persuasion. If the point of a theory of justice is to inspire readers to become better citizens (as opposed to commentators), then Rawls's fares miserably—he certainly doesn't teach people how to become better political actors, only perhaps to hold each other to the original spirit of fair gamesmanship.

The Final Position teaches, if anything, accountability to others. What that means for the shades is not altogether clear, for it can not be spelled out and scripted in advance. For shades-to-come, because the theory, unlike origin accounts, is prospective rather than retrospective (anticipating a retrospective look on lives that were), it is better positioned to prompt the view of persons as evolving over the course of their lives. It is thus more adaptive to changing circumstances, more respectful of contingency, ambiguity, and multiplicity, not to mention human fallibility. Finally, although it champions discussion, the Final Position replaces argument with interpersonal, on-the-ground accountability. Witness that nothing Aeneas could say would convince Dido—but Aeneas no doubt was transformed by the incident. We might say that the Final Position encourages a shame culture over a guilt culture, replaces judgmental gods or godlike logic with democratic challenges and confrontations. The respect for others and otherness must be forged through messy and trying negotiations. If justice is to be won, it will be won on the ground (or under the ground), not, as it were, in the pages of a book.

Advantages over Public Realm Accounts

A number of political theorists—Hannah Arendt and Jürgen Habermas are the most talked about—have forwarded conceptions of a political "public realm" as an antidote to the kind of theorizing that attempts to define the political from an originary position and thus, in the process, tends to write politics out of the equation altogether. Such theorists seek a conception of a uniquely political realm for the late modern world, a sphere of uncoerced debate and free discussion that will help combat the instrumentality and creeping technicism of modernity. These theorists, like state of nature theorists, attempt to delineate a notion of political space, but their impressive efforts at spatiality tend to overshadow comparable considerations of political temporality. Time is a problem. The public realm theorists, Arendt and Habermas in particular, shift focus from a never-never world state of nature to an allegedly more worldly account of agonistic politics; accordingly, they shift from prefixed, contractarian concerns to more open-ended conceptions of political interaction. Under their pen, the political becomes a site for pluralistic, performative, contestatory speech—which, in the end, makes life worth living and death almost tolerable. Yet neither Arendt nor Habermas leaves these free speech zones entirely unprescripted. They employ the same basic binary division between the natural and the political bequeathed to them by state-of-nature theorists; their main innovation, besides shifting the focus from a rarefied speech zone somehow prior to history to one that is somehow located in history, is now to insist on the integrity of a fully denatured political realm. The denaturing, in turn, makes them extremely uneasy about death.

Arendt tries to carve out in theory a realm of artificial, humanly constructed "equality"—an equality that levels so-called natural inequalities while leaving such inequalities intact and unscathed. Under such conditions of artificial equality humans can enact political performances—they can talk, see and be seen, tell stories, undertake initiatives, contribute to worldliness. Arendt's political realm that theoretically equalizes the unequal is defined not mainly in terms of a freestanding human capacity for performance and creation but, rather, on that which it is not, namely, the supposedly unconstructed category, the natural. Arendt describes the political mostly by what it is not, by the realm of the natural and the necessary, the sphere of the *oikos*, the arena of the private, mundane, repetitive, and animalistic. Arendt thus, by indirection, clears out a theoretical space for free political performance, but she doesn't leave in her wake a complete void. She tries to fill in some of the vagaries in her conception by gesturing toward both the ancient Greeks and other real-world referents; these free political actors left memorable stories for us, and maybe such stories can inspire us as well. Still, for all of her talk about the importance of storytelling in politics, Arendt wants her own narrative to belong to the genre of nonfiction: no utopian, she. She strongly implies that her notion of political worldliness is still recoverable even in this depoliticized world of ours.

Habermas likewise conjures up a vision of an ideal demilitarized zone in speech that nonetheless battles instrumental rationality and subject-centered reasoning and other scourges of our epoch. The public realm of discursive rationality, a sphere of distortion-free communicative action, is our last gasp hope for down-to-earth liberation. Habermas's public realm, while idealized, is supposedly no utopia or academicized pipe dream, even if he sometimes almost admits that the odds are great against its realization in the near future.[9] Perhaps because the public realm doesn't make reference to transcendentalism or to irrationalism, Habermas strongly entertains the hunch that it is accessible and practicable.[10] Like Arendt, Habermas urgently depicts his little vision as situated squarely in the this-worldliness of the world at hand (*Lebenswelt*); it is no mere figment of the imagination, no will-o'-the-wisp. Habermas grounds his vision by aligning it with the project of modernity—which is to suggest that the vision has a history behind it and maybe a future, an emancipatory teleology in front of it. But where exactly are these public realms of Arendt and Habermas, especially since they are fighting a hostile epoch that doesn't appreciate such spaces?

For all of their insistence that the public realm is worldly, not originary or imaginary, Arendt and Habermas produce conceptions that become mired in nostalgia. They try to resurrect a lost (though not original!) world by re-membering older accounts, and they hold out the hope that new actors can participate freely in these projects—indeed, they charitably maintain that actual human participation is necessary for such resurrections. But should such political actors appear, as self-proclaimed Arendtians and Habermasians, surely their activity would be mimed and parodic (the Eighteenth Brumaire returns!), a post-farcical, third-order reconstruction of Greek or modernist projects now long gone.[11] If only some group, somewhere, would actually move into and inhabit their public spaces! Alas, Arendt's and Habermas's theories of the public realm have inspired scholarly commentaries on the political, but no politics as such. While both call for a reconciliation of theory and practice, a theory that doesn't write politics out of the textual picture, something about these bookish theories still replicates the problems they work so hard to avoid on paper.[12]

By contrast, the above depiction of a Final Position shifts the site of the agora from a putative real world to an admittedly imaginary land of shades in an afterworld. The theory still borrows much from public realm theory but now imagines the public space and the enclosed political discussion as situated in Hades, in a land where time no longer presents a problem within the space theorized. For shades-to-be, the focus on a public realm in Hades prompts a theoretical outlook that is forward-looking and prospective (again, anticipating a retrospective glance-to-come), rather than backward-looking and nostalgic, nostalgic in the way worldly public realm theory tends to be. As such, the death agora presents some clear advantages for political theory as compared with the more literalist accounts of Arendt and Habermas.[13]

Noninstrumentality of the dialogue: This general feature of public realm speech is hailed by Arendt and Habermas as the key to political integrity. The agonistic, antiessentialist, antidecisionist discussion isn't supposed to produce anything; it is neither producing objects nor serving some extracurricular goal. Although that position may be hard to imagine for real human beings (theorists cite Aristotle heavily in order to make it sound credible), it certainly applies to shades in the Final Position. No one can accuse them of trying to effect some outcome through their discourse—if only because there is simply nothing more to be done. Arendt, by contrast, must explain why the goal of story production doesn't contaminate the noninstrumental, self-referential, purely performative character of the activity in her public space. The stories must live on, or else the lives don't mean much.[14] Habermas must assume the burden of explaining to his critics how his notion of noninstrumental reason is truly universalist, available to all humans without recourse to a telescoped teleology. In the Final Position, however, one needn't lay down ground rules for the character of talk among shades—they talk for the sake of talking, forced to be free, because they have nothing else to do!

Liberal consensus questions: The notion of the public realm is vulnerable to Foucault's claim that it serves theory as a regulative ideal, that it presupposes the norm of consensus, that it requires the idea of liberal volunteerism, that it reinforces the grammar of free subjectivity and human agency. For the shades, consensus is never the goal, the talk is truly unregulated, and one can imagine the shades, if one wishes, as defying unitary conceptions of subjectivity (perhaps multiple personalities are represented by multiple shades, for instance). Such talk doesn't presuppose some recovered common world nor an intersubjective lifeworld; it requires rather the less implausible notion that all shades (and shades-to-be) are subject to death and can talk about it and reflect upon their previous lives.

Power problems: The notion of a purified public realm, situated in the world but somehow separated from some of the messier features of that same world, is extremely vulnerable to power critiques. Arendt and Habermas must maintain the integrity of the public realm by presenting it as largely impervious to outside powers that be, immune to the critiques of Foucault, Marx, Freud, or feminism, or else as itself constituting a higher or more binding form of power. For shades, speech is truly stripped of all power (except that of persuasion)—and precisely because these power considerations have abated (the goal of all public realm theorists), shades are better positioned to confront and talk about former power issues. They can confront some of the ghosts haunting liberalism, exposing the dark otherness that Arendt, and to some extent Habermas, try to take off the table of discussion. For shades-to-come, the specter of a Socrates in hell might prompt the internalization of a new kind of Foucaultian self-surveillance, according to which shades-to-be discipline themselves by imagining confrontations, discussions, and days of accounting with other shades-to-be; but such disciplining tendencies may not be such a bad thing for present political purposes: the theory internalized will likely produce behavior that is not greatly at odds with the theory itself. Imagining accountability is liable to produce behavior that resembles the real thing.

Appearance/reality problems: Public realm theorists face a range of tough questions mostly stemming from the deconstructionist critique of logocentrism and ocularcentrism: Why should we privilege speech over writing, the immediacy of face-to-face and visual communication over deferred meanings? Arendt and Habermas tend to theorize on the polis model, but shades are not so parochial. They have no problem with meaning deferred; they are willing to wait for they have all the time in the world to hear different accounts. They also harbor no illusion that they are not dead and that their apparent world is not the former one, and that the dead world at hand must therefore suffice. Hence any nostalgia they feel for the past world does not unduly color their current discursive performances. Theirs is as free a free speech zone as can be imagined—the ulterior point isn't revelation or liberation; the point rather is pure intercourse in a shared world of appearances.

The Final Position avoids other problems of temporality that plague public realm theory. By attaching an extended notion of time to the purified conception of space, some of the speech impediments encountered by finite human beings in worldly public realm theory can be surmounted.

For instance, public realm theorists depict an idealized vision of uncoerced talk and discussion for all concerned, but they usually don't admit an all-too-conspicuous feature of this game, namely, that advocates of public realm discourse, such as Arendt and Habermas, would probably be very adept at persuading and influencing others, given the proper forum. Talk is their strong suit, and the game is rigged in their favor. Public realm theory is the academic theorist's fantasy: the dream of good thinkers, many of whom are good talkers as well, becoming political actors. The liberal thinker generally tries to popularize this latter-day version of philosophers becoming kings by presenting the vision as democratic and the procedure as neutral (whatever persuades, persuades; and pluralism is the new variation upon Rawlsian fairness). But the dice are loaded. The construct of political equality allows rich and poor to discuss at the same table, but no measures are introduced to accommodate the less literate, the less voluble, the intimidated. The purified public realm, in actual practice, often degenerates into demagoguery and sound-bitism or filibustering. Quiet people, or persons with longer stories to tell, or persons who suffer from "tip of the tongue" problems (remembering only later what they should have said at the time), are not given their due.[15] The agora contains no bill of rights for the speech-impaired or for those who do most of their talking through body language.

Shades, however, are hampered by no such limitations. They have the time to listen to many sides, to longer stories, to give more taciturn types their due. Participation in a public realm is not limited by nagging time considerations—an issue that is usually not confronted by most worldly public realm theorists (except by those who consider electronic bulletin boards, talk radio programs, and interactive television as possible technological fixes for a depoliticized world—but these cyberpunk theorists have already left behind the face-to-face polis model of public intercourse). Shades must also adopt a language that speaks to other shades who are not former academics. Arendtian and Habermasian theorists, the shades know, will discount as silly any theory that departs from worldliness and displaces the agora into an imaginary afterworld; but they also suspect that they, the shades, will have the last laugh. The prospect of death mocks and probably defeats the theories of Arendt and

Habermas, throwing their wonderfully rarefied conceptions into question. Reading Arendt or Habermas means participating in a waiting game, which, if time catches up, soon enough becomes an end-game.

The extraordinary benefit of theorizing a public realm from the vantage of death is that such theory tends to inculcate an anticipatory posture that can favorably infiltrate the politics of the present (even as one reads). The vision of interpersonal, mutual, or collective accountability—those days to come of nontranscendental reckoning—can transform the way citizens view and treat others in the here-and-now. This evolving vision provides no fulcrum for judgment, no formula, no script for commonality; but it tends to make the rehearsal for the future a full dress rehearsal—for as one wonders in anticipation about what one would say to others in an afterworld, one is already enacting a now-transformed politics of the present.

Advantages over Eternal Return Accounts

Notorious for his unforgivable insistence that God is dead, Nietzsche isn't simply an outspoken messenger of divine demise. He attempts to teach human beings, perhaps only certain human beings, how to begin to pick up the pieces and reconstruct a world in an age of religious disenchantment. Indeed, the occasion of God's death affords an opportunity for "great politics."[16] The problem that lingers after the death of God is that formidable moral systems still in place, centuries-long inheritances left by Socrates and Christ, encourage—with insufficient self-awareness—a practice that potentially leads to culturally destructive death wishes. Too many persons participate in ways of valuing the world that lead them, ultimately, to prefer in principle dying to living. Death becomes generally viewed as a form of relief, an antidote to life itself, a compensation for life's sufferings—but that perverse valuation presupposes, and in time promotes, a debilitating attitude toward life in the present. Nietzsche, to speak sweepingly, wants to teach or to help to find new ways of attaching to life as such,[17] new ways of accepting and even affirming what formerly were lamented as human limitations. Indeed, perhaps the largest obstacle to a new value system may be the sneaking presumption that human finitude itself is a shortcoming to be resented.[18]

At times Nietzsche speaks directly to concerns about death: "The certain prospect of death could sweeten every life with a precious and fragrant drop of levity—and now you strange apothecary souls have turned it into an ill-tasting drop of poison that makes the whole of life repulsive."[19] But (assuming that it is fair to speak of Nietzsche's project in such life-or-death terms) Nietzsche usually writes more obliquely, employing other stratagems and devices en route to a new, life-affirming moral outlook. One such device, perhaps not central to his overall project but surely crucial nonetheless, is the idea of eternal recurrence. The term is sprinkled throughout his major writings and notebooks. Commentators have had a tough go at explicating this concept, if only because the textual evidence is cryptic and thin. Some have construed eternal recurrence into a full-fledged cosmological metaphysics;[20] others have claimed that it is a mere "thought-experiment" to drive home a point.[21] Some have contended that the point of eternal recurrence is to insist upon a view of life as presenting infinite change, novelty, and "becoming"; others have sensed a more fatalistic view of repetition therein. Still others have tried to view eternal recurrence as reconciling radical subjectivity with a more fateful historicity.[22]

No matter what one's final interpretation of Nietzsche's notion of eternal recurrence, clearly it is an idea that makes *time* into an issue. The background question informing eternal recurrence might be put this way: How, as finite creatures, can we reattach to existence as such, that is, without recourse to transcendental devices such as Socratic rationalism or Christian eschatology? Nietzsche knows that trying to revalue the value of mortal existence purely from within the frame of mortality presents epistemological problems. Usually mortality is understood from without, through reference to that which it supposedly is not: *Sub specie aeterni* (from the point of view of eternity).[23] Eternal recurrence—notwithstanding all of those commentators who conclude quickly that this idea provides a non-transcendentalist mode of human self-interpretation—surely prompts one to look at issues of finitude from, as it were, without, from the perspective of eternity.

Nietzsche adopts the notion of eternity, but he doesn't use it in quite the same way as previous moral philosophers and Western theologians. His notion of eternity in "eternal recurrence" is circular or cyclical, not linear. In one place he defines eternal recurrence as "the unconditional and infinitely repeated circular course of things."[24] Whereas Christian eternity, as *sub specie aeterni*, takes the linear stretch of a finite life span and projects it forward and outwards to some indefinite sense of infinity, Nietzsche has chosen a different design providing a decidedly different long-term perspective on earthly life spans. Now a finite, linear life is subsumed into the larger cycle of things (and one can debate, as commentators have, the precise sense of the eternal recurrence of the same '*das ewige Wiederkunft des Gleiches*'). The point for our purposes is that Nietzsche's peculiar geometry, however intriguing, virtually obscures the usual boundaries between life and death. Christian heaven/hell opposition insisted on a stark spatial distinction between life and afterlife, attended by a strong dualism between life and death (and that dualism echoed Platonic dualism); Nietzsche's eternal recurrence drops all spatial divisions and transforms finitude into a function of eternal circularity. The result is that death gets soft-pedaled.

The Christian distinction between worldliness and otherworldliness transformed eschatological Christianity into an acutely calculating form of utilitarianism: Faith became subjected to cost-benefit analyses assessing otherworldly rewards and punishments. Perhaps at some original moment of inspiration the notions of heaven and hell were merely points of emphasis intended to underscore the intrinsic merits of good versus bad actions. But the payoff soon became the point. Nietzsche apparently wants to find some device reclaiming a nonutilitarian, nonconsequentialist moral stance, a stance that he calls variously in connection with the idea of eternal recurrence "pantheism," "Dionysian," "*amor fati*," and "the European form of Buddhism."[25] What strange view of eternity, then, can prompt one to be more accepting of human finitude? What grandly consequentialist scheme of things provokes a truly "anticonsequentialist" outlook? With the notion of eternal recurrence, Nietzsche successfully combats Christian utilitarianism, and he offers a view that is widely affirmative rather than invidiously judgmental, but he does so at a cost. He tends to write death out of the cycle, in much the same way that classic Buddhism posits an end to the cycle of physical deaths. At times he even cautions against giving much spatial recognition to any boundary between life and death: "Let us beware of saying that death is opposed to life. The living is merely a type of what is dead, and a very rare type."[26] In offering the prospect of recurring eternally, Nietzsche removes some of the lingering resentment over human mortality essentially by erasing the idea of death as a threshold between two very different modes of spatial existence.[27]

By contrast, the theory of the Final Position reinforces a spatial distinction between human life and human death, and in the process insists on a difference between former lives under finitude and the current existences as shades. The purposes of the Final Position echo many of Nietzsche's apparent goals: to offer a view of life, *sub specie aeterni*, that introduces a potentially nontranscendentalist mode of human self-interpretation and evaluation; a view that doesn't ignore plurality, contingency, and contestability; a valuation that doesn't simply rechannel resentment. But the Final Position offers a better image (for shades-to-be) of the future as negotiable, whereas there is a slight drift in Nietzsche's cyclical pantheism toward prefigured futures.

Eternal recurrence as a thought-experiment or as a cosmology tends to speak to select individuals; it is not a vision that expressly incorporates the presence of others. The new, supposedly intrinsic attachment to existence as such is won by means of self-assertion; affirmation is a form of self-entitlement.[28] Overreacting to Christian reactive-morality, Nietzsche sketches a moral outlook that makes the presence of others into an afterthought at best. Eternal recurrence dares the assertive, solitary individual to accept finitude but not necessarily politics, or at least not politics in the sense of interpersonal accountability. The Final Position, by contrast, stakes the vision of the future, be it heavenish or hellish, directly on one's relations with others. No attitude or moral ethos, however robust, affirms life intrinsically; such positions are rather constructed and negotiated with others.

In sum, the notion of eternal recurrence can effectively capture our imaginations by depicting an extended vision of pure temporality. It superimposes one temporal scheme upon another, resolving finite, linear lives into larger, eternal circulars. Whereas Nietzsche is better able to appeal to our imaginative outlooks than can the more pedestrian-minded public realm theorists (who desperately try to affirm political worldliness from within), he fails to create room for a new public space and for transfigured lives with others.[29] The Final Position maintains perspective on the distinction between life and death, with perhaps a heightened sense of finitude, and also offers an extended vision of both space and time to supplement and abet the politics of the present.

Plutonic Justice

The theory of the Final Position may enjoy all of the above characteristics and advantages over rival theories, but it still faces an enormous uphill (downhill?) battle. Some readers are likely to resist,

even fiercely resist, this manner of theorizing. Death is far too speculative, critics will cry, and imaginative death accounts are impracti-
cal. To what uses, real world uses, can such theory be put?

Original Position theorists, public realm theorists, and theological theorists usually do not face the same objection. Readers are
quite willing, for instance, to accept the surreal conditions required
for thinking logically about state-of-nature accounts. They do not
object that it is simply impossible even to imagine a bunch of untutored, parentless, but property-owning wolf-boys who enjoy basic
rights in a natural state that never was; in fact, many theorists are
eager to stake the entire political economy of America on such
murky grounds. To think that so many intelligent people take those
state-of-nature accounts seriously and find them credible is enough
to cause shortness of breath. One wonders about the health of the
profession.

It is no time, however, to proclaim, yet again, the death of political theory. There is much work to be done that can be done. At the
end of a book titled *The Idea of Political Theory*, Tracy B. Strong
claims that the modern, bureaucratized world (one could add, the
world of democratic liberalism) has unleashed dehumanizing,
Weberian forces to the extent that persons are no longer recognizable to each other as human beings: "If to be a person is to be seen
by another—as philosophers from Hobbes to Rousseau and Hegel
to Wittgenstein tell us—then the modern city—I do not call it a
polis—makes it unnecessary to be a person."[30] Strong doesn't return
to the Greek polis but still longs for a "parochial" politics operating
within and against the big, bad modern world.

But if we throw out the nostalgia for a face-to-face mode of
knowing and acknowledging others, if we finally concede that a return to localism provides no credible model for large-scale liberalism, then with what are we left? Academic political theory has created a kind of public realm among scholars, but the politics of those
exchanges do not translate readily into a model for a politics outside
of the classroom or professional journal. We need a kind of political
theorizing that is easily, widely, and democratically accessible.[31] Participatory politics, if localism is no answer, can become psychological—or a better term—imaginative.[32] Imaginative theory allows individuals to interact as directly as possible given the scale of things
without continuous recourse to mediating scribes, priests, represen-
tatives, officials, institutions, parties, or technologies. An after-
deathly account like the one above can help persons to recognize

others without slipping into transcendentalism or groping for transparency. It provides a thoughtful mechanism, a mental reminder, for trying to see things from others' points of view. It also helps persons see their own self-investment in the lives of others.

Like other Orphic endeavors, the theory of the Final Position outlined above exploits a seemingly consequentialist scenario for the sake of an ultimately anticonsequentialist moment of reflection and maybe valuation. One can begin to imagine rewards for interpersonal conduct that may never actually accrue but are still, in a way, tallied nonetheless. One adopts criteria for judgment that take neither the gods nor godlike rules but, rather, other finite human beings, into account. Literature, as Richard Rorty has argued, can extend the reach of human sympathy and human solidarity. Imagine an unromantic, nonpastoral politics, "in lonely rooms and mid' the din of towns and cities," that could still encourage persons, fully modern, disillusioned, and cleverly calculating, to value, in the words of the poet:

> feelings too
> Of unremembered pleasure: such, perhaps,
> As have no slight or trivial influence
> On that best portion of a good man's life,
> His little, nameless, unremembered, acts
> Of kindness and of love.[33]

I fear that too many political theorists today distrust and even despise literary attempts at building new political communities. Literature is silly, soft, unscholarly, sentimental. It is the antithesis of earnest political theory. Perhaps we have wandered too far from our own Western tradition, which begins with a politics constructed by way of imaginative dialogues, and in particular dialogues with the dead (and death, mused Schopenhauer, is the muse of philosophy). Nonetheless, the appeal to imaginative literature and poetry is admittedly vague. It doesn't provide clear political direction. It may well be asked of the above sketch of an alternative theory of justice as *Plutonic*: What good, what practical contribution, what difference, can this theory make? The notion of a Final Position perhaps offers an interesting gestalt shift in our thinking, but where will it get us? Good intentions alone will not pave our road to hell.

John Rawls did more than merely outline a theory of justice as fairness based on the Original Position, he also explained how that conception might lead toward a redistribution of goods within society. That latter elaboration has generated much commendable commentary and subsequent scholarly dialogue; yet I have suggested in the above critique that Rawls as a theorist might have accomplished too much, for his masterful theory tends to preempt the democratic participation of actual political agents. Philosophical justification is won at the expense of politics.[34]

Having learned that lesson, we are tempted to withhold all speculation about what decisions actual shades in the Final Position might someday arrive upon. We do not want to set in advance too many restrictions upon their free speech. Yet for the sake of illuminating or fleshing out the theory, it would be helpful to proffer a few remarks about what I see as plausible practical consequences for the theory applied in today's context, with respect to a few policy issues. I am not presenting these speculations as definitive; they do not apply across all space and time contexts; they are not immune to challenge, review, and reinterpretation. I shall proceed tentatively.

I will get to my eventual points by culling and modifying ideas from the three main theorists mentioned above, Rawls, Arendt, and Nietzsche. First, two points I take from Rawls, and a bit of setup is required. At the very end of *A Theory of Justice*, Rawls notes that if justice as fairness is more convincing than older contract theories, it is because the Original Position "unites in one conception a reasonably clear problem of choice with conditions that are widely recognized as fitting to impose on the adoption of moral principles."[35] The conception preserves clarity about ethical constraints while avoiding "attributing to the parties any ethical motivation." Thus Rawls explains that he can exploit the idea of "rational prudential choice," allowing his parties to make their decisions "solely on the basis of what seems best calculated to further their interests so far as they can ascertain them." Contemporary rational choice theory owes much to Rawls.

Rawls makes a second point, less noticed, at the end of the book. In the last paragraph, Rawls asks and answers the question: Why does this hypothetical conception matter? Why should anyone take any interest in it? His answer is that the standpoint of the Original Position offers us a perspective on society that is both contextualized, that is, informed by situations that we do in fact accept; as well as decontextualized, thus offering a quasi-detached and thus "objective" perspective. That combination of construction and prior investment, he reveals, best affords the possibility of an intergenerational outlook:

Once we grasp this conception, we can at any time look at the social world from the required point of view. . . . Without conflating all persons into one but recognizing them as distinct and separate, it enables us to be impartial, even between persons who are not contemporaries but who belong to many generations. . . . Thus to see our place in society from the perspective of this position is to see it *sub specie aeternitatis*: it is to regard the human situation not only from all social but also from all temporal points of view.[36]

We might respond to Rawls by drawing upon Nietzsche. First, Rawls's notion of rational choice fails conspicuously to consider death, especially suicide and self-sacrifice, as a possible distributive good in life. Compare that oversight with Nietzsche's referring in numerous writings to suicide as "rational death"[37] and his contending that, as a matter of morality, one should choose the "right time to die."[38]

Second, Nietzsche, too, speaks of *sub specie aeternitatis*, but in such places he notably features an imaginary dialogue about death and a commentary about "posthumous people."[39] By contrast, Rawls's notion of *sub specie aeternitatis* entertains the perspective of "eternity" as effecting an intergenerational outlook "from all temporal points of view" which rational persons can adopt "whatever their generation"—but curiously, in no place does Rawls explicitly mention death as a consideration in his intergenerational political perspective. Rather, Rawls's intergenerational purview is confined to the mundane issue of ensuring that a fair scheme of material resources is distributed from one generation to the next; he thereby wants to set in place an appropriate rate of capital savings, respect for the environment,[40] and a perpetuation of just institutions (p. 137). The parties in the Original Position do not know into what generation they will be born (p. 137); but for most matters, they are assumed to be contemporaries; and Rawls favors a "present entry theory of interpretation" (pp. 140, 292). To effect an intergenerational perspective he must alter "the motivational assumption" (p. 140) by introducing a special "just savings principle" (p. 286); but he is quite clear that the intergenerational concern works in one direction only, as concern for successor generations. "It is a natural fact that generations are spread out in time and actual exchanges between them take place only in one direction. We can do something for posterity but it can do nothing for us. This situation is unalterable, and so the question of justice does not arise" (p. 291). His *Theory of Justice* hence can say nothing about either past obligations or the need to remedy injustices in the past, especially those realized only after the fact. Rawls probably could have avoided this problem had he brought the dead to the bargaining table in the Original Position, so that agents in that position would not know whether they have already lived and thus will never be born again. To extend the sense of intergenerational justice, Rawls should have included shades, ghosts, spirits and zombies as parties to the Original Position—but then the originary sense of the Original Position would have been rendered absurd. That reveals a fatal flaw in the overall theory: Rawls does not utter a peep about the most primary of primary goods, namely, about the relative importance of looking forward to being among the living as opposed to being among the dead.

(Ben Okri begins *The Famished Road* with a depiction of an Original Position of sorts, a land of conscious and calculating spirit children existing prior to birth, a depiction which, as the novel develops, turns out to be a political allegory about Nigeria. The plot twist for Okri is that the spirit children do not wish to be born. Rawls's bold claim that his Original Position effects an impartial outlook from all points of view, *sub specie aeternitatis*, fails, for one example, to take into account the originary outlook of Nigerian spirit children.)[41]

The theory of Plutonic justice can correct these oversights. It can enhance the idea of rational choice and liberal consent theory by offering death as an additional distributive good; and it can offer an enlarged, cross-generational perspective that doesn't write death out of the picture.

Moreover, it can improve upon public realm theory in demonstrable ways, again by offering death as an option. The Plutonic agon among the shades described earlier borrows heavily from public realm theory, especially Arendt's, although it shifts the imagined site of the agonal interaction to a nether world. As I mentioned previously, the Final Position features an equalized agon admitting of multiple perspectives and plural points of view. But because the Final Position offers a perspective from the vantage of death, it takes into consideration the span of entirely lived lives and thus offers greater flexibility than either Rawlsian originalism or Arendtian publicity can afford. The Rawlsian agent in the Original Position—or even the Rawlsian reader recalling that position—looks forward to his or her postcontractural status (as it were) with a fore-shortened perspective. The relative blindness of the veiled Original Position offers some wiggle room for rational calculation about one's future, and some consideration of future mobilities and uncertainties; but an aspect of that determination, the enforcing stakes of that decision, depend upon the strong presumption that once one's cards in life are dealt, one more or less keeps that hand. One is virtually stuck with one's (preassigned but unknown) lot in life—and the generosity of the Original Position is to prompt persons to see those future lots as hypothetically interchangeable. One adheres to the fairness of the blind calculus of the Original Position in large part *because* there will be no radical renegotiation of the distribution of certain goods, interests, and desires in the postoriginal society. Fair is fair.

By contrast, the Final Position offers more flexibility for current contractors, precisely because death throws all prior calculations into relief. The prospect of an equalizing agon can prompt actors to talk about the conditions that gave rise to unequal conditions in life, and it might prompt them to renegotiate the terms of life under which they now find themselves. Current contractors find themselves contemplating the Final Position in the perspective of what Derrida calls the "future anterior"[42]—and because the moment of theoretical justification is regarded as occurring off in the future, circumstances in the present remain up for grabs and are viewed as evolving and possibly alterable. By contrast, Rawls's Original Position promotes a review of current affairs from a past prospective point of view; and because that moment of justification is functionally retrospective, reflecting upon agreements already struck, it doesn't admit the flexibility to invite radical renegotiation of current structural arrangements. Still, the advantage of ongoing contractural renegotiation belongs more to public realm theory in general than to the death perspective of the Final Position in particular; the death vantage simply underscores that everpresent possibility.

The salient advantage of the Plutonic agora over the (worldly, i.e., Arendtian) public realm theory is that the Final Position offers a conception of democratic dialogue and pluralistic exchange now freed of battlefield imagery. It can thus showcase multiplicity without memorialism, challenge without competitiveness, contingency without contestation. The shades in the Final Position talk and confront each other's points of views—they are primarily historians—but since they have no further interests to pursue in the nether world, they are not vying with each other with the purpose of achieving glory by having one story emerge as victorious—more memorable—over another. An advantage is that death is not repressed as it is in the Arendtian contestatory agon; thus the subject of death need not be relegated to the margins of public discourse, as a dark, individuating, private matter. It need not be viewed as providing closure, as putting an end to conversation or as a necessarily tragic aspect of existence that must be transcended through immortalizing activities. Death can be forthrightly politicized, it can be incorporated openly into political calculations. In turn, political debate can be disrupted and revitalized through multiple outlooks on death. In particular, the Plutonic agora can be used to militate against a Hobbesian politics, a politics that erects political order by invoking allegedly universal fears of death.

Let us put these reflections into motion. First, let us ponder whether the theory of Plutonic justice can be of any use in promoting peaceable civil order, especially since it abandons the claim to Hobbesian fearfulness as the hegemonic inducement toward life preservation. How can we stop persons from killing one other (that is, assuming that the victims do not wish to be killed)? If there is no blanket aversion to killing, no prior wholesale agreement prohibiting murder, if all important moments of political justification are deferred to the distant future, then wouldn't the prospect of a Final Position encourage cynicism, fatalism, even murderous anarchy?

My own qualified speculation is that the answer would be generally no. The Final Position would encourage respect for life and discourage the wanton taking of life—but it wouldn't provide any fail-safe guarantees or binding contracts or enforcement mechanisms to those effects. The prospect of confronting one's victim in a democratic land of the shades would, I believe, provide a mental reminder about the ultimate consequences of one's actions—not consequences in the sense of punishments or material losses but the prospect of a face-to-face encounter, after the fact, with one's victim who is now inquiring into the rationale for the earlier life-taking. That scenario would provide a prospective reminder to would-be assassins that the loss of life would be irretrievable, it would emphasize the contingency of the murderer's action, it would underscore the dramatic life-and-death stakes of the action; all in all it would perhaps conspire to prompt one toward preventative accountability, it might thus provide a trip mechanism against violent killing. One would be advised (i.e., self-advised) against the taking of life only in the terms of that other person's wishes—not because human life is inherently precious, not because life is necessarily sacred or God-given, not because premature death is always regrettable, and not because the killings weren't perhaps justified on other grounds. Rather, one would contemplate having to answer to one's victim, and that may or not work; but the enhanced image of having to answer for one's actions under the external, equalized conditions of a democratic agora in the nether world would at least forestall the impression that one could engage in murder without any consequence whatsoever, with total interpersonal impu(g)nity. ("We live with all the dead: this is what murder denies in vain.")[43]

The case of discouraging killing against another's will is relatively easy, because the Plutonic agora basically adopts public realm theory's liberal tendencies toward voluntarism, consent, pluralism, and subject-centered reasoning. But what are the implications of a theory of Plutonic justice for self-inflicted killing or consensual killing? What about the cluster of ethical-political issues regarding suicide, self-sacrifice, euthanasia, and assisted-suicide?

It would be another easy matter if one had only oneself to answer to for one's life, for then the shade of a successful suicide would merely have to declaim a retrospective version of Hamlet's famous soliloquy ("To have been, or not to have been"), and no other shade need listen in. The advantage of the Plutonic conception is that such matters can be put, if need be, to political review. On this score, the decision about whether a particular suicide is warranted could go either way, depending on circumstances. Which is to say: the prospect of a Plutonic agora does *not* provide a blanket sanction against suicide, for instance, on the grounds that such life taking is a theft from God or that such an act is categorically untenable according to transcendental logic. In the case of suicide we begin to see the way in which death can be viewed as a distributive good among the goods of life, a good with political dimensions over which the rational individual has some jurisdiction, accountable perhaps to a larger constituency as well.

When is the right time to die? What is the *kalos thanatos*, the good death?[44] Ronald Dworkin has recently taken up the agonizing issues of suicide, abortion, and euthanasia; and he has forwarded an impassioned, eloquent plea for viewing all life as sacred and precious.[45] But unpredictably, he contends that the principle of life's sacredness doesn't ban outright all suicide, euthanasia, and abortion. He doesn't settle every one of these issues, but he concludes generally that whatever the outcome of a particular policy with life-or-death stakes, that act in question must uphold or attest to the sanctity and dignity of life. Allowing a suffering or physically incapacitated person to die may well do that; allowing a depressed or demented person to commit suicide would contravene such principles.

But why? Why not allow depressed or demented persons to kill themselves? Why bristle at the thought of healthy, efficacious persons taking their own lives? Simply because such deaths are preventable or are premature, which entails the idea that there is more life to be lived, would not necessarily be compelling to all concerned in the Final Position. In fact, there may be good reasons to commit early death. Perhaps one would want time to get one's affairs in order and to say a proper farewell. Perhaps one would think it best to live life with a healthy body and to leave well before ailments take their toll. Perhaps one simply didn't enjoy living much at all from the get-go, even if that condition didn't produce clinical depression or impairment. Perhaps one might want to leave precisely in one's prime, at the top of one's game (the Joe Louis/Michael Jordan theory of early retirement). Perhaps one would want to make a political point that could be persuasively justified to others, or perhaps one might want to die in order to denigrate the value of living, as an ultimate way of condemning current arrangements. Roman senators' preference of suicide to political exile,[46] Japanese hara-kiri, Indian suttee,[47] and Chinese martyrdom[48] are examples of the ways in which early death might be rationally chosen in service of arguable political positions. We in the West tend to view suicide as pathological, irrational, or fanatical; if chosen, it is chosen only under extreme, exogenous, life-threatening, terminal conditions. If it must be justified, we include the Dworkin-like rider insisting that it indirectly attest to life-affirming principles.

Admitting the possibility of deliberately seeking death, committing suicide, as a fully rational act—a position better viewed from the posterior vantage of a death agora[49]—may be stepping on a slippery slope toward increased suicide rates in our culture. For some, that prospect might seem alarming. But more suicide, or the threat of more suicide, may well be the cost of ratcheting downward some of the Hobbesian anxiety about death. Breaking the taboo on self-death may, however, radically reconfigure existing power relations; as Jean Baudrillard has argued, the powers-that-be accrue power by manipulating and legislating various economies of death.[50] The recognition of rational suicide, the right to die, restores to the individual a power of sorts, a power at least of ultimate exemption from objectionable conditions. For instance, an individual's power of suicide provides an escape valve from ultimate state control; a state cannot compel involuntary conscription in war when individuals hold the final trump card (this principle is already widely recognized on death row, where suicide watches must be maintained so that life-imprisoning punishments may be successfully carried out).

Suicide rates, however, are already on the rise. Jean Bethke Elshtain points out that while the forces of democracy are ascendant in this post–Cold War period, the suicide rate among young white men in America, age fifteen to nineteen, has jumped over 200 percent in the past decade.[51] She recommends restoring the family as the best structural protection, over the long term, against this youthful self-destruction. Yet I wonder whether there is any way in the interim to make an appeal for life in terms that make some sense to these suicidal fifteen year olds, a way that doesn't redeem or deny or patronize their flirtations with death. Invoking an older cultural fear of death, or older notions of Christian hell, or appealing to the coercive powers of the state, does not seem very auspicious; such tactics probably won't make a purchase on these youth. Neither can you really ask these children to imagine themselves potentially as rational parties to a bargaining session in an Original Position. They need an expanded sense of time, an abstraction that helps them to imagine the long-term effects of their actions, the lost opportunities weighed against the prospect of self-induced death. A version of the Final Position might prompt the following logic: "If you kill yourself, how will you live with yourself as a shade?" Or, "What will you say to your mother when you eventually meet up with her in the land of the shades?" While such language performs at a register admittedly close to Christian invocations of an afterlife, it should be noted that one is invited to be accountable not to a god, but rather to one's mother or else to oneself, now imaginatively doubled in time.

Thus the Final Position might be used *either* to condone or to discourage suicide. Preserving that possibility as a freestanding choice holds broader cultural implications. Imagine how the economy would be transformed if labor markets were not held hostage to the naked (or symbolic) threat of competitive survival?[52] What would be the cost of health care if desperate individuals refused to allow themselves to be subjected to extortionist price gouging? Can one imagine an environmentally minded person willfully dying, a noble self-squandering, for the sake of future generations, refusing on principle to exhaust scarce natural resources? Aren't doomsday devices the most robust and most cost-efficient deterrent for national security? The theory of Plutonic justice doesn't provide an ordering vision that will settle all of these huge issues; it is, however, more open to raising some of these deathly questions and putting them into credible currency than previous contractural models and perhaps offers greater promise for imagining a democratic response to them.

Death and Taxes

Entertaining a Plutonic narrative can help put more hidebound political theories to the test. It can serve as a foil to these theories by helping to tease out hidden agenda, background assumptions, existential resentments, foreshortened notions of the self, buried compensation fantasies, borrowed-time frameworks, flattened topographies of political spatiality. It can help expose the deathly dimensions of a theory that purports to speak exclusively about lively matters. In the final analysis, however, the theory of Plutonic justice need be offered here neither as a complete and authoritative guide to underworldly affairs nor as the only—nor even as the best—death account that might serve liberal democratic theory and practice. In the *Phaedo* Socrates expresses doubt about Aeschylus's claim that the path to Hades is straightforward and instead proposes that "it is neither straightforward nor single." In the same way that Socrates pits one death image against another, so might we suppose that the greatest benefit that the present Plutonic theory might offer the field of political theory is to set itself in respectful competition with other death models and other models of political temporality and spatiality. The Plutonic theory borrows freely from pagan, Platonic, and cyborgian accounts but admittedly bears a distinct family resemblance to Christian models of death as well. By introducing an explicit discussion of the nether world into contemporary politics, we might be able to show secularists how some Christian conceptions of death remain installed in their collective sensibilities; thus it might be revealed how deeply invested, how very implicated secularism is in the Christian culture it pretends to bracket. As well, Christian theorists might take advantage of this death conceit to reexamine how many of their political positions depend upon, because they might derive from, an unchecked commitment to a particular image of death. Set in speculative competition with the Plutonic version, the Christian account might need to defend its supposed monopoly or the fairness of its afterworldly conception. Offering itself in turn as a rival conception of an afterlife, the Plutonic model helps to level a discursive playing field; it can thus strike some unexpected common ground between secularists and eschatologists who might otherwise talk right past one another.

These considerations, comparisons, competitions, and confrontations can make a real difference in politics, mundane or not. Back to Rawls, for example: Rawls's rational actor model, which instills respect for persons by imagining that a simple bargaining procedure can be extended universally through an abstraction toward noble ignorance, has made an enormous contribution in recent decades toward resuscitating "normative" political theory and suggesting real-life imperatives that follow from the theory. Naysayers, many postmodern and Nietzschean theorists, have taken exception to the applicability of the rational-actor model, arguing that it can hardly suffice for renewing our collective attachments to life as such in the late-modern world. The model is Procrustean: Persons must fit the image of a rational actor or must be *imagined* as potentially fitting that model (or as having a sympathetic Rawlsian philosopher mediating on their behalf); and in recent years that Rawlsian legerdemain has been called into question.

By contrast, netherworldly theorists—especially the pagan and Platonic—characteristically include in their depictions of hell all sorts of life forms: fragmented souls, deformed bodies, unborn innocents, infants and children, unclassified creatures, and numerous animals (bees, wasps, ants, dogs, swans, lions, lambs, eagles, apes). The Orphic tradition in particular features the presence of animal life in the underworld. Rawls's rational model has been of tremendous benefit in attempting to teach us how to use our wits to gather intelligible respect for one another; but as a tool for generating an even more expansive reverence for life beyond rational agents, it is rather clumsy. Many pet owners imagine themselves as carrying on deferred dialogues with their beloved pets in a reconfigured future existence that can't quite be described as Christian heaven. Many parents carry on loving relations with their children that can't simply be plotted as a function of a time-sequenced, multiple-equilibria bargaining model. The Rawlsian worldview has difficulty in accommodating, let alone taking seriously, these other forms of interpersonal accountability or interlife forms of respect. Small wonder that contemporary liberal democratic theory has been able to say virtually nothing, for or against, the growing social and legal movements propounding animal rights, children's rights, and the right to die.

Put in a similar comparative light, it can be noted that Christian models of heaven and hell have been widely compelling (to say the least) and have certainly influenced many Western conceptions of justice. The ideas of heavenly reward or hellish just deserts are very powerful and not easily abandoned. Justice in this afterworldly sense is dispensed after the fact; it is deferred to a day of reckoning: "Thy Kingdom come/ Thy will be done." The Christian model offers the flexibility of combining distributive and retributive dimensions of justice into one ordering vision, through the twin but intertwined options of heaven and hell. Rawls, compared with the Christian model, has great difficulty in bringing distributive and retributive notions of justice under one conceptual roof. Rawls, as Allan Bloom points out, eliminates fear of death as a consideration in his quasi-state-of-nature contractarian account; and thus he eliminates any natural sanction against breaking the law, and likewise eliminates Hobbes's solution for contracting allegiance to the state against Christianity's rival claim to a more important afterlife. "With the disappearance of the fear of death as the primary motive, the sanction for breaking the contract also disappears."[53] Rawls thus has to introduce secondary punishments and sanctions, as part of "non-ideal" and "partial compliance" theory. His proposed reconciliation reads, however, as something of an afterthought—"stabilizing sanctions" are written backwards into the Original Position.[54] Lately Rawlsians have been criticized for being sanctimonious about their punitive tendencies,[55] even though Rawls insists that "to think of distributive and retributive justice as converses of one another is completely misleading."[56] A disinterested observer who compares Rawlsian and Christian images of justice (both of which downplay death) might well conclude, looking backward at the Original Position as opposed to looking forward to a Day of Reckoning, that the Christian vision of justice indeed offers a more compelling package deal.

By further contrast, the Christian heaven/hell model operates rather crudely, at least in one regard, compared with the Plutonic model. These two models feature different forms of decision making, separate afterworldly images that often infiltrate a political cal-

culus. The Christian verdicts of redemption or damnation issue decidedly from a providential edict; the Plutonic model as limned earlier features democratic, unscripted, face-to-face, agent-to-agent
confrontations and judgments. That difference need not be viewed
merely as a difference between the sacred and the secular; it could
be described rather in Georges Bataille's terminology as a difference
between a decision-making process based on a restricted (i.e., limited, bounded, productive) economy versus a general (i.e., unlim-
ited, unbounded, consumptive) economy.[57] A restricted Christian
economy of ethical judgment has been used, for instance, to declare
that all abortion is morally wrong, since all human life, which issues
from a creationist God, is sacred (a labor theory of productive
value). The faithful Christian does not reason, in larger theological
circles, that an accelerated squandering of fetuses will expedite and
virtually ensure that those aborted souls will be reunited blissfully
with their creator; abortion is not promoted as a luxurious theological gift to the fetus. By contrast, the Plutonic narrative might
prompt the following speculation about the abortion issue. It would
imagine the kind of conversation or explanation a mother might
have with her aborted fetus in a land of the shades, should they
eventually meet up with one another (again, a kind of deliberation
that does not fit the Rawlsian model very well). It might also imagine other parties as participating in that conversation. I am in no
position at this point to decide how that encounter might go for any
particular mother or all mothers or all mothers and fathers and
fetuses, why they might say that the destruction was or was not
necessary. (For instance, giving the gift of life could be viewed, following Bataille, as potlatch.) The scenario of a woman speaking to
her fetus after the fact possibly interjects a haunting element of
indeterminacy into that issue, whereas the Christian model offers a
sometimes attractive aspect of blanket settlement. Still, the Plutonic
model is more down-to-earth and case-specific, whereas the Christian version refuses to recognize extenuating circumstances. The
Plutonic model throws the burden of interpretation and judgment
upon the participants, whereas the Christian model demands accountability foremost to God. The Plutonic model, because it is an
imaginative death model, is the only version that can feature fetuses
speaking in a way for themselves (or at least as mutely self-repre-
sentative) without construing them as potentially full-born human
beings. I mention these reflections not to suggest that the Plutonic
theory of justice can adjudicate once and for all the trying issue of

abortion; but it can introduce another dimension into the discussion that might otherwise be difficult to articulate. It can shed some light on that ethical gray zone inhabited by those who experience death but never experience birth into a public world.

In addition, I am well aware of the comparative proximity of the Plutonic model to much contemporary public realm theory, which similarly features a discursive agon as a vital model of politics— even though public realm theory, as argued above, frequently eschews death as a political variable. The discussion-intensive nature of the Final Position eerily resembles the agon that public realm theorists end up defending; yet because the shades are dead, there is no compelling reason for them to take up arms and do real battle, as in a *real* agon: hence they turn to discussion as a last resort. Public realm theorists have no such excuse. To this extent, such theorists often simulate death, viewing faculty meetings and symposia as battlefield struggles by other means. While they probably should be congratulated for attempting to emulate the dead, they also ought to be rebuked for attempting to usurp the political station of the dead. From the Plutonic vantage, the good of death is being unjustly and fraudulently distributed in liberal societies by zombified theorists who presume to speak from the standpoint of the underworld, albeit without proper attribution. These theorists should be exposed as charlatans: They may appear to be dead, but in fact they are not! How would we living theorists like it if the dead masqueraded as the living? In short, the implicit irony of the Plutonic theory recommends that we respect the political division between life and death, even while we entertain imaginative border crossings. The purpose of such infernal forays, we must remind ourselves, is not simply to teach ourselves how to be dead in theory while alive in fact (even if the dead make for a good captive audience).

Parting words: We live in an age when governments bomb and maim civilian populations for reasons quite removed from national self-defense, when proponents of market mechanisms coolly justify making human health into a consumer commodity, when terrorists blow up buildings, airplanes and subways, when teenagers kill each other in the streets without blinking an eye. What is our political theory to do in such an age? Is Hobbes still helpful? How do we reestablish the dignity of the individual in an age when killing and daily violence no longer shock and disturb? What political theory do we bring out of the ivory tower and into, as it were, the streets:

Plato's *Republic*? The Christian Bible? Rawls's *A Theory of Justice*? Derrida's *On Grammatology*? In the foregoing chapter I have been entertaining a sneaking suspicion that Virgil's *The Aeneid*, drawing as it does upon death, or something similar in an updated version,[58] might engage the present age better: What would you say to those persons you have killed or neglected should you meet up with them in the land of the shades? (And the Aeneas-Dido episode dramatizes the difficulties in and yet underscores the abandoned vision of building cross-cultural, cross-gendered, cross-racial communities.) The above political theory neither offers a new version of the golden rule or the categorical imperative or ascetic guilt or provides any guarantee of success. Rather, it pursues the modest thesis that art can sometimes heal wounds; that a little fictional play can sometimes bring people together to talk who would otherwise never speak to one another. Liberal interaction presupposes a great leap of the imagination, namely, the premise that people will want to hear one another out, even as rivals. Perhaps the spirit of modern Orphism can help them to start talking with each other, which may help them to start recognizing each other as persons, which might help them to start putting an end to some of the self-inflicted bloodletting and human carnage that sadly but all too conspicuously characterize our particular epoch in history.

Acknowledgments

A
s one might expect, the foregoing book is the result of many conversations. I've enjoyed the benefit of learning from some remarkable persons, and I want to take the time to acknowledge many of them by name. Most of the writing took place during a year in which I was residing at the Humanities Center at Stanford University, on sabbatical from Pomona College owing to the generosity of a Steele Grant. The Stanford Humanities Center created the perfect climate for writing a book, the perfect combination of solitude and sociability. I express my great appreciation to Wanda Corn, Charles Junkerman, Herbert Lindenberger, and the staff at the Center for creating this little academic nirvana. Daily discussion with my fellows there provided stimulation and good cheer, and I miss them all: Ted Andersson, Rachel Cohon, Whitney Davis, Michael Fellman, Roland Greene, Harry Harootunian, James Ketelaar, Linda Lomperis, Andrea Nightingale, Colin Palmer, Andrew Parker, Patricia Parker, Marleen Rozemond, and Lyman Van Slyke. Joseph Brodsky and Peter Sellars passed on insights into the artistry of death. David and Sue Riggs provided friendship and more.

Several of the ideas first percolated in a multidisciplinary reading group—a seminar sponsored by the Pew Foundation—which drew faculty from Scripps, Pitzer, and Pomona Colleges: Jud Emerick, Michael Harper, Natalie Rachlin, Dan Segal, and Lynn Thomas. Periodic exchanges with Kathy Ferguson and Henry Kariel also provided early provocations and inspirations.

I wrote a good chunk of the Plato chapter on the sly, lucubrating at night, while attending during the day, along with twenty-eight Goethe scholars, a six-week NEH conference devoted entirely to one text, namely *Faust*. To the conference organizers—Jane Brown, Cyrus Hamlin, and Paul Hernadi—I apologize for my being at times somewhat distracted and also for donning a pair of red devil horns about four weeks into the conference. It seemed like the thing to do.

Chapter 4 began as a panel paper for an American Political Science Association annual conference. For their collaborative support, I thank the other panelists, Jane Bennett, Valerie Hartouni, Carolyn Di Palma, and Donna Haraway (who revealed to the audience that her given name is indeed Madonna).

My students at Pomona College have offered many ideas along the way, and for particular contributions I thank Jeanette Cruz, Josh Karant, Christine Koh, Linda Lee, Sheila Réjouis, Belle Richmond, and Anita Seth.

Major editorial labors have fallen on William E. Connolly and Daniel W. Conway. I am deeply grateful for their Herculean efforts. I'm afraid that I haven't adopted all of their excellent suggestions, if only because they were sometimes at odds with one another. In general, one of them, in a Nietzschean mood, wanted me to announce my own decadence more, and the other, in a Foucaultian mood, advised me to take better care of my self. In an infernal project, one often finds oneself between a rock and a hard place.

Several other persons read the entire manuscript in various stages of completion, and I am tremendously indebted to them for their superb ideas and helpful criticism: Terrell Carver, Bill Chaloupka, Marc Ehrlich, Bronwyn Lebaw, George Kateb, Lee McDonald, Bob Meister, and an anonymous reviewer. W. T. Jones read several working chapters and provided his usual wit and wisdom. David S. Meyer offered sound e-mail advice on a daily basis.

Roger Haydon kept the entire project in perspective.

Many thanks to each and all. Errors, oversights, and stupidities that remain are mine and mine alone. I can be stubborn.

Finally, Kim, Molly Marie, and Brownie made life worth living in a suburban desert.

J. E. S.

Claremont, California

Notes

1. The Academy

1. Greetings. Welcome to the nether world of notes. I am as guilty as the next chronic footnoter in overdoing the source citation, but I have tried to restrain myself somewhat in the following material. The supporting documentation is selective because the available literature is vast; hence I make no claims to scholarly exhaustion.

2. See Harvey Goldman's account of Weber on the meaning of specialized academic activity with respect to death: *Politics, Death, and the Devil: Self and Power in Max Weber and Thomas Mann* (Berkeley: University of California Press, 1992), pp. 51–86.

3. Jean Bethke Elshtain has recently called for a greater awareness of "our ongoing dialogue with the dead": *Democracy on Trial* (New York: Basic, 1995), pp. 135–138. Note also: "Communication with the dead—that has to be learned. . . . ," in Hannah Arendt, *Hannah Arendt Karl Jaspers Correspondence 1926–1969*, ed. Lotte Kohler and Hans Saner, trans. Robert and Rita Kimber (New York: Harcourt Brace Jovanovich, 1992), p. 686.

4. Hannah Arendt, "On Violence," *Crises of the Republic* (New York: Harcourt Brace Jovanovich, 1969), p. 165.

5. I am not contending here, however, that Hobbes subscribes to a theory of "motivational reductionism." Cf. Stephen Holmes, "Introduction," in *Behemoth, or The Long Parliament*, ed. Ferdinand Tönnies (Chicago: University of Chicago Press, 1990), pp. xi–xiii.

6. Thomas Hobbes, *De Cive*, ed. Howard Warrenden (Oxford: Clarendon Press, 1983), chap. 2, section 18, pp. 58–59.

7. Norman Jacobson, *Pride and Solace: The Functions and Limits of Political Theory* (New York: Methuen, 1986), esp. pp. 58–59. William E. Connolly has similarly argued that Hobbes manages to control the implications to which the reader consents (he is, in Connolly's words, a "textual bureaucrat"): *Political Theory and Modernity* (1988; Ithaca: Cornell University Press, 1993), p. 34.

8. Carole Pateman, "'God Hath Ordained to Man a Helper': Hobbes, Patriarchy and Conjugal Right," *Feminist Interpretations and Political Theory*, ed. Mary Lyn-

196   Notes to Pages 7–9

don Shanley and Carole Pateman (University Park: Pennsylvania State University Press, 1991), pp. 53–73; Carole Pateman, *The Sexual Contract* (Stanford: Stanford University Press, 1988); Christine Di Stefano, *Configurations of Masculinity: A Feminist Perspective on Modern Political Theory* (Ithaca: Cornell University Press, 1991), pp. 66–104, esp. p. 81; Nancy C. M. Hartsock, *Money, Sex, and Power: Toward a Feminist Historical Materialism* (New York: Longman, 1983), esp. pp. 174–175; Susan Griffin, *Pornography and Silence: Culture's Revenge against Nature* (New York: Harper and Row, 1981).

9. Michael J. Shapiro, influenced by Georges Bataille, offers a superb challenge to the prevailing politics of death that is built on anxiety: "The linguistic economies within which we officially or unofficially give meaning to life and death have a paralyzing effect; we become stingy and afraid to spend—that is, to live. Our different discourses of death—juridical, medical, even statistical/chance—are all discursive economics within which death is a force to be held off by the exercise of a kind of parsimony." Shapiro, *Reading the Postmodern Polity: Political Theory as Textual Practice* (Minneapolis: University of Minnesota Press, 1992), p. 154.

10. Thomas Hobbes, *Leviathan* (Harmondsworth: Penguin, 1968), part 3, chap. 38, p. 478.

11. Ibid.

12. Francis Bacon, "Of Death," in *The Essayes or Counsels, Civill and Morall*, ed. Michael Kiernan (Cambridge: Harvard University Press, 1985), pp. 9–10; cited in Holmes, "Introduction," p. xxix.

13. The "ultimate good is eternal life, and . . . the ultimate evil is eternal death" (Augustine, *The City of God*, vol. 6, book 19, chap. 4, p. 122); cited in Holmes, "Introduction," p. xxxix.

14. Cf. Leo Strauss, *The Political Philosophy of Hobbes: Its Basis and Its Genesis*, trans. Elsa M. Sinclair (Oxford: Clarendon Press, 1936), p. 16.

15. Ibid., p. 17.

16. Thomas Hobbes, *De Homine*, in *Man and Citizen: Thomas Hobbes*, ed. Bernard Gert (Atlantic Highlands, N.J.: Humanities Press, 1972), chap. 11, pp. 48–49; cited in Richard E. Flathman, *Thomas Hobbes: Skepticism, Individuality and Chastened Politics* (Newbury Park, Calif.: Sage, 1993), p. 77.

17. Thomas Hobbes, *A Dialogue between a Philosopher and a Student of the Common Laws of England*, ed. Joseph Cropsey (Chicago: University of Chicago Press, 1971), pp. 116–117; cited in Flathman, *Thomas Hobbes*, p. 91.

18. Richard Flathman contends that Hobbes isn't concerned simply with the right to self-preservation and mere survival but, in key passages, reveals his concern for felicity and living well. See Flathman, *Thomas Hobbes*, esp. chap. 5.

19. David Johnston argues that Hobbes's discrepancies issue from his method of scientific modeling: *The Rhetoric of Leviathan: Thomas Hobbes and the Politics of Cultural Transformation* (Princeton: Princeton University Press, 1986), pp. 93–94.

20. Hobbes, *Leviathan*, part 1, chap. 14, p. 200.

21. See Strauss, *The Political Philosophy of Hobbes*, esp. p. 167; Johnston, *The Rhetoric of Leviathan*, esp. 149–150.

22. Hobbes, *De Cive or The Citizen*, in *Man and Citizen*, ed. Gert, chap. 6, p. 11.

23. See J. G. A. Pocock, "Time, History and Eschatology in the Thought of Thomas Hobbes," in his *Politics, Language and Time: Essays on Political Thought and History* (Chicago: University of Chicago Press, 1989); Patricia Springboard, "*Leviathan* and the Problem of Ecclesiastical Authority," *Political Theory* 3 (August 1975), 289–303; Tracy B. Strong, "How to Write Scripture: Words, Authority, and Politics in Thomas Hobbes," *Critical Inquiry* 20 (Autumn 1993), 128–159;

and A. P. Martinich, *The Two Gods of Leviathan: Thomas Hobbes on Religion and Politics* (Cambridge: Cambridge University Press, 1992).

24. See Norman T. Burns, *Christian Mortalism from Tyndale to Milton* (Cambridge: Harvard University Press, 1972); Strong, "How to Write Scripture," pp. 137–139; Martinich, *The Two Gods of Leviathan*, pp. 262–266.

25. Martinich points out that Luther held that humans are not conscious after death: *The Two Gods of Leviathan*, p. 5; Burns, *Christian Mortalism*, pp. 27–32.

26. Hobbes, *Leviathan*, part 3, chap. 38, p. 484.

27. Ibid.

28. Ibid., chap. 43, p. 610.

29. See Martinich, *The Two Gods of Leviathan*, pp. 257–260.

30. Michael Rogin and others have interpreted the mortal god to be the author of *Leviathan*, Thomas Hobbes himself. Commentators frequently see the phrases "mortal god" and "artificial person" as somehow interchangeable. Rogin, *Ronald Reagan, the Movie and Other Episodes in Political Demonology* (Berkeley: University of California Press, 1987), pp. 299–300.

31. Some gods die and are reborn; but most are immortal. See Elena Cassin, "The Death of Gods," in *Mortality and Immortality: The Anthropology and Archaeology of Death*, ed. S. C. Humphreys and Helen King (London: Academic Press, 1982), pp. 317–325.

32. That the Leviathan is subject to dissolution is addressed in chapter 29, and in his introduction Hobbes mentions that the dissolution of the sovereign is one of the topics of the book overall.

33. Jacobson, *Pride and Solace*, see pp. 56–67.

34. Compare this point with Sheldon Wolin's reading of Hobbes, wherein Hobbes allays political anxieties so that citizens can attend to economic energies: *Politics and Vision* (Boston: Little, Brown, 1960).

35. George Kateb, "Hobbes and the Irrationality of Politics," *Political Theory* 17, no. 3 (August 1989), 355–391.

36. Hobbes, *Leviathan*, part 2, chap. 30, p. 386.

37. Jan H. Blits, "Hobbesian Fear," *Political Theory* 17, no. 3 (August 1989), 417–431.

38. "His most general power, however, consists in getting us to wonder whether any value can ever justify losing and taking life, even if we choose some other way of valuing life than by reference to an unrenounceable right." Kateb, "Hobbes and the Irrationality of Politics," p. 387.

39. Hannah Arendt, *The Life of the Mind* (New York: Harcourt Brace Jovanovich, 1977), part 2, p. 43.

40. Hannah Arendt, *On Revolution* (New York: Viking, 1962), p. 285.

41. George Kateb, *Hannah Arendt: Politics, Conscience, Evil* (Totowa, N.J.: Rowman and Allanheld, 1984), p. 1.

42. Hannah Arendt, *The Human Condition* (Chicago: University of Chicago Press, 1958), pp. 96–97.

43. Ibid., p. 8.

44. Bonnie Honig contends that Arendt's references to political birthing and re-birthing motifs are metaphorical, distinctly severed from biological being: "But we can be reborn only if we sever the umbilical cord that ties us to the womb of our biological and natural existence." As Honig's book impressively demonstrates elsewhere, such claims of complete severance are difficult to sustain: *Political Theory and the Displacement of Politics* (Ithaca: Cornell University Press, 1993), p. 81.

45. Arendt, *The Human Condition*, p. 9.

46. See also Arendt's discussion of death as a political force in "On Violence," *Between Past and Future: Eight Exercises in Political Thought* (New York: Viking Press, 1968), pp. 164–165. To the extent that she admits here any political importance for death, it is only insofar as the idea of death and mortality prompts the political actor to strive for some kind of deathlessness.

47. Arendt insists on a distinction between "eternity" and "immortality." Politics strives for the latter: "Immortality means endurance in time, deathless life on this earth and in this world as it was given, according to Greek understanding, to nature and the Olympian gods." Ibid., p. 8; cf. p. 55.

48. Arendt tussles with a problem in her notion of politics as self-revelatory public action when she in effect acknowledges that the space of the polis must confront time-lag issues: "the light that illuminates processes of action, and therefore all historical processes, appears only at their end, frequently when all the participants are dead. Action reveals itself fully only to the storyteller, that is, to the backward glance of the historian, who indeed always knows better what it was all about than the participants." Ibid., p. 192. The outcome of revelatory action and speech is "unpredictable," hence the ancients reserved the word *eudaimon* for dead people (p. 192). And thus the heroic Greeks sought a short life and premature death (p. 193).

49. "If left to themselves, human affairs can only follow the law of mortality, which is the most certain and the only reliable law of a life spent between birth and death. It is the faculty of action that interferes with this law because it interrupts the inexorable automatic course of daily life, which in its turn, as we saw, interrupted and interfered with the cycle of the biological life process. The life span of man running toward death would inevitably carry everything human to ruin and destruction if it were not for the faculty of interrupting it and beginning something new, a faculty which is inherent in action like an ever-present reminder that men, though they must die, are not born in order to die but in order to begin." Ibid., p. 246.

50. "The task and potential greatness of mortals lie in their ability to produce things—works and deeds and words—which would deserve to be and, at least to a degree, are at home in the everlastingness, so that through them mortals could find their place in a cosmos where everything is immortal except themselves." Ibid., p. 19.

51. Henry David Thoreau, "Civil Disobedience," in *Henry David Thoreau: Essays, Journals, and Poems*, ed. Dean Flower (Greenwich, Conn.: Fawcett, 1975), p. 116. Note that Arendt dismisses this stand ("Here, as elsewhere, conscience is unpolitical"): Arendt, "Civil Disobedience," in *Crises of the Republic* (New York: Harcourt Brace Jovanovich, 1972), p. 60.

52. "Without this transcendence into a potential earthly immortality, no politics, strictly speaking, no common world and no public realm, is possible." Arendt, *The Human Condition*, p. 55.

53. George Kateb, "Death and Politics: Hannah Arendt's Reflections on the American Constitution," *Social Research* 54, no. 3 (Autumn 1987), 612.

54. Hannah Arendt, "Public Rights and Public Interests," in *Small Comforts for Hard Times*, ed. Michael Mooney and Florian Stuber (New York: Columbia University Press, 1977), p. 106.

55. Kateb, "Death and Politics," p. 616.

56. Friedrich Nietzsche, "Homer's Contest," in *The Portable Nietzsche*, trans. Walter Kaufmann (New York: Penguin, 1959), p. 36.

57. Hanna Pitkin and Sheldon Wolin have both raised various questions about the competitive features of the Arendtian agon. See Hanna Fenichel Pitkin, "Jus-

tice: On Relating Private and Public," in *Hannah Arendt: Critical Essays*, ed. Lewis P. Hinchman and Sandra K. Hinchman (Albany: State University of New York Press, 1994), pp. 261–288; Sheldon Wolin, "Hannah Arendt: Democracy and the Political," in ibid., pp. 289–306.

58. Arendt, *The Human Condition*, p. 41.

59. In *The Human Condition* Arendt cites Nietzsche on promising, and she writes that she regrets that Nietzsche scholars don't relate promising to Nietzsche's concept of "will to power"; yet she fails to emphasize that Nietzsche's analysis of promising and contract in *The Genealogy of Morals* involves an elaborate pre-history of pain and violence: *The Human Condition*, p. 245n.

60. Ironically, Arendt cites Nietzsche contra modern scholars who yearn to incorporate violence into their works. Ibid., pp. 203–204n.

61. Seyla Benhabib writes eloquently about the death purposes to which Arendt puts much of her theorizing: "There is little question that Arendt's thinking on this matter was clouded less by her polis-inspired vision of public space than by her historical memory of Jewish emancipation and the paradoxes it entailed, creating parvenus, pariahs, or total social conformists. . . . And it is these tensions which inspire the method of political theory as storytelling, a form of storytelling which, in Arendt's hands, is transformed into a redemptive narrative, redeeming the memory of the dead, the defeated and the vanquished by making present to us once more their failed hopes, their untrodden paths, and unfulfilled dreams." Benhabib, "Hannah Arendt and the Redemptive Power of Narrative," in *Hannah Arendt: Critical Essays*, ed. Hinchman and Hinchman, p. 131.

62. Elisabeth Young-Bruehl suggests that Arendt emphasized the themes of birth, love, and natality in reaction to Heidegger's focus on death: *Hannah Arendt: For Love of the World* (New Haven: Yale University Press, 1982), p. 76.

63. Pitkin, too, questions Arendt's undue fascination with political immortality given her bloodless conception of political life: "Public life, by contrast, is the quest for secular immortality, the hope of being remembered after one's death so that one's name and fame live on. Yet, given the curious emptiness of content characterizing Arendt's image of the public sphere, it is hard to see why such immortal fame should be so important and attractive. It is one thing to hope for heavenly immortality, but the early immortal fame Arendt has in mind seems no good once one is dead. Why should I care—and care *so much*—about whether my name and deeds will be remembered after I am dead and gone?" Pitkin, "Justice: On Relating Public and Private," pp. 271–272.

64. At the end of *The Order of Things*, Foucault calls for an "analytic of finitude"; and he opens *The Birth of the Clinic* by saying the book is about "space, about language, about death." Michel Foucault, *The Order of Things: An Archaeology of the Human Sciences* (New York: Random, 1970), p. 315; *The Birth of the Clinic: An Archaeology of Medical Perception*, trans. A. M. Sheridan Smith (New York: Pantheon, 1973), p. ix. In the essay "What Is an Author?" Foucault takes up the issue of the relation of writing with death. *The Foucault Reader*, ed. Paul Rabinow (New York: Pantheon, 1984), pp. 101–120.

65. I've omitted from this hasty survey two prominent postwar theorists, namely Carl Schmitt and Leo Strauss, mainly on the grounds that their death work falls mostly within, if by commenting upon, the Hobbesian model. See John P. McCormick, "Fear, Technology, and the State: Carl Schmitt, Leo Strauss, and the Revival of Hobbes in Weimar and National Socialist Germany," *Political Theory* 22, no. 4 (November 1994), 619–652.

66. "Wars were never as bloody as they have been since the nineteenth century, and all things being equal, never before did regimes visit such holocausts on their

own populations." Michel Foucault, *The History of Sexuality*, vol. 1, *An Introduction*, trans. Robert Hurley (New York: Vintage, 1980), pp. 136–137.

67. Jean Baudrillard makes a similar point regarding the camouflaging of death in today's exchange economy, a death drive trying to eliminate death itself: "Today, we have made the vertigo of politics that Benjamin denounces in fascism, its perverse aesthetic enjoyment, into the experience of production at the level of the general system. We produce the experience of a de-politicized, de-ideologised vertigo of the rational administration of things, of endlessly exploding finalities. Death is immanent to political economy, which is why the latter sees itself as immortal." Baudrillard, *Symbolic Exchange and Death*, trans. Iain Hamilton Grant (London: Sage, 1993), p. 186.

68. Foucault, *The History of Sexuality*, 1:143.

69. See James Miller on Foucault's preoccupation with death: *The Passion of Michel Foucault* (New York: Simon and Schuster, 1993).

70. Foucault, "Truth and Power," *The Foucault Reader*, ed. Rabinow, p. 63.

71. I deliberately include passing mention of Derrida in this short survey of those connecting death and politics, since Derrida makes an explicit linkage between the two in his book *Aporias*. Yet I also deliberately withhold a longer treatment of his thesis. In the book he brilliantly raises questions concerning all discourse about death and thereby attests to the indeterminacy of talking about death; and he suggests that an incoherent, unspecific "anthropo-thanatology" is contained in much fundamentalist discourse. Moreover, many deathly presuppositions apparently inform political identities, cultures, nationalisms, border-keeping and boundary enforcement in general—and thereby he politicizes Heidegger's "existentialist" (i.e., nonpolitical) treatment of death. While I appreciate his keen awareness of (and throwing into question) the whirl of connections between death and politics, his project is more about poking holes in what he sees as various death theorists' presumptuousness in speaking and writing about death. He doesn't stick his own neck out, however: Jacques Derrida, *Aporias*, trans. Thomas Dutoit (Stanford: Stanford University Press, 1993). I might also note that in 1952 Kenneth Burke attempted to distinguish among the many vague ways the term *death* is used in writing. See Burke, "Thanatopsis for Critics: A Brief Thesaurus of Deaths and Dyings," *Essays in Criticism* 2 no. 4 (1952), 369–375.

72. Cf. John Bowker, *The Meanings of Death* (Cambridge: Cambridge University Press, 1991).

73. In fact, it could be argued that the theme of death is what brings together so many of the writers associated with deconstructive and poststructural movements; a quick name-dropping survey of prominent death writers reads as a list of today's favorites: Barthes, Bakhtin, Benjamin, Cixous, Blanchot, Bataille, Derrida, de Man, Foucault, Kofman, Kristeva, Lacan, Nancy. See *Death and Representation*, ed. Sarah Webster Goodwin and Elisabeth Bronfen (Baltimore: Johns Hopkins University Press, 1993); and Ronald Schleifer, *Rhetoric and Death: The Language of Modernism and Postmodern Discourse Theory* (Urbana: University of Illinois Press, 1990). For a survey of recent work on death in philosophy, see J. M. Fischer, "Recent Work on Death and the Meaning of Life," *Philosophical Books* 34, no. 2 (April 1993), 65–75; also see F. M. Kamm, *Morality, Mortality* (New York: Oxford University Press, 1993); and Hillel Steiner, *An Essay on Rights* (Cambridge: Blackwell, 1994), pp. 249–261.

74. See William E. Connolly, "Freedom and Resentment," *Identity\Difference: Democratic Negotiations of Political Paradox* (Ithaca: Cornell University Press, 1991),

pp. 16–35; George Kateb, "Thinking about Human Extinction (I): Nietzsche and Heidegger," *Inner Ocean: Individualism and Democratic Culture* (Ithaca: Cornell University Press, 1992), pp. 107–126.

75. See Norman O. Brown, *Life against Death* (New York: Vintage, 1959); Jacques Lacan, "The Function of Language in Psychoanalysis," in *The Language of the Self*, trans. Anthony Wilden (Baltimore: Johns Hopkins University Press, 1968); Richard Boothby, *Death and Desire: Psychoanalytic Theory in Lacan's Return to Freud* (New York: Routledge, 1991); Ellie Ragland, "Lacan, the Death Drive, and the Dream of the Burning Child," in *Death and Representation*, ed. Goodwin and Bronfen, pp. 80–102; Laurence A. Rickels, *Aberrations of Mourning: Writing on German Crypts* (Detroit: Wayne State University Press, 1988).

76. Bronislaw Malinowski, *Magic, Science, and Religion* (London: Faber and West, 1948); Emile Durkheim, *Suicide* (London: Routledge and Kegan Paul, 1952).

77. Robert Hertz, "A Contribution to the Study of the Collective Representation of Death," in *Death and the Right Hand*, trans. R. and C. Needham (New York: Free Press, 1960), pp. 27–86.

78. Philippe Ariès, *Western Attitudes toward Death: From the Middle Ages to the Present*, trans. Patricia M. Ranum (Baltimore: Johns Hopkins University Press, 1974). Another famous historian of death is Jacques Choron; see his *Death and Western Thought* (New York: Collier, 1963).

79. Charles O. Jackson, *Passing: The American Vision of Death* (Westport, Conn.: Greenwood, 1977); Elisabeth Kübler-Ross, *On Death and Dying* (New York: Macmillan, 1969); R. M. Harmer, *The High Cost of Dying* (New York: Collier, 1963); Evelyn Waugh, *The Loved One* (London: Chapman and Hall, 1948); Herman Feifel, ed., *The Meaning of Death* (New York: McGraw Hill, 1959); Jessica Mitford, *The American Way of Death* (London: Hutchinson, 1963); Geoffrey Gorer, *Death, Grief, and Mourning* (New York: Doubleday, 1965).

80. Arnold van Gennep, *The Rites of Passage* (Chicago: University of Chicago Press, 1960).

81. James George Frazer, *The Golden Bough* (London: Macmillan, 1890); *The Belief in Immortality and the Worship of the Dead* (London: Macmillan, 1913).

82. Victor Turner, *The Forest of Symbols* (Ithaca: Cornell University Press, 1967); Jane Harrison, *Themis* (Cambridge: Cambridge University Press, 1912); *Death and the Regeneration of Life*, ed. Maurice Bloch and J. Parry (Cambridge: Cambridge University Press, 1982); Mircea Eliade, *The Myth of the Eternal Return, or, Cosmos and History*, trans. Willard R. Trask (Princeton: Princeton University Press, 1971); Mary Douglas, *Purity and Pollution* (London: Routledge and Kegan Paul, 1966).

83. "It is no coincidence that we have chosen to concentrate on the rituals of death; in our view they provide one of the clearest windows on Chinese society." *Death Ritual in Late Imperial and Modern China*, ed. James L. Watson and Evelyn S. Rawski (Berkeley: University of California Press, 1988), p. xv.

84. See especially Richard Huntington and Peter Metcalf, *Celebrations of Death: The Anthropology of Mortuary Ritual* (Cambridge: Cambridge University Press, 1979).

85. Cf. Gary L. Ebersole, *Ritual Poetry and the Politics of Death in Early Japan* (Princeton: Princeton University Press, 1989), pp. 266–271.

86. Huntington and Metcalf, *Celebrations of Death*, p. 1; cited in Bowker, *The Meanings of Death*, p. 20.

87. Douglas N. Walton, *On Defining Death: An Analytic Study of the Concept of Death in Philosophy and Medical Ethics* (Montreal: McGill-Queen's University Press, 1979).

88. Sigmund Freud made the same plaint: "The notion of 'natural death' is quite foreign to primitive races; they attribute every death that occurs among them to the influence of an enemy or of an evil spirit. We must therefore turn to biology in order to test the validity of the belief. If we do so, we may be astonished to find how little agreement there is among biologists on the subject of natural death and in fact that the whole concept of death melts away under their hands." Freud, *Beyond the Pleasure Principle*, trans. James Strachey (New York: W. W. Norton, 1961), p. 39.

89. Baudrillard insists that we distinguish between a biological linkage between sex and death and a symbolic linkage: *Symbolic Exchange and Death*, pp. 190–191, n. 23.

90. Beth Ann Bassein, *Women and Death: Linkages in Western Thought and Literature* (Westport, Conn.: Greenwood Press, 1984); Christine Di Stefano, *Configurations of Masculinity*, p. 158; Bloch and Parry, "Introduction," in *Death and the Regeneration of Life*, ed. Bloch and Parry, pp. 1–44; and Maurice Bloch, "Death, Women and Power," in *Death and the Regeneration of Life*, ed. Block and Parry, pp. 211–230.

91. George Wald, "The Origin of Death," in *The End of Life*, ed. John D. Roslansky (Amsterdam: North-Holland, 1973), pp. 3–20; Alfred G. Killilea, *The Politics of Being Mortal* (Lexington: University Press of Kentucky, 1988), p. 52; Georges Bataille, *Death and Sensuality: A Study of Eroticism and the Taboo* (New York: Walker, 1962). See also Jacques Lacan, *The Four Fundamental Concepts of Psycho-Analysis*, ed. Jacques-Alain Miller, trans. Alan Sheriden (New York: Norton, 1978), pp. 150, 177.

92. See Jonathan Parry, "Sacrificial Death and the Necrophagous Ascetic," in *Death and the Regeneration of Life*, ed. Bloch and Parry, pp. 74–110.

93. Ivan A. Lopatin, *The Cult of the Dead among the Natives of the Amur Basin* (The Hague: Mouton, 1960), pp. 26–27.

94. See S. C. Humphreys, "Death and Time," in *Mortality and Immortality*, ed. Humphreys and King, esp. pp. 271–272.

95. Cf. Fred Feldman, *Confrontations with the Reaper: A Philosophical Study of the Nature and Value of Death* (New York: Oxford University Press, 1992). Several authors in Goodwin and Bronfen's *Death and Representation* collection attest to the difficulties of (and yet necessities for) *representing* death.

96. Sigmund Freud, "Our Attitude towards Death," *The Standard Edition of the Complete Psychological Works of Sigmund Freud*, ed. James Strachey, vol. 14 (London: Hogarth, 1964).

97. Ludwig Wittgenstein, *Tractatus Logico-philosophicus*, trans. D. F. Pears and B. F. McGuinnes (New York: Humanities Press, 1961), 6.4311.

98. Quotes from La Rochefoucauld, Choron, and Becker are from Alfred G. Killilea, *The Politics of Being Mortal* (Lexington: University Press of Kentucky, 1988), pp. 14–31; Jacques Choron, *Death and Modern Man* (New York: Collier, 1964); Ernest Becker, *The Denial of Death* (New York: Free Press, 1973).

99. Foucault, *The History of Sexuality*, vol. 1.

100. Greil Marcus, *Dead Elvis: A Chronicle of a Cultural Obsession* (New York: Doubleday, 1991).

101. Lopatin, *The Cult of the Dead among the Natives of the Amur Basin*, pp. 35–37.

102. Herbert Marcuse, "The Ideology of Death," in *The Meaning of Death*, ed. Herman Feifel (New York: McGraw-Hill, 1959), pp. 68–70.

103. "Recognition that life is short encourages the self to contribute to the crys-

tallization of its own individuality." Connolly, *Identity\Difference*, p. 17; cf. pp. 164–171.
104. Although I find his book extremely thoughtful and useful, Alfred Killilea tends to use death in this way. He contends that it is a mistake to denigrate death, and if we revalue the value of death, then, he concludes, we would be able to confirm the dignity of human beings, we would better appreciate community, and we would foster a greater participatory ethic in politics. Killilea, *The Politics of Being Mortal*.
105. Or, to the extent that one views society as more or less individuated, one looks to van Gennep—and his rituals of separation and incorporation—for resolving the individual into larger societal and political orders: *The Rites of Passage*.
106. For a fine attempt to extend such sociological analysis to contemporary liberalism, see Michael C. Kearl and Anoel Rinaldi, "The Political Uses of the Dead as Symbols in Contemporary Civil Religions," *Social Forces* 61, no. 3 (March 1993), 693–708.
107. Ernst Kantorowicz, *The King's Two Bodies: A Study in Medieval Political Theory* (Princeton: Princeton University Press, 1957), p. 394.
108. Cf. James J. Farrell, *Inventing the American Way of Death, 1830–1920* (Philadelphia: Temple University Press, 1980).
109. W. Lloyd Warner, *The Living and Dead* (New Haven: Yale University Press, 1959); Vanderlyn R. Pine, *Caretaker of the Dead: The American Funeral Director* (New York: Irvington, 1975).
110. Mitford, *The American Way of Death*; Geoffrey Gorer, "The Pornography of Death," *Encounter* 5 (October 1955), 49–52; Christopher Lasch, *The Culture of Narcissism* (New York: Norton, 1978).
111. Jackson, *Passing*, p. 232.
112. Cf. Garry Wills's account of Edward Everett, Emerson, and the rural cemetery movement in America: *Lincoln at Gettysburg: The Words That Remade America* (New York: Simon and Schuster, 1992).
113. Philippe Ariès, "The Reversal of Death: Changes in Attitudes toward Death in Western Societies," in *Death in America*, ed. David E. Stannard (Philadelphia: University of Pennsylvania Press, 1974), pp. 134–158.
114. Derek Humphrey, *Final Exit: The Practicalities of Self-Deliverance and Assisted Suicide for the Dying* (Eugene, Ore.: Hemlock Society, 1991); Sherwin B. Nuland, *How We Die: Reflections on Life's Final Chapter* (New York: Knopf, 1994).
115. Max Weber, *Economy and Society*, vol. 1, ed. Guenther Roth and Claus Wittich (Berkeley: University of California Press, 1978), p. 405; for an application of Weber's idea of "legitimate" property transactions and their relation to death, see Jack Goody, *Death, Property and the Ancestors: A Study of the Mortuary Customs of the Lodagaa of West Africa* (Stanford: Stanford University Press, 1962), esp. 304–327.
116. Orlando Patterson, *Slavery and Social Death* (Cambridge: Harvard University Press, 1982).
117. Derrida, *Aporias*, p. 24 and passim.
118. Following Maurice Freedman, Humphreys distinguishes between ancestor worship and memorialism; "Death and Time," pp. 269–270.
119. Jean Baudrillard, *America*, trans. Chris Turner (London: Verso, 1989), p. 51; Ariès, *Western Attitudes toward Death*, pp. 78–82.
120. Thomas Paine, *Rights of Man* (1791) (New York: Viking Press, 1984), p. 42.
121. See Bloch, "Introduction," p. 11.
122. Andrew Carnegie, "The Gospel of Wealth," in *The Gospel of Wealth, and Other Timely Essays*, ed. Edward C. Kirkland (Cambridge: Belknap Press, 1962), p. 29.

123. Aristotle, *Nicomachean Ethics*, 1100a–1101b.

124. Jean-Jacques Rousseau, *The First and Second Discourses*, ed. and trans. Victor Gourevitch (New York: Harper and Row, 1986), p. 139.

125. There are a number of return narratives in "non-Western" sources (Quetzalcóatl, Seraphis, Mithra, Krishna, Thoth, Isis and Osirus, Tammuz and Ishtar, Baal, Lo Pah, Kubaiko, Nishan, Izanami and Izanagi, Mataora and Nuvarahu, Hiku, Malekulan, Le-Heu-Hen), as well as a great number of Western descents besides the Orphic (Bacchus, Dionysus, Heracles, Persephone, Theseus, Aphrodite, Demeter, Odysseus, Lemminkainen).

126. On the Orphic tradition, see Raymond J. Clark, *Catabasis: Vergil and the Wisdom-Tradition* (Amsterdam: B. R. Grüner, 1979); Charles Segal, *Orpheus: The Myth of the Poet* (Baltimore: Johns Hopkins University Press, 1989); Ake Hultkrantz, *The North American Indian Orpheus Tradition* (Stockholm: Caslon Press, 1957), pp. 183–206; W. K. C. Guthrie, *Orpheus and Greek Religion* (New York: W. W. Norton, 1966); Vittorio D. Macchioro, *From Orpheus to Paul: A History of Orphism* (New York: Henry Holt, 1930); John Block Friedman, *Orpheus in the Middle Ages* (Cambridge: Harvard University Press, 1970); John Warden, ed., *Orpheus: The Metamorphoses of a Myth*; John Evan Seery, *Political Returns: Irony in Politics and Theory from Plato to the Antinuclear Movement* (Boulder, Colo.: Westview, 1990), chap. 1; Jean Paul Sartre, *Black Orpheus*, trans. S. W. Allen (Paris: Présence africaine, 1963); Robert Garland, *The Greek Way of Death* (Ithaca: Cornell University Press, 1985), p. 150; Alice K. Turner, *The History of Hell* (New York: Harcourt Brace, 1993).

127. Kenneth Burke writes that no one can "write of death from an immediate experience of it, the imaging of death necessarily involves images not directly belonging to it. . . . [It lies]beyond the realm of such images as the living body knows." "Thanatopsis for Critics," pp. 369–75; quoted in Goodwin and Bronfen, "Introduction," in *Death and Representation*, ed. Goodwin and Bronfen, p. 4.

128. "Nothing is told us about Sisyphus in the underworld. Myths are made for the imagination to breathe life into them." Albert Camus, *The Myth of Sisyphus and Other Essays*, trans. Justin O'Brien (New York: Vintage, 1955), p. 89.

129. Richard Rorty, "Robustness: A Reply to Jean Bethke Elshtain," in *The Politics of Irony: Essays in Self-Betrayal*, ed. Daniel W. Conway and John E. Seery (New York: St. Martin's Press, 1992), pp. 219–223.

130. Richard Rorty, *Contingency, Irony, and Solidarity* (Cambridge: Cambridge University Press, 1989), p. 195.

131. Harold Bloom, *The Anxiety of Influence* (New York: Oxford University Press, 1973), p. 80; quoted in Rorty, *Contingency, Irony, and Solidarity*, p. 24n.

132. Rorty, *Contingency, Irony, and Solidarity*, p. 24n.

133. Aristophanes, *The Wasps, The Poet and the Women, The Frogs*, trans. David Barrett (New York: Penguin, 1964), p. 208.

134. Sebastian de Grazia, *Machiavelli in Hell* (Princeton: Princeton University Press, 1989), p. 320.

135. Niccolò Machiavelli, "Letter to Vettori," *The Chief Works and Others*, trans. Allan Gilbert, 3 vols. (Durham: Duke University Press, 1965), 2:927–931.

136. Ibid., p. 929.

137. De Grazi, *Machiavelli in Hell*, p. 340.

138. On the need for *poesis*, see Daniel W. Conway, "Parastrategesis; or, Rhetoric for Decadents," *Philosophy and Rhetoric* 27, no. 3 (1994), 179–201.

139. Laurence A. Rickels locates the cult of death and theory in "California," in *The Case of California* (Baltimore: Johns Hopkins University Press, 1991).

140. "Thus, even though theorists who call themselves 'contractarians' have all supposedly begun from the same reflective starting point—namely, what people could 'agree to'—these differences and disagreements among people who are supposedly in the same philosophical camp show that contractarians are united not by a common philosophical theory but by a common *image*. Philosophers hate to admit it, but sometimes they work from pictures rather than ideas." Jean Hampton, "Feminist Contractarianism," in *A Mind of One's Own: Feminist Essays on Reason and Objectivity*, ed. L. Antony and C. Witt (Boulder, Colo.: Westview, 1992), p. 232.

141. See Allan Bloom's critique of Rawls on this score in *Giants and Dwarfs: Essays 1960–1990* (New York: Simon and Schuster, 1990), p. 323.

142. There could be yet another reason: It could be a bad career move. Terrell Carver has pointed out to me that Ludwig Feuerbach published a book on death and it cost him his job and ruined his career. See Feuerbach, *Thoughts on Death and Immortality*, trans. James A. Massey (Berkeley: University of California Press, 1980).

143. John Adams expresses this down-to-earth view of politics: "A death bed, it is said, shows the emptiness of titles. That may be. [However] . . . shall laws and government, which regulate sublunary things, be neglected because they appear baubles at the hour of death?" "Discourses on Davila," *The Works of John Adams*, ed. Charles Francis Adams (Boston: Little, Brown, 1850–1856), vol. 6, p. 242; cited in Arendt, *The Life of the Mind*, part 1, p. 162.

144. Arendt, "Civil Disobedience," p. 62; "Truth and Politics," in her *Between Past and Future*, p. 228.

145. Aristotle, *Protreptikos*, B43, ed. Ingemar Düring (Frankfurt: n.p., 1969); cited in Arendt, *Life of the Mind*, part 1, p. 84. But Arendt, again dismissive of any real embrace of death, tends to read this remark in the way that she reads Kant's *Fiat justicia, et pereat mundus*, namely, as part tongue-in-cheek, rhetorical, merely metaphorical.

146. See Michel Foucault, "About the Beginning of the Hermeneutics of the Self," *Political Theory* 21, no. 2 (May 1993), 198–227.

147. I much appreciate a countertendency toward ironical self-subversion that sometimes sneaks into the Christian tradition, a strain that runs from Augustine to Dante to Cervantes. See John Freccero, *Dante: The Poetics of Conversion* (Cambridge: Harvard University Press, 1986).

2. The Cave

1. This chapter extends and refashions a reading of the *Republic* that I presented in "Spelunkers of the World, Unite!" in *The Politics of Irony: Essays in Self-Betrayal*, ed. Daniel W. Conway and John E. Seery (New York: St. Martin's, 1992), pp. 7–29.

2. Gregory Vlastos, *Socrates: Ironist and Moral Philosopher* (Ithaca: Cornell University Press, 1991).

3. G. W. F. Hegel, *Lectures on the History of Philosophy*, vol. 1, trans. E. S. Haldane and Frances H. Simson (London: Routledge and Kegan Paul, 1974); Hegel, *The Philosophy of Right*, trans. T. M. Knox (Oxford: Clarendon Press, 1952).

4. Hegal, *Lectures on the History of Philosophy*, vol. 1, p. 386.

5. Ibid., pp. 373, 411; cf. G. W. F. Hegel, *The Philosophy of History*, trans. J. Sibree (New York: Dover, 1956), p. 269.

6. I have consulted and cross-checked numerous translations of all Platonic dialogues under discussion in this chapter, and have settled upon these translations to present my case: Hugh Tredennick's *Apology* in *The Collected Dialogues of Plato*, ed. Edith Hamilton and Huntington Cairns (Princeton: Princeton University Press, 1961); *Phaedo* in *Four Texts on Socrates*, trans. Thomas G. West and Grace Starry West (Ithaca: Cornell University Press, 1984); and *Plato: The Republic*, ed. and trans. Desmond Lee (New York: Penguin, 1974).

7. See West and West's note on *timasthai*. The evident play upon value or price could be read as Socrates' way of ironizing his sophistic opponents. *Four Texts on Socrates*, p. 90, n. 66.

8. Ibid., p. 95, n. 79.

9. West and West point out these four poets are mentioned in the same order in Aristophanes' *Frogs*, with an emphasis there on their respective benefit to humankind. Ibid., p. 96, n.81.

10. Friedrich Nietzsche, *The Gay Science*, trans. Walter Kaufmann (New York: Vintage, 1974), p. 272.

11. Friedrich Nietzsche, *Twilight of the Idols*, in *The Portable Nietzsche*, trans. Walter Kaufmann (New York: Penguin, 1959), p. 479.

12. See Friedrich Nietzsche, *Birth of Tragedy*, trans. Walter Kaufmann (New York: Vintage Books, 1967), pp. 103–104.

13. Ibid., p. 18.

14. C. D. C. Reeve also discounts the importance of irony in the *Apology*. See his *Socrates in the Apology: An Essay on Plato's Apology of Socrates* (Indianapolis: Hackett Publishing, 1989).

15. Michel Foucault, Collège de France lecture, February 15, 1984, trans. Michael Behrent; cited in James Miller, *The Passion of Michel Foucault* (New York: Simon and Schuster, 1993), pp. 461–462, n. 11, n. 15; for a transcript in English, see Thomas Flynn, "Foucault as Parrhesiast: His Last Course at the Collège de France (1984)," in *The Final Foucault*, ed. James Bernauer and David Rasmussen (Cambridge: Cambridge University Press, 1988), pp. 102–118; see also Foucault, "About the Beginnings of the Hermeneutics of the Self," *Political Theory* 21, no. 2 (May 1993), 198–227.

16. "Throughout the dialogue the invisibility of *noeta* is related by way of a pun to Hades": Jacob Klein, *A Commentary on Plato's Meno* (Chapel Hill: University of North Carolina Press, 1965), p. 137.

17. Cf. Burger's reading of the *Phaedo*. Burger deftly views the dialogue not as a "treatise" but as a "conversation," and as an ironic one at that; and she nicely challenges a conventional reading of Platonism; but in the end she views Plato's written dialogue as reinforcing a literalist *logos*, which, to my mind, makes her reading too close to a traditional Platonism. Ronna Burger, *The Phaedo: A Platonic Labyrinth* (New Haven: Yale University Press, 1984).

18. For a homoerotically affirmative reading of these last words to Crito, see Eva C. Keuls, "Socrates' Last Words as a Phallic Joke," *The Reign of the Phallus: Sexual Politics in Ancient Athens* (Berkeley: University of California Press, 1985), pp. 79–82.

19. Sigmund Freud writes: "Even in the early Babylon cult, god is 'the excrement of Hell,' Mammon = ilu manman." And he explains in a footnote that "Mammon is Babylonian Manman, another name of Nergal, the god of the underworld." See Freud, "Character and Anal Eroticism," in *Collected Papers*, vol. 2 (London: Hogarth Press, 1953), pp. 49, 49–50, n. 3.

20. Alexander Nehamas, "Socratic Reflections: Echoes and Images, from Plato and Xenophon to Nietzsche and Foucault," Sather Lectures, University of California, Berkeley, March 17, 1993 (University of California Press, forthcoming).
21. Luce Irigaray presents a lively alternative reading of the deathliness of *The Republic.* With a bit of interpretive license (for instance, she assumes that the cave dwellers' genitals all face the same direction, and thus their unmarked sex must be male), she claims that the cave myth is a male-hysterical myth about the womb, and thus it is a myth about male rebirthing; and it is also a death-cave. The holes, cracks, tears, and long passages suggest the dark presence of vaginas and hymens. Throughout, the text reveals an anxiety about feminine otherness, and male regeneration is an attempt to recover doubleness in a way that erases the feminine and allows a return to all-male sameness. See Luce Irigaray, "Plato's Hysteria," *Speculum of the Other Woman,* trans. Gillian C. Gill (Ithaca: Cornell University Press, 1985), pp. 243–365. Blanchot is another writer who suggests a strong reading of the death imagery of the *Republic.* See Maurice Blanchot, *The Writing of the Disaster,* trans. Ann Smock (Lincoln: University of Nebraska Press, 1986).
22. Eric Voegelin, *Plato and Aristotle,* vol. 3 of *Order and History* (Baton Rouge: Louisiana State University Press, 1966), p. 53.
23. Voegelin cites here K. Kérenyi in K. Kérenyi and C. G. Jung, *Essays on a Science of Mythology,* trans. R. F. C. Hull (New York: Pantheon, 1949), p. 164. See also Alexander Sesonske, "Plato's Apology: *Republic* I," in *Plato's Republic: Interpretation and Criticism,* ed. Alexander Sesonske (Belmont, Calif.: Wadsworth Publishing, 1966), pp. 40–47.
24. Socrates' underworldly concerns are parodied by Aristophanes in *The Clouds.* Students at the Thinkery are bent over, staring at the ground, in an attempt to study phenomena under the earth.
25. Connop Thirlwall, "On the Irony of Sophocles," in *The Philological Museum,* vol. 2 (Cambridge: J. Smith, Printer, 1833), pp. 483–537.
26. Julia Annas, *Introduction to Plato's Republic* (Oxford: Clarendon Press, 1981), p. 18.
27. Sesonske similarly detects Plato's irony in the opening book of the *Republic:* "Plato's Apology: *Republic* I," pp. 40–47.
28. Jacques Derrida, "Plato's Pharmacy," *Disseminations,* trans. Barbara Johnson (Chicago: University of Chicago Press, 1981), pp. 61–172.
29. "Like [Harry] Berger (and Stanley Rosen), then, I read Plato in opposition to Derrida not as a metaphysical dogmatist but as a kind of deconstructionist *avant la lettre,* a cunning writer fully alive to the doubleness of his rhetoric who embraces *différance* and who actively courts in his writing an effect of undecidability." David M. Halperin, "Plato and the Erotics of Narrativity," in *Oxford Studies in Ancient Philosophy: Methods of Interpreting Plato and his Dialogues,* ed. Julia Annas, James C. Klagge and Nicholas D. Smith (Clarendon Press: Oxford, 1992), p. 118.
30. Friedrich Schlegel, "On Incomprehensibility," *Friedrich Schlegel's Lucinde and the Fragments,* trans. Peter Firchow (Minneapolis: University of Minnesota Press, 1971), p. 267.
31. See Charles L. Griswold, Jr.'s excellent discussion of the irony of Plato's written text: *Self-Knowledge in Plato's Phaedrus* (New Haven: Yale University Press, 1986).
32. A few commentators have recently attempted to venture beyond Strauss's dramatic reading of Platonic irony. See Drew A. Hyland, "Taking the Longer

Road: The Irony of Plato's *Republic*," *Revue de Metaphysique et de Morale*, 93, no. 3 (July–Sept. 1988), 317–335; Charles L. Griswold, Jr., "Plato's Metaphilosophy: Why Plato Wrote Dialogues," in *Platonic Writings, Platonic Readings*, ed. Charles L. Griswold, Jr. (New York: Routledge, 1988), pp. 143–167.

33. I do not mean to play into Derrida's hand here, as if I were oblivious to his elaborate critique of "logocentrism." My position rather is that Derrida shares (maybe even borrows without proper attribution) Plato's concern that readers continue to pose questions of texts and not presume that written meaning is stable and unitary. Derrida, on my account, has tried to exaggerate the distance between himself and Plato precisely because their projects are so similar. What else can explain Derrida's failure to address Plato's irony? Cf. Albert Cook, "Dialectic, Irony, and Myth in Plato's *Phaedrus*," *American Journal of Philology* 106, no. 4 (Winter 1985), 427–441.

34. First, there is the evident paradox that the *Republic* is a *written* dialogue. Then, several references raise, at least implicitly, the question of writing: the letters of the individual and politics (368d, 402a); the baskets of instruction books by Orpheus and Musaeus (364e); the sketch of a city in words (369a); the question of the writings of the poets (e.g., 380a).

35. For the connection to the Aeschylus myth (and much more), I am indebted to Eva T. H. Brann and her fabulous essay, "The Music of the *Republic*," *St. John's Review* 29, no. 1, 2 (1989–1990), 1–103. Brann also mentions irony in connection with the descent motif and in general observes playful aspects of the *Republic*, all of which help us "to remind ourselves that while Socrates is speaking to Glaucon, the dialogue itself is speaking to us" (p. 96). Where we depart is that she emphasizes the esoteric music of the *Republic*, and I emphasize the mock-visual aspects; she traces the *katabaino* moments mainly to Hermes' descent, whereas I tend to emphasize Orpheus's descent.

36. *Gorgias* 524d.

37. As mentioned above, in addition to the opening Pireaus scene, the cave allegory, and the myth of Er, the ring of Gyges (359d), the divided line (511b), and the helmet of Hades (612b) are *katabaino* stories. It might also be noted that the myth of the metals features a descent into a poetic underground in order to receive vital political orientation. This Phoenician tale (413c) probably refers to Hesiod's *Works and Days*.

38. 521c, 534d.

39. The Straussian "ironic" reading of the Republic, which regards the pursuit of justice in this world as a joke, seems to make far too much of this one passage (517a–b) as the basis for an interpretation of the entire book.

40. Clearly Plato conflates Aeschylus's cave with Pythagorean imagery. Brann contends that Socrates in *Philebus* (16c) intimates that Pythagoras is the true Prometheus.

41. As mentioned above, it should be noted (but I haven't noticed this observation in any of my reading about the famous censorship of the poets) that the banned poetry in the *Republic* is poetry primarily about death and stories about Hades (386–388c). Socrates says that people should instead commend Hades and not fear death, because otherwise people will not be sufficiently dedicated to fighting. This strikes me as another gentle ironization of people who are motivated mainly on the basis of a consequentialist ethic.

42. Here I think Plato has already anticipated and responded to Foucault's themes of the "death of the author" and the disciplining power of the prison. Plato's ironic play on the Pythagorean notion of imprisonment and bodily death

makes Foucault's twentieth-century insight seem somewhat pedestrian and belated.

43. See Lee's excellent notes on visual imagery: *Plato: The Republic*, pp. 312, n. 2, p. 314 n. 1, p. 315 n. 4. James Robert Peters warns against attending exclusively to visual imagery, but I don't think he considers the possibility that the visual devices can serve an ironic reading: "Reason and Passion in Plato's *Republic*," *Ancient Philosophy* 9, no. 2 (Fall 1989), 173–188.

44. The contemporary critique of "gazing" and "ocularcentrism" seems to preclude an appreciation of Plato's irony. See Martin Jay, "In the Empire of the Gaze: Foucault and the Denigration of Vision in 20th Century French Thought," in *Postmodernism: ICA Documents*, ed. Lisa Appignanesi (London: Free Association, 1989), pp. 49–87.

45. Brann points out that Plato never supplies us with an explicit account of the Good. "The Music of the *Republic*," pp. 50, 56.

46. Ibid., p. 48.

47. Socrates mentions that fighting over shadows is the cause of civil war (520d), and later he refers to Helen of Troy as a phantom (586c). Elsewhere he likens the pursuit of wealth as a two-dimensional shadow (587d).

48. Jowett senses irony in this analogy: *Plato's Republic: The Greek Text*, ed. B. Jowett and Lewis Campbell, 3 vols. (Oxford: Clarendon Press, 1894), 3:322.

49. Those who asseverate that Plato privileges "mind over body" seem to be reading this passage as if it contained no hint of irony. Cf. John Clardy Kelley, "Virtue and Inwardness in Plato's *Republic*," *Ancient Philosophy* 9, no. 2 (Fall 1989), 173–188.

50. 522e–523b. "Do you *see* what I *see* in this learning?" "It seems to be one of the studies we're *looking for*." "Observe how I distinguish the things that lead up there from the ones that do not and agree or disagree so we'll *clearly see*." "*Show* them." "I will if you *watch*." (My italics.)

51. Jowett senses irony also in this passage: *Plato's Republic: The Greek Text*, 3:330.

52. Later (533e), Socrates says that they shouldn't haggle over this word for the faculty of understanding.

53. Plato makes a similar shift from two-dimensional to three-dimensional figures at 587e. For a discussion of this passage, see my *Political Returns: Irony in Politics and Theory from Plato to the Antinuclear Movement* (Boulder, Colo.: Westview, 1990), p. 127.

54. Jowett points out that those who conceive "nobly" of things above are said in the *Timaeus* (91d) to be destined hereafter to enter on another life in the form of birds: *Plato's Republic: The Greek Text*, 3:339.

55. Too often commentators presume that this antivisibility motif serves merely to enforce a distinction between the sensible versus intelligible worlds, as if the intelligible exists in some straightforward sense. While the irony of the dialogue, to my mind, detracts from such an interpretation, its function is not simply to subvert or mock entirely a visionary glance (as some readers of irony would have it).

56. See my *Political Returns*, pp. 124–128.

57. On Hades, see especially Robert Garland, *The Greek Way of Death* (Ithaca: Cornell University Press, 1985), pp. 48–76, 149–160.

58. Karl Marx, *Karl Marx, Friedrich Engels: Collected Works* (Moscow: Progress Publishers, 1975), 1:489–500.

59. See Garland on Er's story; *The Greek Way of Death*, pp. 100–101.

60. Note that all three of the major *katabaino* scenes involve "spectacles" (327b, 515d, 619e). As I argue in *Political Returns*, what unifies these spectacles is not the visual imagery of up or downward worlds but, rather, the concept of returning to the political world: pp. 121–122, 139–140.
61. "What is especially striking about this parallel between the journeys to Hades by Odysseus and Socrates is that in both cases the journeys seem to be required before a city can be founded. Put another way, the foundation of a city, the most complete human association for the Greeks, the most complete expression of Greek life and culture, requires the founder to have journeyed to the 'city of the dead.'" Klonoski similarly sees Socrates' descent into the Pireaus as a "re-performance" of the Homeric journey to Hades. Richard J. Klonoski, "The Preservation of Homeric Tradition: Heroic Re-Performance in the Republic and the Odyssey," *Clio* 22, no. 3 (Spring 1993), 251–271.
62. If I seem to be borrowing an esoteric/exoteric distinction as a rough basis for interpretation, then I want to recast that distinction in terms of choice (cf. 617e) rather than one's natural endowment of *nous*. Hence if an elite is formed, it is a self-selecting elite: Everyone in principle has the possibility of making such a choice (cf. 518d).
63. Certainly the passage (619d) on the soul who came from a well-governed state (which owed its goodness to habit and custom and not philosophy) would militate against such a conclusion. Also the fact that the souls represent a great variety of lives overall, rather than conforming to a single mold.

3. The Tomb

1. A. N. Wilson, *Jesus* (London: Sinclair-Stevenson, 1992), p. vii.
2. Niccolò Machiavelli, *The Prince*, trans. Allan H. Gilbert (New York: Hendricks House, 1964), pp. 149–150.
3. A few notable works: John H. Yoder, *The Politics of Jesus: Vicit Agnus Noster* (Grand Rapids, Mich.: William B. Eerdman's Publishing, 1972); Jean-Marie Paupert, *The Politics of the Gospel* (New York: Holt, 1969); Reinhold Niebuhr, *Interpretation of Christian Ethics* (New York: Harper, 1935); Jacques Maritain, *Man and the State* (Chicago: University of Chicago Press, 1951); Reginald Stackhouse, *Christianity and Politics* (London: English Universities Press, 1966); Richard J. Cassidy, *Jesus, Politics, and Society: A Study of Luke's Gospel* (Maryknoll, N.Y.: Orbis, 1978); *Jesus and the Politics of His Day*, ed. Ernst Mammel and C. F. D. Moule (Cambridge: Cambridge University Press, 1984); *Political Issues in Luke—Acts*, ed. Richard J. Cassidy and Philip J. Scharper (Maryknoll, N.Y.: Orbis, 1983); Glenn E. Tinder, *The Political Meaning of Christianity* (Baton Rouge: Louisiana State University Press, 1989).
4. See Hendrikus Boers, *Who Was Jesus? The Historical Jesus and the Synoptic Gospels* (San Francisco: Harper and Row, 1989); and John Dominic Crossan, *The Historical Jesus: The Life of a Mediterranean Jewish Peasant* (San Francisco: Harper, 1991); Robert W. Funk, Roy W. Hoover, and the Jesus Seminar, *The Five Gospels: The Search for the Authentic Words of Jesus* (New York: Macmillan, 1993); Raymond E. Brown, *The Death of the Messiah: From Gethsemane to the Grave*, vols. 1 and 2 (New York: Doubleday, 1994); John P. Meier, *A Marginal Jew: Rethinking the Historical Jesus* (New York: Doubleday, 1991). Note that Meier distinguishes between the "real" Jesus and the "historical" Jesus; the latter, for Meier, is the Jesus found through texts and documentary evidence.

5. Burton L. Mack presents curiously bold and sweeping statements discounting the Gospel's and later accounts of Jesus' life and death on the basis of nine pages of supposed ur-texts confined to Jesus' "sayings." Out of those nine pages Mack extracts 275 pages of commentary. He claims, among other things, that Jesus did not seek to be a messiah, and that his death was not divine, tragic, or saving in any way: *The Lost Gospel: The Book of Q and Christian Origins* (San Francisco: Harper, 1993).

6. Compare Wilson's "historical" debunking of resurrection with Derrett's account. Wilson, *Jesus*; J. Duncan M. Derrett, *The Anastasis: The Resurrection of Jesus as an Historical Event* (Warwickshire, England: P. Drinkwater, 1982).

7. John Shelby Spong, *Born of a Woman: A Bishop Rethinks the Birth of Jesus* (New York: Harper, 1992).

8. Meier discounts this idea on the grounds that the virginal conception is, according to the texts, performed by God's spirit: *A Marginal Jew*, pp. 221–222.

9. Mary Daly, *Gyn/Ecology: The Metaethics of Radical Feminism* (Boston: Beacon Press, 1978), pp. 83–89.

10. Oscar Cullmann, *The State in the New Testament* (New York: Charles Scribner's Sons, 1956), 8–23.

11. In his attempt to focus relentlessly on Jesus qua man, Wilson misses, I think, the heart of Dostoyevsky's interpretation: "The profundity of Jesus's Temptations in the Wilderness is quite lost if we imagine that the Devil is whispering into the ear of a divine being. . . . By his persistent 'If-you-are-the-Son-of-God' questions in the Gospel accounts of the Temptations, Satan is not testing the idea of Jesus's divinity. He is testing the kind of man that *Jesus* is": *Jesus*, pp. 109–110.

12. Max Weber, *Economy and Society*, ed. Guenther Roth and Claus Wittich (Berkeley: University of California Press, 1978), pp. 498–499.

13. Ibid., p. 633.

14. Ibid., p. 592.

15. Jay Haley, *The Power Tactics of Jesus Christ and Other Essays* (Rockville, Md.: The Triangle Press, 1986).

16. Mark 6:5; see Weber, *Economy and Society*, p. 564.

17. Wilson points out that in the Gospels Jesus is always particularly rude to and about his mother: *Jesus*, p. 86.

18. Weber, *Economy and Society*, p. 510.

19. Wilson insists that the dates are all wrong for the Last Supper to be a Passover seder, but his claim that the meal was just a meal among friends seems a bit contortionist in the attempt to disassociate Jesus the man from the Pauline myths: *Jesus*, pp. 191–206.

20. This parable is discussed in Julia Kristeva, *Powers of Horror: An Essay on Abjection*, trans. Leon S. Roudiez (New York: Columbia University Press, 1987), p. 122.

21. Schweitzer contends, based on Mark, that Jesus spoke the words "this is my body" while the disciples were eating and the words "this is my blood" after they had all drunk of the cup. Albert Schweitzer, *The Problem of the Lord's Supper according to the Scholarly Research of the Nineteenth Century and the Historical Accounts*, vol. 1, *The Lord's Supper in Relationship to the Life of Jesus and the History of the Early Church*, trans. A. J. Mattill (Macon: Mercer University Press, 1982), p. 135.

22. A number of writers try to dispute the notion of a divine presence in the Eucharist by attending to the ambiguities of Aramaic in the phrase "this is my blood." In response to this line of argument see Martin Chemnitz, *The Lord's Supper*, trans. J. A. O. Preus (St. Louis: Concordia Publishing, 1979), pp. 28–30.

23. H. K. Ringgren, *Sacrifice in the Bible* (New York: Association Press, 1962).
24. Dennis D. Hughes, *Human Sacrifice in Ancient Greece* (New York: Routledge, 1991); R. K. Yerker, *Sacrifice in Greek and Roman Religion and Early Christianity* (New York: Charles Scribner's Sons, 1952); Robert Garland, *The Greek Way of Death* (Ithaca: Cornell University Press, 1985). Garland mentions that there is no evidence for blood sacrifices after Homer (p. 168); nowhere in Burkert's volume do I find a bloody ancient Greek precursor to the idea of a God-to-God sacrifice. See also Walter Burkert, *Homo Necans: The Anthropology of Ancient Greek Sacrificial Ritual and Myth*, trans. Peter Bing (Berkeley: University of California Press, 1983).
25. See Robert J. Daly, *Christian Sacrifice: The Judaeo-Christian Background Before Origin* (Washington, D.C.: The Catholic University of America Press, 1978); Daly, *The Origins of the Christian Doctrine of Sacrifice* (Philadelphia: Fortress Press, 1978); Cheryl A. Brown, "The Peace-Offerings and Pauline Soteriology," *Immanuel* 24/25 (Jerusalem: Ecumenical Theological Research Fraternity, 1990), pp. 59–76; Frances M. Young, *The Use of Sacrificial Ideas in Greek Christian Writers from the New Testament to John Chrysostom* (Philadelphia: Philadelphia Patristic Foundation, 1979); Bruce Chilton, *The Temple of Jesus: His Sacrificial Program within a Cultural History of Sacrifice* (University Park: Pennsylvania State University Press, 1992).
26. Friedrich Nietzsche, *On the Genealogy of Morals*, trans. Walter Kaufmann (New York: Vintage, 1967), essay 2, sec. 21, p. 92.
27. Ringgren distinguishes between and among the different sacrifices of the Old Testament (*zebakh, kalil, shelem*), but he also notes evidence of human sacrifice that crept into Israelite religion (Lev. 18:21, 20:2f; 2 Kings 21:6, 23:10; Jer. 7:30f, 32:35). He contends that no consistent teaching concerning sacrifices can be extracted from the New Testament (Mark 1:44; Luke 2:24; Acts 21:26, 24:17; Matt. 5:23f, 9:13, 12:7; Mark 12:33). Moreover, he and several other commentators note that no precise word for "sacrifice" is used, but the implication in the Gospels is clear (e.g., "ransom" in Mark 10:43 and "consecrate" in John 17:19). Ringgren, *Sacrifice in the Bible*, pp. 12, 73. See also D. R. Jones, "Sacrifice and Holiness," in *Sacrifice and Redemption: Durham Essays in Theology*, ed. S. W. Sykes (Cambridge: Cambridge University Press, 1991), pp. 9–21.
28. Patricia Vicari, "Sparagmos: Orpheus among the Christians," in *Orpheus: The Metamorphoses of a Myth*, ed. John Warden (Toronto: University of Toronto Press, 1982), pp. 63–83.
29. Eleanor Irwin, "The Songs of Orpheus and the New Song of Christ," in *Orpheus: the Metamorphoses of a Myth*, ed. John Warden (Toronto: University of Toronto Press, 1982), pp. 51–62.
30. Mary Daly notes that Piers Paul Read's book *Alive*—the story of the Andes survivors who ate the frozen bodies of their dead companions—tells how survivors justified their eating human flesh on the basis of the Gospels and the ritual of the Catholic mass: Daly, *Gyn/Ecology*, p. 81.
31. Wilson's argument about the mere symbolism of the Eucharist isn't convincing, for his reading ignores the need for an extraordinary and shocking act to bind the disciples to Jesus: "It is even less likely that, at a Passover meal, a devout Jew such as Jesus would have handed around a chalice of wine and told his friends that if they drank from it, they would be drinking his blood. This smacks strongly of the mystery cults of the Mediterranean, and has little in common with Judaism": *Jesus*, p. 21.
32. Commentators who have objected to Schweitzer's reading of the Eucharist as a "messianic banquet" often make recourse to Judaic conventions and practices of

the day and thus overlook the possibility that the event is supposed to be peculiar and extraordinary. Loyalty tests are often tests conducted under extreme and trying circumstances. See Chilton, "The Sacrifice of Jesus," *The Temple of Jesus*, 137–141.

33. Kleist draws on the *Didache* to suggest that early Christians invoked a code of secrecy surrounding the hidden meaning of the Eucharist: "'Do not give to dogs what is sacred' (9.5). In their original context (Matt. 7.6) these words of Our Lord are a general injunction not to divulge (much less, to give) to infidels what is sacred to Christians. Are they not the forerunner of the later *disciplina arcani*? Pliny's report to the emperor Trajan confirms our impression. Spies had been sent out to investigate the strange behavior of the Christians at their services; but all they were able to ascertain was that they ate *cibum promiscuum et innoxium*, 'Just ordinary and harmless food.' They saw that bread and wine were given to the communicants, but were unable to learn that they were the Body and Blood of Christ." James A. Kleist, "Introduction," *The Didache or Teaching of the Twelve Apostles* (Westminister, Md.: The Newman Press, 1948), p. 8.

34. Daly, *Gyn/Ecology*, pp. 81–83.

35. Weber, *Economy and Society*, p. 490.

36. Ibid., p. 489. Cf. p. 529.

37. Max Weber, *The Religion of India: The Sociology of Hinduism and Buddhism*, trans. Hans H. Gerth and Don Martindale (New York: Free Press, 1958), p. 137.

38. Ibid., p. 138.

39. Weber, *Economy and Society*, p. 423.

40. Ibid., p. 531.

41. Nietzsche, *On the Genealogy of Morals*, essay 2, sec. 19, pp. 88–9.

42. Ibid., p. 89.

43. Friedrich Nietzsche, *Daybreak: Thoughts on the Prejudices of Morality*, trans. R. J. Hollingdale (Cambridge: Cambridge University Press, 1982), p. 218.

44. Joseph L. Henderson and Maud Oakes, *The Wisdom of the Serpent: The Myths of Death, Rebirth and Resurrection* (New York: G. Braziller, 1963), p. 17.

45. Jacques Derrida, "The Politics of Friendship," *Journal of Philosophy* (1988), 632–644.

46. "This ['The Martyrdom of St. Polycarp'] is the oldest record of the ancient Christian concept which regarded death (and especially a martyr's death) as a birth, and the day and anniversary of death (especially of a martyr) as a birthday; but the underlying sentiment, that death is in reality a passage to life, is already indicated in Ignatius of Antioch, *Rom.* 6.I ('The birth *pangs* are upon me'), 2.2 ('May I *rise* in His presence'), and 7.2 ('There is in me a *Living* Water'). In the Roman Martyrology the word *natalis* (*dies*) denotes the day of a martyr's death. See the very interesting discussion of this subject by A. C. Rush, *Death and Burial in Christian Antiquity* (Stud. in Christ. Ant. I, Washington 1941), Ch. 4: "Death as a Birth. The Day of Death as *Dies Natalis*." 'The heroes': see Clement of Rome, n.25: ACWI.105." Kleist, *Didache*, p. 203 n. 51.

47. Norman O. Brown, *Love's Body* (New York: Random House, 1966), p. 164.

48. Caroline Walker Bynum alludes to this unpleasant theological problem, but she doesn't follow through with an analysis of this particular point: "The eucharistic host, fragmented by human teeth and digestive processes yet in every minute crumb the whole body of Christ is, argued Guibert, the guarantee that wholeness—non-partibility and non-passibility—is God's ultimate promise to humankind." Bynum, *Fragmentation and Redemption: Essays on Gender and the Human Body in Medieval Religion* (New York: Zone, 1991), p. 12.

49. My argument here is similar to that of Leo Steinberg, who attends to the genital focus of much Christian painting in the Renaissance. Such paintings displaying Christ's sexuality, at birth and at death, "confess the mystery of the dual nature of Christ, and the leasing of his humanity to mortal suffering": *The Sexuality of Christ in Renaissance Art and in Modern Oblivion* (New York: Pantheon, 1983), p. 42.

50. See Norman O. Brown, *Life against Death: The Psychoanalytic Meaning of History* (New York: Vintage, 1959), p. 339, n. 13.

51. Erik H. Erikson, *Young Man Luther: A Study in Psychoanalysis and History* (New York: Norton, 1958); Brown, "Studies in Anality," *Life against Death*, pp. 179–306; Martin Pops, "The Metamorphoses of Shit," *Salmagundi*, no. 56 (Spring 1982), 26–61.

52. François Rabelais, "How Gargantua was born in a strange manner," *Gargantua and Pantagruel*, vol. 1 (London: J. M. Dent and Sons, 1932–33), 18.

53. Medievalists, however, have been drawing this connection. See Sarah Beckwith, *Christ's Body: Identity, Culture, and Society in Late Medieval Writings* (London: Routledge, 1993); Miri Rubin, *Corpus Christi: The Eucharist in Late Medieval Culture* (Cambridge: Cambridge University Press, 1991); and Caroline Walker Bynum, *Holy Feast and Holy Fast: The Religious Significance of Food to Medieval Women* (Berkeley: University of California Press, 1987).

54. S. W. Sykes, "Introduction," *Sacrifice and Redemption*, ed. S. W. Sykes, p. 1.

55. Julia Kristeva comes close in her explication of A. Nygren's analysis of Pauline agape as a particularly *theocentric* act of love: "God is Love," in *Tales of Love*, trans. Leon S. Roudiez (New York: Columbia University Press, 1987), pp. 139–150; Anders Nygren, *Eros et Agapè, La Notion chrétiene de l'amour et ses transformations* (1930; Paris: Aubier, 1962). Other psychotheological accounts, notably those of Freud and Money-Kyrle, in which sacrifice symbolically reenacts an infanticidal wish by fathers to kill their sons, also come close to recognizing a theocentric notion of sacrifice—but psychologizing the event returns the focus to humans. Many classic accounts of sacrifice—by E. B. Tylor, W. Robertson Smith, James George Frazer, Edward Westermarck, M. Alfred Loisy, Henri Hubart, and Marcel Mauss—explore relations between gods and victims; but none focuses in particular on the God-to-human sacrifice in the Christian account; rather, they all ask how Jesus might occupy both divine and victim roles. The problem is that the Christian trinity complicates traditional understandings of sacrifice—as gift, communion, magic, expiation, ritual, and so forth.

56. Albert Schweitzer, *The Quest of the Historical Jesus: A Critical Study of Its Progress from Reimarus to Wrede*, trans. W. Montgomery (London: Black, 1954).

57. Hannah Arendt, *The Life of the Mind* (New York: Harcourt Brace Jovanovich, 1978), part 2, p. 65.

58. For Paul's views on sexual control, see Peter Brown, *The Body and Society: Men, Women and Sexual Renunciation in Early Christianity* (New York: Columbia University Press, 1988), esp. pp. 51–57. Brown also points out that opponents of Paul had linked procreation with community regeneration, and, in that sense, resurrection of the dead. Ibid., p. 7.

59. See Leo Steinberg on the Christian phallus as an instrument of salvation: "But the organ of the God-man does better. By dint of continence, through the willed chastity of the Ever-virgin, it obviates the necessity for procreation since, in the victory over sin, death, the result of sin, is abolished. In such orthodox formulation, the penis of Christ, puissant in abstinence, would surpass in power the phalli of Adam or Dionysus. And it is perhaps in this sense that the old

connotation of the phallus as anti-death weapon is both adapted to the Christ context and radically converted." Steinberg, *The Sexuality of Christ in Renaissance Art*, p. 46. Witness also his discussion of the erection motif in depictions of the dead Christ, pp. 82–96.

60. Robin Lane Fox makes the point that it was easier for women to convert to Christianity since they did not have to go through the pain of circumcision: *Pagans and Christians* (New York: Knopf, 1987), p. 271.

61. See Steinberg's superb discussion of the salvational dimensions of Christ's circumcision: *The Sexuality of Christ in Renaissance Art*, pp. 49–65.

62. That circumcision should be connected to sacrificial death themes is not so unusual if one consults cross-cultural anthropological sources. Note, for instance, that Maurice Bloch makes precisely this connection in observing the Merina people of central Madagascar: "The circumcision ceremony is another major Merina ritual. . . . Circumcision is made to stand symbolically in opposition to biological birth, which is defined in the ritual as polluting, as associated with women and individual houses. . . . The same kind of pattern is therefore acted out in the circumcision ceremony as is dramatized in the funerary ceremony. . . . .The circumcision ceremony, the sociomoral birth, as opposed to the defiling biological birth, is thus equated in a number of ways to the social death, entry into the tomb, which like social birth is the source of fertility since it is the source of blessing. . . . One can say, therefore, that in Merina ideology the concept of birth and death are systematically collapsed in these rituals and made one by opposing them to an antithesis acted out by women, biological birth and biological death." Maurice Bloch, "Death, Women and Power," *Death and the Regeneration of Life*, ed. Maurice Bloch and Jonathan Parry (Cambridge: Cambridge University Press, 1982), pp. 219–220; see also the connection between the Dowayo death rituals and circumcision, Nigel Barley, "The Dowayo Dance of Death," *Mortality and Immortality: The Anthropology and Archaeology of Death*, ed. S. C. Humphreys and Helen King (London: Academic Press, 1981), pp. 149–159. Approaching this issue from another angle is Caroline Walker Bynum, who, in contesting Leo Steinberg's assumption that the penis and sexuality go hand in hand, claims that medieval religious people "saw all bodily fluids as reducible to blood and saw bleeding basically as purging, bleeding was an obvious symbol for cleansing or expiation, and all Christ's bleedings were assimilated." Thus they associated Christ's penis with pain and blood and therefore tied the circumcision directly to salvation. Bynum, *Fragmentation and Redemption*, p. 87. See also Walter Burkert on the phallic connections between sex and death in ancient Greek ritual: *Homo Necans*, pp. 58–70.

63. Daly, *The Origins of the Christian Doctrine of Sacrifice*, p. 42.

64. Ibid., pp. 43–44.

65. Brown, *Life against Death*; Sigmund Freud, "Character and Anal Eroticism," in *Collected Papers*, vol. 2, ed. J. Riviere and J. Strachey (New York: The International Psycho-Analytical Press, 1924), pp. 45–50; "On the Transformation of Instincts with Special Reference to Anal Eroticism," in *Collected Papers*, vol. 2, ed. Riviere and Strachey, pp. 164–171.

66. Brown, *Life against Death*, p. 100.

67. Ibid., p. 281.

68. Ibid., p. 285.

69. Ibid., p. 292.

70. Kristeva, following Bataille and resisting a theory of anal eroticism, also attempts to link death, rebirthing, eating, and excreting; yet she reads the link

between defilement and rebirthing as stemming from the maternal and the fear of feminine generative power. Specifically she associates Christian food narratives— the abolition of dietary taboos, the dining with pagans and lepers, the commingling of bodies and breads, the tamed cannibalism—with an archaic relation to "the first pre-object (ab-ject) of need: the mother." See Kristeva, *Powers of Horror*, esp. pp. 2–4, 71–71, 94–97, 113–132.

71. Brown, *Life against Death*, p. 294.

72. Note how Augustine grapples with this dilemma in the sections, "The meaning of 'shaped into the likeness of God's Son'" and "Will women retain their sex in the resurrected body?" Augustine, *The City of God*, trans. Henry Bettenson (New York: Penguin, 1972), pp. 1056–1058.

73. Brown, *Life against Death*, pp. 308–309.

74. Although Weber points out that Christianity militates against a democratic universalism: "Nothing was further from Jesus' mind than the notion of the universalism of divine grace. On the contrary, he directed his whole preaching against this notion. Few are chosen to pass through the narrow gate, to repent and to believe in Jesus": *Economy and Society*, p. 632.

75. "I see, Diognetus, that you are very much in earnest about investigating the religion of the Christians and make very exact and careful inquiries concerning them. Who is the God in whom they trust—you wonder—and what kind of cult is theirs, because one and all, they disdain the world and despise death? They neither recognize the gods believed in by the Greeks nor practice the superstition of the Jews! And what is the secret of the strong affection they have for one another?" "The Epistle to Diognetus," *The Didache*, p. 135.

76. Although Girard's applying his notions of mimetic desire and scapegoating to the Gospels is highly suggestive, and although he is of course very adept at reading the double aspects of sacrificial agents/victims, he doesn't consider anywhere in his provocative account the idea of a God-to-God sacrifice; and thus he is too quick to exonerate Jesus in favor of a sociological reading of the violent mob. René Girard, *Violence and the Sacred*, trans. B. Gregory (Baltimore: Johns Hopkins University Press, 1977).

77. Friedrich Nietzsche, *The Will to Power*, trans. Water Kaufmann and R. J. Hollingdale (New York: Vintage, 1968), p. 116.

78. Friedrich Nietzsche, *Thus Spoke Zarathustra*, trans. Walter Kaufmann (New York: Penguin, 1978), p. 73.

4. The Womb

1. See Virginia Held, "Birth and Death," in *Feminism & Political Theory*, ed. Cass R. Sunstein (Chicago: University of Chicago Press, 1982), pp. 87–113.

2. Annie Leclerc, "Parole de femme," in *French Feminist Thought*, ed. Toril Moi (New York: Basil Blackwell, 1987), p. 77.

3. "Men love death. In everything they make, they hollow out a central place for death, let its rancid smell contaminate every dimension of whatever still survives." Andrea Dworkin, "Why So-Called Radical Men Love and Need Pornography," in *Take Back the Night: Women on Pornography*, ed. Laura Lederer (New York: Morrow, 1980), p. 148.

4. Mary Daly, *Gyn/Ecology: The Metaethics of Radical Feminism* (Boston: Beacon Press, 1978), p. 59.

5. Kathy E. Ferguson tends toward this position in her superb critique of my position on death and irony. *The Man Question: Visions of Subjectivity in Feminist Theory* (Berkeley: University of California Press, 1993), pp. 93–95.

6. Eva C. Keuls, *The Reign of the Phallus: Sexual Politics in Ancient Athens* (Berkeley: University of California Press, 1985), p. 129. See also Turner: "Liminality is frequently likened to death, to being in the womb, to invisibility, to darkness, to bisexuality, to an eclipse of the sun or the moon." Victor Turner, "Death and the Dead in the Pilgrimage Process," in *Religious Encounters with Death*, ed. Frank E. Reynolds and Earle H. Waugh (University Park: Pennsylvania State University Press), p. 95; cited in Elisabeth Bronfen, *Over Her Dead Body: Death, Femininity, and the Aesthetic* (New York: Routledge, 1992), p. 203. See also Eliade's discussion of the Kogi joint terms for womb and the grave (the reason the fetal position is common to both). Mircea Eliade, "Mythologies of Death: An Introduction," in *Religious Encounters with Death: Insights from the History and Anthropology of Religions*, ed. Frank E. Reynolds and Earle H. Waugh (University Park: Pennsylvania State University Press, 1977), p. 16.

7. Maurice Bloch, "Death, Women, and Power," in *Death and the Regeneration of Life*, ed. Maurice Bloch and Jonathan Parry (Cambridge: Cambridge University Press, 1982), pp. 211–230.

8. Beth Ann Bassein, *Women and Death: Linkages in Western Thought and Literature* (Westport, Conn.: Greenwood Press, 1984), p. 205.

9. Julia Kristeva, *Powers of Horror: An Essay on Abjection*, trans. Leon S. Roudiez (New York: Columbia University Press, 1982), p. 159.

10. Virginia Held, "Feminism and Moral Theory," *Women and Moral Theory*, ed. Eva Feder Kittay and Diana T. Meyers (Totowa, N.J.: Rowman and Littlefield, 1987), p. 124.

11. Walter Burkert, *Homo Necans: The Anthropology of Ancient Greek Sacrificial Ritual and Myth*, trans. Peter Bing (Berkeley: University of California Press, 1983), pp. 70–72.

12. Nancy C. Hartsock, *Money, Sex, and Power: Toward a Feminist Historical Materialism* (Boston: Northeastern University Press, 1983), pp. 186–204.

13. Helen Caldicott, *Missile Envy: The Arms Race and Nuclear War* (New York: William Morrow, 1984).

14. Jessica Benjamin, *The Bonds of Love: Psychoanalysis, Feminism, and the Problem of Domination* (New York: Pantheon, 1988), esp. pp. 66–84.

15. Bataille credits Alexander Kojève with this reading of Hegel. See Georges Bataille, "Hegel, Death and Sacrifice," trans. Jonathan Strauss, *Yale French Studies* 78 (1990), 9–28.

16. "It is interesting to read Hegel's account of the relation of self and other as a statement of male experience: the relation of the two consciousness takes the form of a trial by death. As Hegel describes it, 'each seeks the death of the other.'" Nancy C. M. Hartsock, "The Feminist Standpoint: Developing the Ground for a Specifically Feminist Historical Materialism," in *Discovering Reality: Feminist Perspective on Epistemology, Metaphysics, Methodology, and Philosophy of Science*, ed. Sandra Harding and Merrill B. Hintikka (Dordrecht, Holland: D. Reidel, 1983), p. 296.

17. G. W. F. Hegel, *The Phenomenology of Spirit*, trans. A. V. Miller (Oxford: Oxford University Press, 1977), p. 288.

18. See Seyla Benhabib, "On Hegel, Women and Irony," in *Feminist Interpretations and Political Theory*, ed. Mary Lyndon Shanley and Carole Pateman (University Park: Pennsylvania State University Press, 1991), p. 142.

19. See especially Donna J. Haraway, "Situated Knowledges: The Science Question in Feminism and the Privilege of Partial Perspective," in her *Simians, Cyborgs, and Women: The Reinvention of Nature* (New York: Routledge, 1991), pp. 183–201.

20. Donna Haraway, *Primate Visions: Gender, Race, and Nature in the World of Modern Science* (New York: Routledge, 1989). Subsequent page references to this book appear in the text.

21. Donna Haraway, "A Manifesto for Cyborgs: Science, Technology, and Socialist Feminism in the 1980s," *Feminism/Postmodernism*, ed. Linda J. Nicholson (New York: Routledge, 1990), pp. 190–233.

22. Ibid., p. 190.

23. Haraway uses the term *irony* this way in the chapter on Akeley in *Primate Visions* and she makes that use even more explicit in the cyborgs essay: "Irony is about contradictions that do not resolve into larger wholes, even dialectically, about the tension of holding incompatible things together because both or all are necessary and true. Irony is about humor and serious play." Ibid.

24. Amid all of Haraway's qualifications and explanations, foundationalist language sometimes creeps through: "The detached eye of objective science is an ideological fiction, and a powerful one. But it is a fiction that hides—and is designed to hide—how the powerful discourses of the natural sciences *really work*." Haraway, *Primate Visions*, p. 13; italics added.

25. "*Primate Visions* is replete with representations of representations." Ibid., p. 377.

26. Martin Heidegger, "The Origin of the Work of Art," in *Poetry, Language, Thought*, trans. Albert Hofstadter (New York: Harper and Row, 1971), pp. 17–87; Meyer Schapiro, "The Still Life as a Personal Object—A Note on Heidegger and van Gogh," in *The Reach of Mind*, ed. Marianne L. Simmel (New York: Springer, 1968), pp. 203–209; Jacques Derrida, "Restitutions," in *The Truth in Painting*, trans. Geoff Bennington and Ian McLeod (Chicago: University of Chicago Press, 1987), pp. 255–382.

27. Derrida, "Restitutions," p. 366.

28. Ibid., p. 381.

29. For a fascinating discussion of Rousseau's limited understanding of the orang-utan, see Robert Wokler, "Perfectible Apes in Decadent Cultures: Rousseau's Anthropology Revisited," *Daedalus* 107 (Summer 1978): 107–134.

30. Mary Shelley, *Frankenstein: Or, The Modern Prometheus* (New York: Penguin, 1963), p. vii.

31. In this section Haraway raises the possibility that Carl and Mary Jobe Akeley might have seriously misread the motivations and intentions of the Gikungu, but she doesn't make this observation auto-referential. For instance, Haraway seems quick to pass judgment about the nature of the Akeleys' "well-meaning" intentions: *Primate Visions*, pp. 52–54.

32. Haraway reveals that she shares the progressivist view of science even as she problematizes that view as held by others: One task of the "sign work" of primatology, she notes, is that it can envision a "different order of relationships between people and between people and things"; and she also wants her readers to envision "a different and less hostile order of relationships among people, animals, technologies, and land." Ibid., pp. 5, 15.

33. Haraway does apparently invite her "readers radically to rewrite stories in the act of reading" SF stories, but she doesn't invite us explicitly to subvert radically *her* account. Ibid., p. 15.

34. Haraway is sensitive to the metaphor of texts as bones: "The bones of old papers can be reanimated in the bodies of another generation's professional and political publications, as the bones of fossil hominids can be reanimated in late twentieth century U.S. sexual politics or international anti-racist organizations." Ibid., p. 186.

35. Cf.: "Akeley feared the gorilla would be driven to extinction" (p. 34); "Akeley's was a literal science dedicated to the prevention of decadence, of biological decay" (p. 34); "Akeley had many stories to tell, but they all expressed the same fundamental vision of a vanishing, threatened scene" (p. 4); "All three activities [exhibition, eugenics, conservation] were prescriptions against decadence, the dread disease of imperialist, capitalist, white culture" (p. 55); and "I am writing about primates because they are popular, important, marvelously varied, and controversial. And all members of the Primate Order—monkeys, apes, and people—are threatened" (p. 3).

36. In the cyborg essay, Haraway seems to insist on a difference between *Frankenstein* and her cyborgian fiction, as if the overall point of *Frankenstein* is revealed in the monster's hopes for pastoral coupledom (rather than in Shelley's ultimate dashing of all such notions): "Unlike the hopes of Frankenstein's monster, the cyborg does not expect its father to save it through a restoration of the garden; i.e., through the fabrication of a heterosexual mate, through its completion in a finished whole, a city and cosmos." "A Manifesto for Cyborgs," p. 192.

37. "I have tried to fill *Primate Visions* with potent verbal and visual images." *Primate Visions*, p. 2.

38. René Girard, *The Scapegoat*, trans. Yvonne Freccero (Baltimore: Johns Hopkins University Press, 1986).

39. René Girard, "Generative Violence and the Extinction of the Social Order," trans. Thomas Wieser, *Salgamundi* 63-4 (Spring/Summer 1984), 204-237.

40. See, for example, *Primate Visions*, pp. 9-10.

41. Haraway at times almost explicitly concedes that what she wants to do is to impose upon her readers a new vision-based disciplinary regime by making her textual images strong and disturbing. Shortly after quoting Foucault, for instance, she makes the following admission: "If Akeley's ethos, to be father of the game, is iconically represented in the mounted figure of the Giant of Karisimbi, the image haunting this chapter is. . . ." Ibid., p. 59.

42. Or at least Madonna ranks right up there with the father-figure cyborg, the Terminator, played by Arnold Schwarzenegger.

43. bell hooks sees Madonna's self-exploitation of her image as the quintessential "white girl" and her attempts to "colonize and appropriate black experience for her own opportunistic ends" as "tragically ironic," because, according to hooks, Madonna's transgressions mask racism and phallic domination. *Black Looks: Race and Representation* (Boston: South End Press, 1992), pp. 157-164.

44. Max Horkheimer and Theodor W. Adorno, "The Culture Industry: Enlightenment as Mass Deception," *Dialectic of Enlightenment*, trans. John Cumming (New York: Seabury Press, 1972), pp. 120-167.

45. *Primate Visions*, p. 350; "A Manifesto for Cyborgs," pp. 194, 223.

46. *Primate Visions*, p. 93.

47. Jean-François Lyotard, *The Postmodern Condition: A Report on Knowledge*, trans. Geoff Bennington and Brian Massumi (Minneapolis: University of Minnesota Press, 1984).

48. Though Haraway seems comfortable with popular culture and marginality, she sometimes implies that the real stakes of the political game involve reoccupy-

ing the center or main-(male-) stream: "But in a post-colonial world of the politics of being female, the earlier margins of possibility can become the main story. Not in the margins of the opening chapter, but at the culmination of *Primate Visions*." *Primate Visions*, p. 378.

49. Tania Modleski takes issue with Baudrillard's view of the ironically feminine. "Femininity as mas(s)querade: a feminist approach to mass culture," *High Theory/ Low Culture: Analyzing Popular Television and Film*, ed. Colin McCabe (New York: St. Martin's Press, 1986), pp. 37–52.

50. See the essays in *Out There: Marginalization and Contemporary Cultures*, ed. Fussell Ferguson et al. (Cambridge, Mass.: MIT Press, 1990).

51. *Primate Visions*, p. 35.

52. These multiple strategies of resistance also obviate the search for a single, universalizing response to Habermas's question of Foucault: "Why resist?"

53. See, e.g., Nancy Hartsock, "Foucault on Power: A Theory for Women?" *Feminism/Postmodernism*, ed. Linda Nicholson, pp. 157–176.

54. Haraway even returns at the end to the theme of *monstrous* birthing in Octavia Butler's xenogenetic vision: *Primate Visions*, p. 378.

55. Haraway's brilliantly instrumentalist use of (what she calls) irony, in service of feminist/survivalist storytelling, seems closer to Kierkegaard's notion of "dissemblance": 'Dissemblance, insofar as one wishes to relate it to the subject, has a purpose, an external purpose foreign to dissemblance itself. Irony, on the other hand, has no purpose, its purpose is immanent in itself, a metaphysical purpose. The purpose is none other than irony itself. . . . Irony has, therefore, no external purpose but is self-purposive." Søren Kierkegaard, *The Concept of Irony: With Constant Reference to Socrates*, trans. Lee M. Capel (Bloomington: Indiana University Press, 1965), p. 273. Also, note Kierkegaard's insistence on the difference between irony as a form of writing and irony as a way of life: "Irony is an existential determination, and nothing is more ridiculous than to suppose that it consists in the use of a certain phraseology, or when an author congratulates himself upon succeeding in expressing himself ironically. Whoever has essential irony has it all day long, not bound to any specific form, because it is the infinite within him." Kierkegaard, *Concluding Unscientific Postscript*, trans. David F. Swenson and Walter Lowrie (Princeton: Princeton University Press, 1941), p. 449.

56. Haraway, "Situated Knowledges," p. 195.

57. Haraway, "The Biopolitics of Postmodern Bodies: Constitutions of Self in Immune System Discourse," in her *Simians, Cyborgs, and Women*, p. 215.

58. Haraway, "A Manifesto for Cyborgs," p. 191.

59. Ibid.

60. For a sense of the Leviathan borrowing as ironic, see the exchange between Silver and Strong. Victoria Silver, "A Matter of Interpretation," *Critical Inquiry* 20 (Autumn 1993), 160–171; Tracy B. Strong, "When Is a Text Not a Pretext? A Rejoinder to Victoria Silver," ibid., pp. 172–178.

61. Haraway, "A Manifesto for Cyborgs," p. 192.

62. Ibid., p. 191.

63. I am influenced here by the conversion trajectories suggested by Jacobson and Connolly. See Jacobson, *Pride and Solace*; William E. Connolly, *The Augustinian Imperative: Reflections on the Politics of Morality* (Newbury Park, Calif.: Sage, 1993).

64. Haraway, "A Manifesto for Cyborgs," p. 192.

65. Ibid.

66. Ibid., p. 206.

67. Ibid., p. 217.
68. Ibid., p. 219.
69. Ibid., p. 205.
70. Ibid., p. 222.
71. Ibid., p. 219.
72. Ibid., p. 223.
73. Ibid., p. 222.
74. Haraway describes the cyborg as impure, not innocent, capable of subversion if not destruction; but these are relatively tame descriptions of violence.
75. See the discussion of regenerating as opposed to rebirthing, ibid., p. 223.
76. Bronfen, *Over Her Dead Body*, p. 255.
77. Ibid., p. 403.
78. Haraway is keenly aware and critical of the view of woman as the sustainer of daily life; the issue here is one of slippage. See "A Manifesto for Cyborgs," p. 223.

5. The Agora

1. Virgil, *The Aeneid of Virgil*, trans. Allen Mandelbaum (Toronto: Bantam, 1961), book 6, lines 600–606.
2. Åke Hultkrantz, *The North American Indian Orpheus Tradition* (Stockholm: Caslon Press, 1957), p. 91.
3. John Rawls, "Justice as Fairness: Political not Metaphysical," *Philosophy and Public Affairs* 14, no. 3 (1985), 223–251.
4. John Rawls, *A Theory of Justice* (Cambridge: Harvard University Press, 1971), p. 139.
5. Ibid., pp. 4–5, 453–462.
6. Ibid., pp. 119–120, 454–458.
7. *Republic*, 369d–372d.
8. "The essential point here is that the principles that best conform to our nature as free and equal rational beings themselves establish our accountability." Rawls, *A Theory of Justice*, p. 519.
9. For instance, Habermas assesses the prospects for an effective public sphere in the political realm as something that cannot be disqualified as "simply utopian." Jürgen Habermas, *The Structural Transformation of the Public Sphere: An Inquiry into a Category of Bourgeois Society*, trans. Thomas Burger and Frederick Lawrence (Cambridge, Mass.: MIT Press, 1989), p. 235.
10. "It may be that this provocative threat, this challenge that places the symbolic structures of the lifeworld as a whole in question, can account for why they have become accessible to us." Jürgen Habermas, *The Theory of Communicative Action*, vol. 2, *Lifeworld and System: A Critique of Functionalist Reason*, trans. Thomas McCarthy (Boston: Beacon Press, 1987), p. 403.
11. I am intrigued by Bonnie Honig's important reading of Arendt that contends that an appeal to the past, a beginning or founding, may be creatively disruptive rather than reverentially authoritative. One wonders then, however, why the past must be appealed to, amended, and performed upon at all; why invoke it at all if not to draw largely upon its authoritative legacy? *Political Theory and the Displacement of Politics* (Ithaca: Cornell University Press, 1993), pp. 112–115.
12. Arendt and Habermas are certainly aware of this tension between scholarship and politics. Habermas, for instance, is careful to distinguish between literary

versus political public realms (*The Structural Transformation of the Public Sphere*, pp. 51–56). Arendt throughout her writings is concerned about the tension between the *vita activa* and the *vita contemplativa*; cf. Hannah Arendt, *The Human Condition* (Chicago: University of Chicago Press, 1958), p. 12.

13. For a helpful overview of public realm theory and its discontents, see Dana R. Villa, "Postmodernism and the Public Sphere," *American Political Science Review* 86, no. 3 (September 1992), 712–721.

14. "Without this transcendence into a potential earthly immortality, no politics, strictly speaking, no common world and no public realm, is possible." Arendt, *The Human Condition*, p. 55.

15. See Deborah M. Burke, Donald G. MacKay, Joanna S. Worthley and Elizabeth Wade, "On the Tip of the Tongue: What Causes Word Finding Failures in Young and Older Adults?" *Journal of Memory and Language* 30 (1991), 542–579.

16. Friedrich Nietzsche, *Beyond Good and Evil*, trans. Walter Kaufmann (New York: Vintage, 1966), section 208, p. 131; "Why I Am a Destiny," in *On the Genealogy of Morals and Ecce Homo*, trans. Walter Kaufmann and R. J. Hollingdale (New York: Vintage, 1989), p. 327.

17. George Kateb, "Thinking about Human Extinction (1): Nietzsche and Heidegger," *Raritan* 6, no. 2 (Fall 1986), 1–28.

18. William E. Connolly, *Identity\Difference: Democratic Negotiations of Political Paradox* (Ithaca: Cornell University Press, 1991), pp. 22–23, 164–171.

19. Nietzsche, "The Wanderer and His Shadow," in *On the Genealogy of Morals*, p. 185.

20. Gilles Deleuze, "Active and Reactive," trans. Richard Cohen, in *The New Nietzsche*, ed. David Allison (New York: Dell, 1977), pp. 80–106.

21. Joan Stambaugh, *Nietzsche's Thought of Eternal Return* (Baltimore: Johns Hopkins University Press, 1972).

22. Mark Warren, *Nietzsche and Political Thought* (Cambridge, Mass.: MIT Press, 1988), pp. 196–206.

23. Nietzsche borrows this phrase from Spinoza. *The Gay Science*, trans. Walter Kaufmann (New York: Vintage, 1974), p. 218n.

24. Nietzsche, *Ecce Homo*, pp. 273–274.

25. Cf. Nietzsche, *Beyond Good and Evil*, p. 68; *The Will to Power*, trans. Walter Kaufmann and R. J. Hollingdale (New York: Vintage, 1968), pp. 35–36, 536.

26. Nietzsche, *The Gay Science*, p. 168.

27. "It makes me happy that men do not want at all to think the thought of death! I should like very much to do something that would make the thought of life even a hundred times more appealing to them." Ibid., p. 225.

28. Note that the "means of enduring" the idea of eternal recurrence is the "revaluation of all values," according to which one no longer says "everything is merely subjective," but rather "it is also our work!" Nietzsche, *The Will to Power*, p. 545.

29. Note that Nietzsche ends "Mixed Opinions and Maxims" (1879) with a trip to Hades, but he emphasizes eternal aliveness: *On the Genealogy of Morals*, p. 179.

30. Tracy B. Strong, *The Idea of Political Theory: Reflections on the Self in Political Time and Space* (Notre Dame: University of Notre Dame Press, 1990), pp. 154–155.

31. Here I am intrigued by Jennifer Ring's account of the "portability" of the Arendtian polis. Ring, "The Pariah as Hero: Hannah Arendt's Political Actor," *Political Theory* 19, no. 3 (August 1991), 433–452.

32. On the faculty of imagination and its relevance to politics, see Hannah Arendt, *Lectures on Kant's Political Philosophy*, ed. Ronald Beiner (Chicago: Univer-

sity of Chicago Press, 1982), p. 43; Arendt, "Lying in Politics," *Crises of the Republic* (New York: Harcourt Brace Jovanovich, 1972), p. 5.

33. William Wordsworth, "Lines, composed a few miles above Tintern Abbey on revisiting the banks of the Wye during a tour" (New York: Thomas Y. Crowell, 1892), lines 30–35, pp. 239–244.

34. See Honig on Rawls, *Political Theory and the Displacement of Politics*, pp. 126–161.

35. Rawls, *A Theory of Justice*, p. 584.

36. Ibid., p. 587.

37. Friedrich Nietzsche, *Human, All Too Human*, trans. R. J. Hollingdale (Cambridge: Cambridge University Press, 1986), pp. 47, 355; Nietzsche, *Twilight of the Idols*, in *The Portable Nietzsche*, trans. Walter Kaufmann (New York: Penguin, 1959), pp. 536–537.

38. Nietzsche, *The Will to Power*, p. 484; Nietzsche, *Thus Spoke Zarathustra*, trans. Walter Kaufmann (New York: Penguin, 1978), pp. 183–186.

39. Nietzsche, *The Gay Science*, p. 218; see also pp. 309, 321.

40. Rawls, *A Theory of Justice*, p.137.

41. Ben Okri, *The Famished Road* (New York: N. A. Talese, 1991).

42. Jacques Derrida, *Aporias*, trans. Thomas Dutoit (Stanford: Stanford University Press, 1993), p. 2.

43. Jean-Luc Nancy, *The Experience of Freedom*, trans. Bridget McDonald (Stanford: Stanford University Press, 1993), p. 169.

44. S. C. Humphreys, "Death and Time," in *Mortality and Immortality: The Anthropology and Archaeology of Death*, ed. S. C. Humphreys and Helen King (London: Academic Press, 1982), p. 265.

45. Ronald Dworkin, *Life's Dominion: An Argument about Abortion, Euthanasia, and Individual Freedom* (New York: Knopf, 1993).

46. Humphreys, "Death and Time," p. 265.

47. Rajeswari Sunder Rajan, "Representing Sati: Continuities and Discontinuities," in *Death and Representation*, ed. Sarah Webster Goodwin and Elisabeth Bronfen (Baltimore: Johns Hopkins University Press, 1993), pp. 285–311.

48. Lyman Van Slyke at Stanford University is writing a biography of Liang Chi who wrote a series of letters before his suicide explaining carefully his political purposes behind that act.

49. In their separate attempts to argue that death is bad, the proper object of rational fear (modified by a naturalist "therapy" in Nussbaum's case), Thomas Nagel and Martha Nussbaum view death as an interruption or deprivation, a loss of life's goods, not as a possible good among others. See Thomas Nagel, "Death," *Mortal Questions* (Cambridge: Cambridge University Press, 1979), pp. 1–10; Martha C. Nussbaum, "Mortal Immortals: Lucretius on Death and the Voice of Nature," in her *The Therapy of Desire: Theory and Practice in Hellenistic Ethics* (Princeton: Princeton University Press, 1994), pp. 192–238.

50. Jean Baudrillard, *Symbolic Exchange and Death*, trans. Iain Hamilton Grant (London: Sage, 1993).

51. Jean Bethke Elshtain, *Democracy on Trial* (New York: Basic Books, 1995), p. 7.

52. "Labor power is instituted on death . . . Does capital exploit the workers to death? Paradoxically, the worst it inflicts on them is refusing them death. It is by deferring their death that they are made into slaves and condemned to the indefinite abjection of a life of labour." Baudrillard, *Symbolic Exchange and Death*, pp. 39–40.

53. Allan Bloom, *Giants and Dwarfs: Essays 1960–1990* (New York: Simon and Schuster, 1990), p. 323.

54. "It is clear from the preceding remarks that we need an account of penal sanctions however limited even for ideal theory." Rawls, *Theory of Justice*, p. 241.

55. Cf. Honig, *Political Theory and the Displacement of Politics*, pp. 137–149.

56. Rawls, *Theory of Justice*, p. 315.

57. Georges Bataille, *The Accursed Share: An Essay on General Economy*, trans. Robert Hurley, 3 vols. (New York: Zone, 1988–1991).

58. Cf. James Miller's account of the influence of Hermann Broch's *The Death of Virgil* on Jean Barraqué and Foucault. *The Passion of Michel Foucault* (New York: Simon and Schuster, 1993), pp. 84–85; also see Hannah Arendt on the importance of Virgil's *Aeneid* for rewriting contemporary politics and theory, in *The Life of the Mind*, part 2 (New York: Harcourt Brace Jovanovich, 1978), pp. 204–216.

Index

225

CONTESTATIONS

Cornell Studies in Political Theory

A series edited by

WILLIAM E. CONNOLLY

The Other Heidegger
by Fred Dallmayr

Allegories of America: Narratives, Metaphysics, Politics
by Frederick M. Dolan

united states
by Thomas L. Dumm

Intimacy and Spectacle: Liberal Theory as Political Education
by Stephen L. Esquith

Political Theory and the Displacement of Politics
by Bonnie Honig

The Inner Ocean: Individualism and Democratic Culture
by George Kateb

*The Anxiety of Freedom: Imagination and Individuality in
Locke's Political Thought*
by Uday Singh Mehta

Political Theory for Mortals: Shades of Justice, Images of Death
by John E. Seery

Signifying Woman: Culture and Chaos in Rousseau, Burke, and Mill
by Linda M. G. Zerilli